HENRY HARFORD:
LAST PROPRIETOR OF MARYLAND

By
Vera F. Rollo

With a Foreword by Dr. Morris L. Radoff

THE MARYLAND BICENTENNIAL COMMISSION,
HARFORD COUNTY COMMITTEE
1976

Copyright © 1976, Vera F. Rollo.

All rights reserved. No part of this book may be reprinted by any means, except brief excerpts for review purposes, without the written permission of the author.

Inquiries may be directed to:

> Maryland Historical Press
> 9205 Tuckerman Street
> Lanham, Maryland 20801

Library of Congress Catalog Card Number
76-554-85

ISBM 0-917-882-06-7

Printed in the United States of America

Compliments of The Harford County State Bi centennial Committee
Chairman
    Hazel Whitford Baldwin
      (Mrs. Fred Baldwin)

April 5th, 1978

HENRY HARFORD: LAST PROPRIETOR OF MARYLAND

CONTENTS

List of Illustrations — vi
Foreword by Dr. Morris L. Radoff — vii
Preface — xi

Chapter
- I MARYLAND'S ENGLISH BACKGROUND — 1
- II FREDERICK CALVERT — 17
- III THE SIXTH BARON ACTS TO REMOVE LEGAL OBSTACLES TO HARFORD'S ASSUMING THE PROPRIETORSHIP — 35
- IV GOVERNOR EDEN IN MARYLAND — 47
- V HENRY HARFORD: HIS ENGLISH BACKGROUND — 59
- VI TWO PRECEDENTS: PROPRIETARY HEIRS IN PENNSYLVANIA AND VIRGINIA — 69
- VII HENRY HARFORD'S MARYLAND SOJOURN — 75
- VIII HARFORD APPEALS TO THE BRITISH GOVERNMENT — 91
- IX FRANCES MARY HARFORD — 95
- X HENRY HARFORD'S LIFE IN ENGLAND: 1785–1834 — 107
- XI THE DESCENDANTS OF THE CALVERTS — 117

APPENDICES
- A WILL OF FREDERICK CALVERT, SIXTH LORD BALTIMORE — 131
- B MEMORIAL OF HENRY HARFORD, PUBLISHED BY THE GENERAL ASSEMBLY OF MARYLAND, 1786 — 141
- C CASE OF THE BRITISH–AMERICAN CLAIMANTS — 151
- D WILL OF HENRY HARFORD, ESQUIRE — 165
- E WILL OF ESTHER HARFORD — 195
- F WILL OF FRANCES MARY HARFORD WYNDHAM — 199
- G THE GOVERNORS OF MARYLAND — 203
- H SITES IN ENGLAND ASSOCIATED WITH THE PROPRIETARY FAMILY OF MARYLAND — 207

BIBLIOGRAPHY — 221
INDEX — 235

LIST OF ILLUSTRATIONS

Kiplin Hall in Yorkshire, England	xvii
George Calvert, First Lord Baltimore	5
Cecil Calvert, Second Lord Baltimore	10
Charles Calvert (I), Third Lord Baltimore	12
Benedict Leonard Calvert, Fourth Lord Baltimore	14
Charles Calvert (II), Fifth Lord Baltimore	18
Hester Rhelan of the Kingdom of Ireland	20
Frederick Calvert, Sixth Lord Baltimore	22
Woodcote Park, a Calvert home	24
Sir Robert Eden, Governor of Maryland	50
St. Martin's Parish Church	60
Aerial view of Windsor and Eton	62
Exeter College, Oxford University	64
The Maryland Inn, Annapolis, Maryland	74
Home of Charles Carroll of Carrollton	76
Dr. Upton Scott's house in Annapolis, Maryland	82
St. Anne's Church in Annapolis, Maryland	86
Frances Mary Harford	97
Petworth House	101
Henry Harford's country home, Down Place, near Windsor	109
The Church of St. Michael at Bray	112
The village of Bray	112
Florence M. Harford and Pamela V. Harford	127
Kiplin Hall in Yorkshire	202
Eton, a street scene	214
View of Spa Creek, Annapolis, Maryland	228

FOREWORD

When millions of dollars were appropriated for the Bicentennial celebration by the Congress, it was assumed that it would be easy to use the money. At the head of the entire celebration there was the Bicentennial Commission, established to distribute the funds throughout the country. This was distributed as seed money to the cities and the counties to do whatever they liked to commemorate the great occasion. What had seemed to be a great deal of money at the beginning turned out to be only driblets when the distribution was completed. Most of the local committees took the easy way out. The local militia was pressed into service with muskets and flintlocks of all periods from the Revolution through the Spanish War. The ladies of the patriotic societies were asked to don their so-called colonial costumes, tea was served and gunpowder was expended at a great rate to stage sham battles on the town green. All of this show used up the funds and gave a demonstration of how our forefathers won the Revolution. There was nothing wrong with this kind of celebration except that it was good for a single day and nothing permanent was created for the next year.

The national celebration which was centered in the Library of Congress tried for more. There was the enormous project for writing new histories of all the states. There were also national projects as, for example, an account of all state houses of all fifty states, funded by the National Endowment for the Humanities. There were other miscellaneous projects such as the one by the Newberry Library which consisted of an Atlas of the Revolutionary War.

The counties were left, for the most part, with local history to write or to reprint. Where the committee was especially vigorous and found funds locally, some good work was done. In Maryland, Anne Arundel County was able to reprint Riley's *The Ancient City: A History of Annapolis in Maryland* plus a new topical history of Anne Arundel County. These works were useful, both for the period of the Bicentennial and for later as well. Harford County, Maryland, was both fortunate in the subject they chose and in its accomplishment. Harford County was set up in 1773 at the beginning of the Revolution and named for the last Proprietor of Maryland, Henry Harford. Harford succeeded Frederick, Sixth Lord Baltimore, on the death of the latter in 1771 as Proprietor (but not as Seventh Lord Baltimore).

The Harford County Committee was fortunate in that they found a subject that had not been done before and they also found a distinguished scholar who was prepared to do the work, a rare coincidence. The reader of Maryland history will certainly be aware of Henry Harford, and he will also be aware that he knows little more than the name and the probable dates. He will also be aware, if he reads a bit more, that the reason Henry Harford did not succeed to the title was because he was illegitimate and there were others who shared the inheritance with him. But how the heritage was shared and what events brought him to the proprietorship of Maryland, the student of Maryland history knows little. Perhaps because it was too complicated for him and it was considered better to put the whole problem under the rug, where even scholars have consigned it to this day.

Why has Henry Harford been so neglected by historians? As the author of this book has shown, Harford materials were scarce in America. The task required travel to England to visit numerous sites and to search out descendants and family archives. In finishing this work after having invested so much time and effort in it the author was unable to find correspondence or journals relating to Harford, without which it cannot be said that the book is complete. But everything that could be found at this time about Henry Harford has been found by the author.

When the thought occurred to the members of the Harford County Bicentennial Committee that the life of Henry Harford would make an ideal publication for the county, they found an author ready and willing to do the job, Vera Rollo of Lanham, Maryland. At an early age she took a great interest in writing about Maryland and publishing the results of her study. She attended the University of Maryland where she was awarded the B.A. in History in December 1972 and the M.A. in American History in May 1976. She has also distinguished herself in her minor in sociology. Vera Rollo is, however, essentially self taught in Maryland history which for a long time was neglected in the curriculum of the University of Maryland. Only with the arrival of many young students from the West and from the East was there a renewed interest in the history of the state which has blossomed into full flower during the last ten years.

Mrs. Rollo took advantage of the rich collections of the Maryland Historical Society in Baltimore, of the library facilities at the University of Maryland and of the excellent collection of State archives at the Hall of Records in Annapolis. Her first book was a history of Maryland for elementary and secondary school students, which is now in its third edition. This first book, however, did not demonstrate Mrs. Rollo's scholarship which appears in her later and more mature works. It was the work of a beginner created to a considerable extent from the works of others and was written to provide a book on Maryland history which was lacking for younger people of that time. This was followed by *Maryland's Constitution and Government* which was also prepared for the young reader but shows a real mastery of the subject. This was followed by *Maryland Personality Parade I,* 1970 and *The Negro in Maryland,* 1972. All these books were published at Lanham, Maryland, where Mrs. Rollo maintains the Maryland Historical Press.

All of these earlier works were successful in their way but they did not show Mrs. Rollo's ability to do scholarly work as did her Master's thesis composed in 1976 and devoted to "Henry Harford, Last Proprietor: How he Became Proprietor and Reasons for his Lack of Success in Maryland Following the American Revolution." When the opportunity came to do a book for the Harford County Bicentennial Committee on Henry Harford, she expanded her thesis and consulted sources in Great Britain, and transcribed scores of eighteenth century documents, to finish her work. She presents it now for your edification and to help complete the history of colonial rule in Maryland.

Morris L. Radoff
Archivist Emeritus
State of Maryland

PREFACE

Henry Harford is known best in Maryland as the person for whom Harford County, Maryland, is named. Informed residents of the county and state also know him as the last Proprietor of Maryland and the son of Frederick Calvert, sixth and last Lord Baltimore. Very few persons can tell you more than these sparse facts.

Who, many have wondered, was Henry Harford, and how did he happen to become Maryland's last Proprietor. Are Harford families now in America descended from him?

Turning to accounts of the history of Maryland and of colonial America, we discover very little more about Harford. He is mentioned with astonishing brevity in histories today as the illegitimate son of Frederick, Lord Baltimore, and is described as "as infant" appointed Proprietor of Maryland by the sixth Baron in his will. Harford usually rates an additional sentence or two in these histories, mentioning his lack of success in retrieving Calvert lands or recompense for his losses in Maryland upon application for such restitution to the Maryland legislature after the American Revolution. Able historians Matthew Page Andrews, Charles Albro Barker, Aubrey C. Land, and others, dismiss Harford in this manner.[1]

This poses for the inquiring researcher into Harford's life the additional question: why was Henry Harford, last Proprietor of Maryland, so harshly treated by the General Assembly? He was cut off without a penny willingly given after the Revolution, while to the north and south of Maryland the heirs of the Penn and Fairfax families were allowed to keep many miles of land and to receive other compensation as well.

The nineteenth-century historian, J. Thomas Scharf, offers us a bit more data, yet this information is incomplete, a bit garbled, and in some instances in error.[2]

From Scharf to Land, historians' information is based on two sources, both of which are inadequate to fill the historical gap in our knowledge of Maryland's last proprietorship. The first source is a four-page printed document published January 1786 by the Maryland House of Delegates. The paper gives the text of Henry Harford's memorial to the General Assembly requesting recompense for lands and incomes in Maryland lost to him due to actions of the legislature during the American Revolution. The proceedings of the House and the Senate with regard to his claims are given.[3] The second source of information for historians writing about Maryland during this period are two small books written by a Calvert descendant, Charles Browning, and published in 1821 and 1825.[4] These booklets trace the ownership of land in Maryland and attempt to prove that Browning was entitled to recompense from the Maryland legislature because he was a legitimate descendant of the Calverts. In the two publications Browning makes mention of Harford's illegitimate birth; of a settlement, made with Browning's father in the late eighteenth century; and of Browning's contact with Henry Harford in England in the early nineteenth century.[5] Information given by Browning is not plainly stated, unfortunately, but rather is submerged in a host of polemical and subjective statements.

A brief addition to these two major sources, the Harford memorial and the Browning tracts, surfaced in 1950 when another scrap of information about Henry Harford appeared in the December edition of *Etoniana,* the Eton College magazine. An unnamed writer of a short article added to the published facts about Harford that Henry Harford was educated at Eton and Oxford, was twice married, and was presumed to have had children by both marriages. The article stated that Harford ran once (unsuccessfully) for a seat in Parliament, that he sat for a portrait by Romney, and that he lived in London in the late eighteenth century. The article noted that Harford's date of death was December 1805 but that this date seemed incorrect. It was in error, for Harford died in 1834. A sentence or two about Harford's sister, Frances Mary, completed the short account.[6]

The accounts of both Scharf and the writer of the *Etoniana* article on Harford's life and inheritance are far from complete and both contain errors. Scharf, for example, causes some confusion because he does not quote Frederick Calvert's will in its entirety, which would have been quite possible since it is a fairly short document. Scharf also tells us that funds were paid by the British government to the "two sisters," of Henry Harford, when in fact the amount mentioned was paid to the two sisters of Harford's father.[7] Turning to the *Etoniana* article we find that it states that the State of Maryland paid Harford £10,000, when in fact Maryland volunteered him nothing. The £10,000 was a sum almost confiscated by the British government from Bank of England stock owned by Maryland and held during the Revolution in England. The money was paid to Harford by the British government out of the Maryland stock account, with grudging agreement on Maryland's part, before the matter of the hostage stocks was settled.[8]

The details of the transfer of Maryland to Harford, instead of to the legal heirs of the Calverts, have never been published. Was Harford ever legally recognized in the courts of England as the sole Proprietor of Maryland? If so, one might ask how this dispute was settled between the legal heirs and Harford? One of the most interesting documents to come to light in the course of the writer's research into the life of Henry Harford deals with this settlement, that is, the Estate Act of 1781. In the one hundred pages of this document complete details of the transfer are given.[9] The writer may now offer for the first time the story of how Henry Harford was able to gain legal recognition of his claim to the proprietorship.

Why have historians so neglected the last Proprietor? He lived in a most complex and interesting historical period. His relations with Maryland and with the legal heirs to the proprietorship have never been investigated. The data on his life and proprietorship are obviously incomplete. It is strange, too, that historians have not remarked upon the exceptional harshness of the Maryland legislature with regard to Harford's request for post-Revolutionary recompense for his losses of lands and revenues. It would seem that the dearth of information about Harford would have aroused the curiosity of writers. That it did not is due perhaps to the fact that the major part of the material bearing on his life is to be found only in England. It was to England that this writer was forced to go in order to locate the wills, the depositions, and the various records that document the events in the life of the last Proprietor and provide information relative to his relations with Maryland.[10]

A major part of the purpose of this study then, was to fill in the gaps in Maryland history pertaining to her last proprietor, Henry Harford, and to correct errors regarding his life and proprietorship that have been introduced into the literature. Research has provided us with the details of the transfer of Maryland to Harford rather than to the legal heirs of the Calverts. It has given us, as well, some clues as to why the Maryland legislature refused to honor Harford's request for recompense for his losses in America following the Revolution.

The present account answers many questions and supplies new data and exactness to the interactions between Maryland and the proprietary, both before and after the Revolution. It is to be hoped that at some future date personal letters and papers regarding Henry Harford will also surface to give us a better knowledge of the man, for, as it is, Harford himself remains a somewhat shadowy personality. Still, this study has given us a solid outline of his life. It also offers us a better understanding of the interesting years prior to, during, and following, the American Revolution.

Research into the histories of the Calvert, the Harford, and the Browning families was greatly assisted by materials located in the Manuscript Division of the Maryland Historical Society in Baltimore with the help of Richard Cox, Archivist. The Calvert Papers collection was particularly useful. Further information was found in the Hall of Records, Annapolis; in the Maryland Room, McKeldin Library, University of Maryland; and in the Eisenhower Library, Johns Hopkins University. Additional material was found in the Genealogical Research Room and in the Law Library of the Library of Congress.

The bulk of the materials needed to bring together the details of this life of Henry Harford, however, were located in England. In the summer of 1974 the writer went to London where she found new documentation pertaining to Henry Harford and his contemporaries, and relating to the various reparations paid to Harford by the British government. In the Bodleian Library, Oxford University, she located a first clue as to the existence of the Estate Act of 1781. Further investigation led her to London and the discovery of the actual 100-page document in the Record Office of the House of Lords. This revealed for the first time the exact terms of agreement between the legal heirs to Maryland (Louisa Calvert Browning and Caroline Calvert Eden) and Henry Harford that finally made him the sole Proprietor of Maryland.

Further travel in England led the writer to useful libraries, record offices and private collections of documents. These included the Archives and Manuscripts Sections of the Eton College Library; local history collections in the cities of Windsor, York, Exeter, Exmouth, Epsom, and Chichester. A visit to Kiplin Hall in Yorkshire yielded information on Harford's Calvert family antecedents, thanks to the kindnesses of its Curator and the Friends of Kiplin Hall. Near Windsor at Down Place, which was formerly Harford's county estate, the directors of the Bray Film Studios kindly escorted the writer about the old building. Information regarding Harford's first wife, Louisa Pigou, was located in the Exeter Cathedral thanks to the assistance rendered by the Librarian of the Exeter Cathedral Library. Facts about Harford's Oxford years were gained due to the assistance of the staff of the Bursar's Office, at Exeter College, Oxford University

Details of Harford's Maryland stay and his relations with his sister, Frances Mary Harford Wyndham, were located in the Petworth House Archives near Chichester, courtesy of the present Lord Egremont and with the kind assistance of Mrs. Patricia Gill, West Sussex County Archivist. A journey to Epsom in Surrey revealed physical details of the old Calvert estate, Woodcote Park, and geographical facts of other nearby areas associated with Harford's early years. A visit to the parish church in Epsom gave the writer a view of the churchyard there in which the Calvert family vault is located.

One of the writer's final calls in England was to the last direct descendants of Henry Harford, the Misses Florence and Pamela Harford, located via a series of lucky encounters. These gentlewomen make their home near their father's former estate, "Broadfield," in Buckinghamshire, just a few miles from Windsor. They showed her portraits of family members. One, the portrait of Hester Rhelan, is reproduced in this book. Further, they brought out a large family Bible which had been handed down to them. It contains a handwritten memorandum of the birth of Frederick Calvert, his son Henry Harford, and a listing of all the Harford descendants down to the present day. They confirmed that they were the last of the Harford line and, since neither has married, no direct descendants bearing the name will remain upon their deaths. This answers the question as to the possible connection of present-day Harford families with Henry Harford. (The Harfords in America are descended from an entirely separate English family from Yorkshire. A book, *The Harford Family,* by Alice Harford, gives an excellent account of this family's history. It may be found in the Genealogical Research Room, Library of Congress.) From these two Harford sisters, great-great-granddaughters of the last Proprietor, the writer gleaned many interesting leads to assist her in her search for facts and further documentation pertaining to Henry Harford and his descendants.

After the writer's return to Maryland, many rewarding documents were gathered via correspondence carried on with the London Record Office and the Record Office of the House of Lords, also in London. A microfilm of the Estate Act of 1781, texts photographed from official manuscript copies of various wills, plus other interesting material came by mail. As a result, Maryland historians and scholars of the American Revolution will find valuable information in the documents appended.

As the search progressed, the story that unfolded was an unexpected and fascinating one. Most of the facts and documents are published here for the first time on the life and times of Henry Harford, our almost unknown last Proprietor of Maryland.

The research for this study, the writing of this book, and its publication, have been greatly assisted by many people. The writer tenders thanks to Dr. Morris L. Radoff, for many years Archivist of Maryland, now *Archivist Emeritus,* for reading the manuscript and offering most helpful suggestions for putting it into final form. Thanks are certainly due to Dr. John E. Brown, Professor of History, Harford Community College and a member of the Harford County Committee of the Maryland Bicentennial Commission, for editing assistance and for taking an active interest in the publication of this book. The writer is most grateful to the Harford County Committee, chaired by Mrs. Fred B.

Baldwin, which helped make publication possible in the Bicentennial year.

Vera Rollo
Lanham, Maryland
1976

[1] Matthew Page Andrews, *History of Maryland: Province and State* (New York: Doubleday, Doran & Co., 1929; facsimile reprint by Tradition Press of Hatboro, Penna., 1965), pp. 292, 377, 378; Charles Albro Barker, *Background of the Revolution in Maryland* (New Haven: Yale University Press, 1940), pp. 329, 330, 350; Aubrey C. Land, "Provincial Maryland," *Maryland: A History, 1632-1974* (Baltimore: Maryland Historical Society, 1974), p. 74.
[2] J. Thomas Scharf, *History of Maryland,* 3 vols., (Hatboro, Penna.: Tradition Press, 1967, a facsimile reprint of the 1879 edition), II, pp. 136-139.
[3] Memorial of Henry Harford and related proceedings, a broadside, dated January 6, 1786, published by the Maryland House of Delegates, MS Div., Vertical Files, "Harford, January 6, 1786," Maryland Historical Society. Appendix B.
[4] Charles Browning, *An Appeal to the Citizens of Maryland* (Baltimore: n.p., 1821); Charles Browning, *The Granting of Lands in Maryland,* (Baltimore: "For the Proprietor," 1825).
[5] Browning, *An Appeal* . . . , p. 11.
[6] *Etoniana,* Vol. 109 (December, 1950), pp. 135, 136.
[7] Scharf, II. p. 394.
[8] Scharf, II, p. 506; Morris L. Radoff, *Calendar of Maryland State Papers, No. 2: The Bank Stock Papers* (Annapolis: State of Maryland, Hall of Records Commission, 1947), pp. xxiv, xxv, xxix, xxxii, xxxv, xxxvi, xxxvii.
[9] Estate Act of 1781, microfilm, Record Office, House of Lords, London.
[10] Repositories visited in the United States included: Maryland Hall of Records, Annapolis; Manuscript Division of the Maryland Historical Society, Baltimore; Maryland Room, McKeldin Library, University of Maryland, College Park; Eisenhower Library, Johns Hopkins University, Baltimore; Library of Congress, Genealogical Research Room and the Law Library, Washington, D.C.

Major repositories searched in England included: Manuscript Room, British Museum; Periodicals Room, British Museum; Hall of Record, Chancery Lane, London; Record Office, House of Lords, London. Other collections studied were located at: Bodleian Library, University of Oxford; Archives and Manuscript Collection, Eton College Library, Eton College; and the local history collections in city libraries in Windsor, York, Exeter, Exmouth, Epsom, and Chichester, England.

Private collections, too, were most helpful. Valuable data came to light from the private collection of the Petworth House Archives, available courtesy the present Lord Egremont, Petworth House, and with acknowledgements to the West Sussex Record Office and the County Archivist, Mrs. Patricia Gill. Upon locating the great-great-granddaughters of Henry Harford, the writer was shown portraits, a family Bible, and other documentation which was most helpful in writing this account of the life of Henry Harford.

Kiplin Hall, Yorkshire, England (Author's 1974 photograph)

RULERS OF ENGLAND: 1509–1820

HENRY VIII	1509–1547
EDWARD VI	1547–1553
MARY I	1553–1558
ELIZABETH I	1558–1603
JAMES I	1603–1625
CHARLES I	1625–1649

From 1642–1646 civil war raged in England, followed by a second civil war. In 1653 Oliver Cromwell was made ruler of England as head of the Puritan forces. He was given the title "Protector." In 1658 Cromwell died and his son, Richard, was made Lord Protector of England, 1658–1659.

CHARLES II	(Restored)	1660–1685
JAMES II		1685–1688
MARY II and		1688–1694
WILLIAM III		1688–1702
QUEEN ANNE		1702–1714
GEORGE I		1714–1727
GEORGE II		1727–1760
GEORGE III		1760–1820

CHAPTER I

MARYLAND'S ENGLISH BACKGROUND

Since conditions in England had a direct influence on the founding of Maryland and on subsequent events in Maryland, a short outline is given here of the political situation in Britain in the sixteenth, seventeenth, and eighteenth centuries. Because Maryland was founded by members of the Calvert family and Henry Harford was descended from the Calverts, brief biographies of his antecedents, the six Barons of Baltimore, are provided.

Political and Religious Strife in England

For centuries England had one "established church," the Roman Catholic Church with the Pope in Rome at its head. According to the belief of the times, kings held their power by divine right from God. This gave the Pope and the Church tremendous influence on kings and commoners and on every aspect of the fabric of the society of Europe. The Church was immensely rich. It controlled to a great extent the administration of justice, education, and the emerging press, virtually the entire culture. When it desired, the Church could wield great political power.

Henry VIII, King of England, resented the power held by the Catholic Church, and in 1534, using the pretext that the Pope had denied his right to divorce his Spanish Queen, Catherine of Aragon, he renounced the authority of the Pope and laid the foundation for a new established church in England. He made himself the nominal head of the new Church of England, also known as the Anglican Church, and with great energy Henry confiscated the wealth held by the Roman Catholic Church in England. He took over land, buildings, and every sort of property owned by the Church; assumed the right to appoint bishops and priests; and even prescribed articles of faith!

Henry was not alone in throwing off Catholic control. During the same time period Martin Luther was buffeting the Catholic Church in Germany and Holland; Calvin was doing the same in France and Switzerland—in other words, the Protestant Reformation was on in earnest. Only in Spain did the Crown and the Inquisition join forces effectively to crush any outbreak of revolt against the Roman Catholic Church.

Plain words can scarcely convey the effect of King Henry's actions on his people. A deep conviction, such as a peoples' long-held religion, is not easily cast off. Henry was an extremely forceful person and a powerful king. Those whom he did not "convert by reason," he converted by threat. Those who protested openly he had beheaded or burnt at the stake.

When nine-year-old Edward VII succeeded Henry VIII, the Church of England became even stronger in its influence. Catholic property continued to be confiscated and the persecution of Catholics went on. King Edward, however, was not strong, being very nearly an invalid all his life, and in 1553 he died. Thereupon, Mary I, daughter of Henry VIII and Catherine of Aragon, became Queen of England. A confirmed Catholic like her mother, Mary at once set about restoring England to the Roman Church. She began a relentless extermination of all proponents of the Church of England. During her five-year reign (1553–1558) some three hundred persons were burned at the stake for heresy, for expressing ideas contrary to those supported by the Catholic Church. So vengeful was she that historians named her "Bloody Mary."

When Mary was succeeded by Elizabeth I, a Protestant, once again the wheel of religious struggle made a complete turn. Elizabeth ruled for forty-five years and during this time firmly placed in power the Church of England as the established church. When

Elizabeth died in 1603 she was succeeded by James I. Born of a Catholic mother, Mary, Queen of Scots, who was beheaded for treason by Queen Elizabeth I, James was constantly suspected of favoring the Roman Catholic Church and its members. Yet, since England was so firmly a Protestant country, he was repeatedly forced to deny this preference for Catholicism.

A particularly militant group of Protestants known as Puritans now began to gather strength. They were impatient with the slowness with which traces of "popery" were being eradicated. They kept a watchful eye on the King, whom they suspected of favoring certain Catholics. The Puritans were enraged when James I tried to marry his son to a Spanish (Catholic) princess.

All of this religious strife and political maneuvering made life difficult for both the powerful and the weak in England. Conditions continued to worsen and a terrible four year civil war was fought in England over essentially religious matters.

Other Difficulties in England

The scarcity of land increased the pressure on certain citizens of England to find new homes in the New World. During the reign of King James I and for a hundred years to come, England had almost entirely an agricultural economy. Agriculture requires land, and the Crown, which favored nobles and the Church, owned most of the land. Most of the people in England worked the fields for these landowners and were in truth little better than slaves. They had scant hope of ever owning farms themselves.

Even in wealthy families this lack of land created a difficulty. Often land was held under an entail, and the eldest son inherited the bulk of the family real estate. This excluded younger sons and female family members in many cases. Younger sons were encouraged to join the army, the navy, or to attempt a career in the Established Church. Opportunities were limited among younger sons and almost non-existent, save for the career of marriage among daughters. Wealthy families considered it beneath the dignity of family members to engage in trade. A growing middle class in England as yet had neither great numbers or influence. The lower classes, the laborers and the farm hands were almost entirely at the mercy of the land owners. So an ever greater portion of the English populace yearned for opportunity to better themselves and for land to develop by themselves.

Taxes imposed on English citizens were a heavy burden. England for centuries had been involved in wars against the French, the Spanish, and others, sometimes with one country as an enemy and again with that country as an ally! All these wars were costly. The English people—merchants, nobles, tradesmen, and workers—groaned under the continuous taxation.

All of these pressures inclined many men and women to yearn for a new land. Stories of a fresh, fertile country that was the New World came to England. These were alluring indeed to a people sick of the stifling, brawling homeland. America had its dangers, but it was at least relatively free of heavy taxation. There were opportunities there, and there was land—almost limitless amounts of land.

Hope for land, for less taxation, for opportunity, for gold, for adventure—all were reasons to leave England, however much one loved the green and beautiful motherland.

(Photograph courtesy the Enoch Pratt Free Library)

George Calvert, First Lord Baltimore. Portrait by Daniel Mytens the elder, court painter to both James I and Charles I.

The Calvert Family

Henry Harford was a direct descendant of the Calvert family. As an undistinguished but respectable part of the minor gentry, the Calverts lived for generations in Yorkshire. They believed themselves descended from Flemish weavers drawn to the region by its production of wool, at an early period. The name appears in Yorkshire records as early as 1366.[1] The Calvert name is specifically associated with Kiplin, an estate located near Catterick, Yorkshire, as early as 1570 and even 1565.[2]

George Calvert

High office and wealth were to come to the Calvert family due to the brilliance of George Calvert. He was born around 1580 to Leonard of Kiplin, gentleman, and Alice Crosland Calvert.[3] Leonard of Kiplin was a tenant of Philip, Lord Wharton.[4] Originally, George Calvert's parents were Catholics. The persecution of Catholics in England during the sixteenth and seventeenth centuries profoundly affected young Calvert and would lead him eventually to plan the establishment of a colony in America. While George was yet young, his father yielded to the pressures exerted on him and became a Protestant and a member of the Established Church.

Religious persecution of Catholic families consisted in part of local authorities forcing young Catholics to attend Protestant schools. In this manner Leonard Calvert's two sons were taken from him and enrolled in such a school twenty miles from Kiplin at Linton. George Calvert was listed as a Protestant and remained so until later in his life, as we shall see. By 1593 persecution of the senior Calvert ceased, so it was probably at this time that he became a member of the Established Church.[5] This religious dissension was bound to have an effect on George Calvert, yet his Protestant schooling opened many doors for him in England that would have been closed had he remained a Catholic.

The Kiplin mansion, or hall, at this early time is not recorded in either picture or word, and we can only surmise that it was most probably a medieval, fortified type of house. By 1619 we know that George Calvert managed to return to Yorkshire and to buy from Philip, Lord Wharton, and his son, Thomas, both his old home and a considerable amount of land around it.[6] The mansion built by George Calvert, and said by local lore to incorporate a part of the walls of the old Kiplin house in its fabric, still stands, remote even today. It is 30 miles from York, near the town of Catterick in Yorkshire.

Early in his life George Calvert demonstrated ability and showed a winning personality. He continued his education at All Saints College, Oxford University, entering the college in 1593 and obtaining a degree of Bachelor of Arts in 1597. Eight years later he was created Master of Arts, August 30, 1605. An excellent scholar, he exhibited particular proficiency in his mastery of ancient languages.[7]

After leaving Oxford, he traveled in Europe for several years as was the custom of young men of means. Such tours were designed to polish manners, refine social abilities, widen acquaintanceships, and allow young men to master several foreign languages. Many chose to use the time to sow their wild oats, yet George Calvert diligently applied himself to increase his knowledge of the world and soberly studied and mastered several foreign languages.

During 1602 or 1603 he returned to England at the beginning of the reign of King James I. At this time he was about twenty-six years of age, a man of handsome appearance and pleasing manners. He was to demonstrate that he was also an able man and one who could be trusted.

Calvert became secretary to Sir Robert Cecil (Earl of Shaftesbury) and held several minor governmental posts.[8] In the course of this work he became familiar with the relations between England and Ireland and was soon regarded as something of an expert in Irish affairs. Calvert became a member of the Privy Council of James I, and a member of Parliament. The King liked and trusted him and recognized his linguistic and diplomatic abilities, sending him on several missions to Ireland and to the Continent. Nothing, it seemed, could stem Calvert's rise. He was knighted in 1617 and became principal Secretary of State in 1619. It seemed most likely that he would continue in the good graces of the Crown indefinitely.

Yet, in 1625, Calvert gave up his chances of further preferment and advance—by openly avowing his Catholic faith and by leaving the Anglican church. King James, himself continually suspected of favoring Catholics, could only accept Calvert's resignation as Principal Secretary, yet he kept Calvert as a member of his Privy Council and gave him the title of Baron of Baltimore with estates in Ireland.

George Calvert had long been interested in colonization ventures in the New World with the idea of establishing a haven for Catholics in the lands far west of England. As early as 1620 he bought out English interests in Newfoundland, obtained a charter from the Crown, and attempted to set up a colony there. By 1629, however, he was forced to acknowledge the difficulties in making the colony successful in its frigid climate, and he asked the Crown for a grant of land near Virginia in North America. Since lands to the south of Virginia were not available, lands north of Virginia were ceded to the Calverts by the King of England. Virginians resented this, for they coveted the rich lands to the north and east of the Potomac River.

George Calvert, first Lord Baltimore, had made the granting of land for a colony in North America possible and had done a great deal of the preliminary planning for a settlement, yet he was not to sign the charter, nor was he to be the first Proprietor. Before the charter of Maryland (as the colony was to be named) was ready for signature, both King James and George Calvert were dead. James had died on March 27, 1625, and George Calvert died on April 15, 1632.

Negotiations were subsequently carried on between the sons of these two men. On June 20, 1632, King Charles I met with Cecil Calvert to sign a charter granting the palatinate of Maryland to the Calvert family. Cecil Calvert, second Lord Baltimore, became Maryland's first Proprietor. The new colony was named "Maryland" in honor of the Queen, Henrietta Maria.

Cecil Calvert

It remained the task of Cecil Calvert to direct the settlement of that wild American land, 3000 miles westward of England. His was the work of finding settlers and equipment and of making final plans. His also the work of extricating the expedition, once formed, from political complications in England in order to send his two ships across the Atlantic Ocean.

George and Cecil Calvert parted with some of their Yorkshire lands in order to finance the colonization venture. Many men from Scorton, the "archer's village," near Kiplin Hall in Yorkshire joined the venture to help make up the complement of workers, artisans, ladies, and gentlemen needed to settle Calvert's colony.[9]

Once the expedition had crossed the Atlantic and had established a settlement in Maryland, Cecil Calvert supervised from England the expansion of the colony for over forty years. He sometimes expressed a desire to see his American lands, yet the complex political events in England caused him to remain there to guard the Calvert family interests in both Maryland and in Britain.

Initially, he set up conditions that enabled the colonists to gain a firm foothold in their new land. The two ships carrying the first venture to America were sent off from England, their departure timed so as to arrive in Maryland early enough in the year for the colonists to plant crops, early enough to have the spring and summer months in which to build a fort and snug homes. Thus Calvert hoped his settlers

(Photograph courtesy the Enoch Pratt Free Library)

Cecil Calvert, Second Lord Baltimore, shown holding a map of Maryland, with his grandson and namesake, Cecil, son of Charles Calvert, governor of Maryland. The boy, born in Maryland, was to inherit the title but died in 1681. Portrait by Gerard Soest, court painter to Charles II.

might escape the starvation and other dangers that beset the English colony at Jamestown, just across the Potomac River from Maryland, in its early years. Obviously Calvert profited from the Virginia experience as well as from experience gained from the Calvert colonization ventures in Newfoundland.

Through the years Cecil Calvert managed to keep control of the situation in England and at the same time to guide the free men settling his Maryland colony. These men demanded more of a voice in their government than he had planned that they have, yet he was flexible enough in his viewpoint to see that he had little means of enforcing his will over possibly minor points. Had he succeeded in dictating to the free men of the colony over small matters, he might lose their loyalty and willingness to accede to certain larger demands he made on them. The perspective lent us by the passage of nearly 350 years reveals that Cecil Calvert knew how to strike a balance of power by sometimes yielding, sometimes standing firm.

The complications of early Maryland colonial government are told elsewhere and make a colorful and interesting tale. Lord Baltimore did not always manage to retain complete control of his colony. It is striking to note in those early days how just a few dozen men could take over a government, win or lose a battle, usurp control of a province. Events in England sometimes provided opportunistic men in Maryland with an excuse to take over the government for a time. The first Proprietor eventually prevailed in maintaining his claim to govern Maryland despite political turmoil in the motherland.

Cecil Calvert sent his son, Charles, to govern Maryland from 1661 to 1676. Charles returned to England in 1676, following his father's death in 1675, as the third Lord Baltimore and the second Proprietor of Maryland.

(Photograph courtesy the Enoch Pratt Free Library)

Charles Calvert (I), Third Lord Baltimore. This portrait was signed by Sir Godfrey Kneller, court painter to five English rulers.

Charles Calvert (I)

Born in 1630, Charles Calvert spent more time in Maryland than did any of the other proprietors. He first ruled the colony as its Governor, for an initial period of about fifteen years, and then returned in the dual role of Proprietor and Governor to stay in Maryland from 1679 until 1684. He maintained a lordly life style in Maryland. Charles enjoyed the social events, the hunting, the horse racing, and the sheer beauty of the Maryland countryside.

Charles was Proprietor of Maryland for forty years, from 1675 until 1715. During part of this time he was relegated to the role of landlord of Maryland and was denied his right to govern or to appoint governors to Maryland. Political upheaval in England which was reflected in Maryland caused this loss of control. He was allowed to keep his property rights and revenues, however, and lived in the hope that he might one day regain his full rights of proprietorship.

He also had problems closer to home. His son and heir, Benedict Leonard Calvert, in 1713 announced that he was leaving the Catholic Church and intended to join the Church of England. It is not difficult to see why Benedict Leonard made this decision. Political events in England clearly indicated that a move to the Established Church would meet with great approval. Catholics could not expect to be granted restoration of lands, of powers, or to obtain favors from the government.

The old Lord Baltimore died in England, a staunch Catholic, at the age of 77 in 1715. He had led a full life, married four times, and enjoyed many years of good living.

Benedict Leonard Calvert

Benedict Leonard Calvert, third Proprietor, fourth Lord Baltimore, also led a most interesting life. His actions had a definite impact on the relationship between the proprietary of Maryland and the British

(Photograph courtesy the Enoch Pratt Free Library)

Benedict Leonard Calvert, Fourth Lord Baltimore. Portrait a copy by Boris Luban of the original picture, artist unknown, in the Enoch Pratt Free Library.

government. His cursory treatment by historians may be due to the fact that, after an exceedingly long wait for it, he held his title (and the proprietorship) for only a few months.

Benedict Leonard married in 1698/9 a granddaughter of Charles II. His bride, Charlotte, was the daughter of Edward Henry (Lee), 1st Earl of Lichfield by Lady Charlotte Fitzroy, an illegitimate daughter of Charles II and of "the superb and voluptuous" Barbara Palmer, as that lady was described by Macaulay.[10] (Portraits of Charlotte Lee Calvert and of her father remain on the walls of Kiplin Hall today, as they have for well over two hundred years.) This marriage between Benedict Leonard and Charlotte obviously connected the Calvert family with members of the powerful English aristocracy.

After six years of marriage and seven children, Charlotte and Benedict Leonard separated in 1705.[11]

As noted earlier, late in the reign of Queen Anne (1702–1714) Benedict Leonard converted to the Church of England. With the death of Charles, third Baron, the proprietorship of the province of Maryland was abruptly restored to his son the Anglican, Benedict Leonard Calvert, by Queen Anne's successor, King George I (1714–1727).

Benedict Leonard enjoyed the title of fourth Baron of Baltimore and Proprietor of Maryland for only a few weeks before his death in 1715.

Charles Calvert (II)

Charles Calvert, fifth Lord Baltimore and fourth Proprietor of Maryland, was born in 1699. He was spared the long wait for his title which his father had endured, for Charles inherited his title at the age of sixteen. He was Maryland's Proprietor for over thirty-five years. He, too, experienced marital difficulties, as we shall see in the following chapter, yet his was a rich existence, always close to the Prince of Wales, and always busy with many posts and properties.

[1]John B. C. Nicklin, "The Calvert Family," *Maryland Historical Magazine*, 16:1 (March, 1921), p. 50; James W. Foster, "George Calvert: His Yorkshire Boyhood," *Maryland Historical Magazine*, 55:4, (December, 1960), pp. 261–274.
[2]Foster, p. 263.
[3]Foster, p. 264. Also, John G. Morris, *The Lords Baltimore* (Baltimore: Maryland Historical Society, 1874), p. 7, in which Morris gives her name as "Alicia Crossland."
[4]Foster, p. 264.
[5]Ibid, p. 266.
[6]G. Bernard Wood, "Kiplin: Birthplace of Maryland," *Historic Homes of Yorkshire* (London: Oliver & Boyd, 1957), p. 78.
[7]Clayton C. Hall, *The Lords Baltimore and the Maryland Palatinate* (Baltimore: Nunn, 1904), p. 7.
[8]Ibid, p. 8.
[9]Wood, p. 78.
[10]Hall, p. 22.
[11]After the death of the fourth Lord Baltimore, his widow, Charlotte, traveled abroad where she met and married one Christopher Crowe. Crowe was "so enraptured with Kiplin [Hall] that in 1722 he bought the place from his stepson, Charles, for 7,000 pounds." G. Bernard Wood, "Kiplin," *Yorkshire Illustrated Magazine,* Vol. 11 (July, 1950), p. 14.

CHAPTER II

FREDERICK CALVERT

Upon his father's death in 1751, Frederick Calvert, the sixth Baron of Baltimore, inherited both a title and a great fortune. The fortune was a complex one involving English securities and English lands plus the palatinate of Maryland with its land, incomes, and prerogatives. Maryland was an important part of Calvert's inheritance with substantial annual incomes and miles of unsold lands.[1]

The colony had been established early in the seventeenth century to provide a refuge for Catholics and to serve as a commercial venture as well. The freedom of worship for Catholics lasted only a few years but the expectations for a successful colonial commercial venture fared better.

Maryland's fifth Proprietor, Frederick Calvert, inherited princely powers of government under the terms of the Maryland Charter of 1633. The Proprietor owned all the land and had all executive and judicial powers, and all writs were issued in his name. He appointed the governors of Maryland, the members of the governors' councils, and the magistrates. Further, the Proprietor was empowered to establish courts in Maryland, to set up ports of entry, and to appoint officials to collect duties and fees. The Proprietor could raise an armed force and could declare martial law. Finally, the Proprietor was the last court of appeal.[2]

The English crown exacted only ceremonial taxation from Maryland. The only two checks placed upon the power of the Proprietor were that the laws of the colony should resemble those of England and that Marylanders, free men gathered in an Assembly, must assent to the laws of the province.[3] Maryland men took very seriously this right to assist in the governing

(Photograph courtesy the Enoch Pratt Free Library)

Charles Calvert (II), Fifth Lord Baltimore. This portrait is believed to have been painted by Allan Ramsay, court painter to King George III.

process as it ensued, for despite the property requirements that had to be met in order to vote, a substantial number of men were able to do so. The council members made up the upper house of the Maryland Assembly, the free men the lower house. As the colony grew, not all free men attended Assembly sessions, but sent delegates instead. As the years passed, the lower house of the Assembly gained political leverage by holding the right to approve laws and funds. The lower house claimed, as well, the right to set fees and taxes and this proved to be a continual point of friction between the lower house and the proprietary.[4]

The proprietary garnered income from quitrents, land sales, and tonnage duties. Charles Albro Barker, has shown that the later lord proprietors would have had a much less luxurious mode of living without their personal revenues from Maryland.[5] Barker noted that: "In return for the privilege of being the tenant-in-chief of Maryland, the lord proprietor received, during the years from 1768 to 1774 inclusive, a net income of £10,267 in sterling exchange payable in London."[6]

Charles Calvert, fifth Lord Baltimore and fourth Proprietor of Maryland, also left to his son, Frederick, family lands located near Epsom, England, large holdings in the form of investments in Bank of England stocks and similar conservative securities.

In his will Charles Calvert removed his Irish lands from the inheritance that devolved to Frederick Calvert, choosing to leave those lands and incomes to a Mrs. Cecil Brossan and her two sons, Charles and Augustine. His London townhouse and a block of securities went to Jane Nowton, another mistress.[7]

To his legal heirs, his wife, his son Frederick, and his two daughters, Louisa and Caroline, he left the remainder of the huge Calvert fortune.

It would have been difficult to see how such great inherited wealth and secure social standing could be

(Photograph courtesy Florence M. and Pamela V. Harford)

Hester Rhelan of the Kingdom of Ireland. She was the mother of Henry Harford, last Proprietor of Maryland. The artist is unknown.

appreciably diminished in the sixth Baron's lifetime. By the time of his father's death, Frederick had long since left Eton College and was eager to travel and enjoy his title and wealth.[8]

At twenty-one years of age Frederick Calvert gained control of his great fortune and in that same year married Diana Egerton, daughter of Scrope (Egerton) first Duke of Bridgewater. With suitable pomp and display the wedding took place on March 9, 1753.[9] The marriage produced no children and, in fact, "due to a helpless disagreement of temper . . ." the couple lived separately much of the time.[10] In the summer of 1758 Lady Baltimore and her husband went "for an airing" in an open carriage. There was an accident and Lady Baltimore was thrown from the phaeton. She died shortly thereafter.[11]

Prior to Lady Baltimore's death, a male child was born to Frederick Calvert and an Irish girl, Hester Rhelan, in London, April 5, 1758. The boy was named Henry Harford.[12] He was to be Frederick Calvert's only son. (Frederick Calvert, incidentally, did not marry again so had no legitimate children.) On November 28, 1759, another child was born to Frederick Calvert and Hester Rhelan "Harford," and named Frances Mary Harford.[13] Though he was to take other mistresses in the next few years, Frederick Calvert continued to arrange for the care and support of Hester Rhelan and these two children.[14] (Two mistresses followed, each bearing Lord Baltimore two female children.)

Lord Baltimore enjoyed traveling throughout the Continent and the Near East with his entourage of a mistress, their children, and several servants. He spent considerable time writing ungrammatical poetry and travelogues which, however elaborately printed, bound, and dedicated, aroused only merriment at his expense from the critics of the day.[15]

In England late in 1767 and at odds with his current mistress, Frederick Calvert's eye chanced upon a love-

(Frick Art Reference Library and courtesy the Enoch Pratt Free Library)
Frederick Calvert, Sixth Lord Baltimore. The portrait shows him with books, paper, and a pen to indicate his desire to be remembered as a literary figure. It was painted by Johann Ludwig Tietz of Germany.

ly young woman who ran a small millinery establishment in Epsom, the town outside London which was near the Calvert family estate, Woodcote Park. Her name was Sarah Woodcock, a respectable young woman, who was engaged to be married.

With the aid of disreputable servants Lord Baltimore abducted Mistress Woodcock and seduced her, after several nights of terror in his mansion. Her father engaged legal assistance and sued Lord Baltimore. The trial for rape was widely reported in the journals of the day, and Baltimore's reputation, none too good at this point in any case, was irretrievably ruined. Public opinion of Lord Baltimore's attack upon the young woman declared that it was "an atrocious act of seduction, and the conviction of his guilt was universal."[16] Frederick Calvert addressed the court with "quite a pretty speech for a man universally known to be one of the most licentious of his times."[17] Accounts of the times agree that all that saved Baltimore from conviction was the fact that, having lost her virginity and her reputation, Sarah Woodcock had vacillated in her attempts to escape him.[18] Set free by an acquittal, March 26, 1768, Lord Baltimore quickly prepared to leave England to live on the Continent and escape the opprobrium of English society.

The news of Lord Baltimore's trial for the crime of rape traveled quickly to Maryland in spite of measures taken there to suppress it. Governor Sharpe forbade the printer of the *Maryland Gazette* to publish any account of the trial, but papers in Pennsylvania and other northern colonies provided Marylanders with the full particulars of the sordid adventures of the Proprietor of Maryland.[19] The scandal engendered by the trial confirmed Maryland residents in their poor opinion of their hedonistic Proprietor. His relations with his province up to this time (1768) had in any case furnished Marylanders with little grounds for affection or loyalty toward him.[20]

(From an old print)

Woodcote Park, a Calvert family home near Epsom, Surrey, England.

The estrangement between Maryland residents and the sixth Baron was rooted in a long-standing anti-proprietary movement, yet it was Frederick Calvert's flagrant disinterest in the welfare of the people of the province, his only too-obvious greed, and his mismanagement of provincial affairs that greatly increased tensions between Maryland provincials and the proprietary government. By his behavior the sixth Lord Baltimore loosened ties of loyalty and habit that had bound Marylanders to the proprietary and to England.

During his tenure as Proprietor, Frederick Calvert refused to face issues in Maryland. He let provincial business await his pleasure as he paraded across Europe.[21] During the French and Indian War he exhibited a parsimonious attitude that created much criticism in Maryland.[22] In this same vein, Frederick Calvert sold off his Maryland lands in such a way as to demonstrate his greed and his lack of interest in the province.[23] Unwise appointments of unsuitable men as clergy to Church of England parishes in Maryland likewise revealed Baltimore's greed and and carelessness.[24]

Although once mildly interested in coming to Maryland, if only to attend to his financial interests, Lord Baltimore did not make that journey, thus neglecting an opportunity to build personal connections in the palatinate and to impress some of his provincial planters.[25]

Baltimore obviously wished only to continue a profitable status quo without the expenditure of effort on his part. He refused to allow Maryland to have an agent in England to represent provincial interests, and he failed to oppose measures himself that would not be in the interest of Maryland. Even his governor, Horatio Sharpe, remonstrated with him for failing to oppose the Stamp Act, for example.[26]

It is not surprising, then, that the leaders of the people of Maryland felt less and less loyalty to their Proprietor. The hostile climate generated by Frederick

Calvert was to make it impossible for his son (Henry Harford) to obtain recompense later for proprietary lands confiscated by the Maryland legislature during the Revolution.

The Anti-Proprietary Movement

The beginning of the anti-proprietary movement started with the assembly of 1739. At that time new members of the House of Delegates drew up a formidable catalogue of grievances asserting that the fee proclamation of 1733 violated the Maryland charter; the one-shilling duty of 1704 imposed for the support of the governor was illegal; the tonnage duties collected for his lordship's privy purse operated under lapsed legislation; the collection of alienation fines on land sales was contrary to the terms of the Maryland land grant system; the selling of clerkships tended to ruin the province; and the collection of naval officers' fees in gold and silver was a violation of the paper-money law. As a token of their determination to correct these grievances, the delegates of the assembly of 1739 voted to appeal their case to the king.[27]

During the following years the tensions between the proprietary and the House continued to erupt periodically. Barker in *The Background of the Revolution in Maryland* traces these contests between the government of the Proprietor and the House of Delegates in detail. These tensions, then, existed before Frederick Calvert became Proprietor. When he took over the reins of Maryland's government neither proprietary nor provincial attitudes were altered in any significant way.[28] As the sixth Baron's tenure as Proprietor proceeded, however, he greatly increased the existing tensions. Even the capable governor, Horatio Sharpe, appointed by Frederick Calvert, was not able to conceal from the people of Maryland the fact that their Proprietor was not interested in their welfare, but rather was concerned only with his own.

The Proprietor Neglected Provincial Affairs

Marylanders soon discovered that their Proprietor paid little attention to the business of governing his palatinate, preferring to spend his time wandering about Europe in search of amusement. Cecilius Calvert, the principal Secretary of the province, in letters from England to Horatio Sharpe in the 1760s, was often forced to admit that he had not heard from Lord Baltimore for weeks, even months, nor was he always certain of the sixth Baron's whereabouts. The Secretary had great difficulty in obtaining answers to questions about provincial affairs from Baltimore.[29] Many matters had to await Lord Baltimore's attention. This naturally did little to endear him to Maryland men inconvenienced by these delays.

Baltimore Careless of the Security of Colonists.

The behavior of the sixth Baron during the progress of the French and Indian War was yet another sore point in the relations between the Proprietor and the province. During the early 1760s Maryland lands to the west were under attack by parties of French and Indian allies. Settlers not murdered by the attackers retreated eastward. Others withdrew to the little western frontier town of Frederick. Even this stronghold was saved only at the last possible moment at one juncture by the arrival of munitions and supplies.[30] Some were so terrorized that they fled all the way to Baltimore and rushed aboard ships in the harbor. Yet Lord Baltimore flatly refused, even in the face of the obvious need for stronger defenses of the frontier, to allow his manor and reserved lands in Maryland to be taxed for funds to help pay expenses incurred in the defense of the province. Governor Sharpe, coping with the situation despite the lack of adequate funds, was eventually forced by sheer military necessity to tax these lands, acting in opposition to the specific instructions of the Proprietor.[31]

The war ended in 1763, but Marylanders did not forget the Proprietor's stingy attitude and his lack of concern for their safety during that conflict.

Rapid Sale of Proprietary Lands.

The manner in which Frederick Calvert sold off proprietary lands in Maryland was yet another factor in the widening breach between the Proprietor and the people of Maryland. True, the sale of land in Maryland, and of patents to take up land, had long been a respectable and major source of income for the proprietary family, but the sixth Baron planned a rapid and wholesale relinquishment of land on a very large scale indeed. He exhibited little interest in the welfare of the persons planning to invest in the manor and reserve lands he offered for sale.

In 1766, Lord Baltimore authorized Governor Sharpe, Daniel Dulany, and a Mr. Jordan, to sell all his manor lands and other tracts in Maryland. The land sales commissioners accordingly immediately advertised in the *Maryland Gazette,* offering large tracts in the various counties for sale. This represented an acreage, according to J. Thomas Scharf, 19th-century historian, of about three hundred thousand acres. A large part of this land was sold; indeed the market was saturated with land.[32]

Frederick Calvert's intention was plain to members of the Maryland gentry. He was determined to exploit the province in a greedy and impatient manner in order to place pounds in his pocket. Scharf comments that this peremptory disposal of the proprietary estates, completed to a large extent by 1769," . . . had broken almost the last link between the Calverts and Maryland."[33]

In spite of the sixth Baron's best efforts to sell off his American acres, close to a quarter of a million acres of land were left unsold. This land represented a financial reserve and an important source of future income to the proprietary family.[34]

Inappropriate Church of England Appointments.

A continual grievance against Frederick Calvert during his proprietorship resulted from his penchant for making wildly inappropriate appointments of ministers to Church of England parishes in the province. All taxpayers, regardless of their religious affiliation, were required to pay a poll tax to support the Anglican Church and its ministers. There were a great many non-Anglican Marylanders. In spite of the fact that the Established Church had the weight of both the Proprietor and the English government behind it, it was unpopular in Maryland.

By the 1770s, "Complaints filled the *Maryland Gazette,* describing the corruption and the lack of divine reverence among the ministers. Some of the clerics' actions were so patently vile that even the Dulanys (entrenched in high office in the proprietary government) denounced them."[35] The issue of his appointment of such clergymen was not forgotten in Maryland after the American Revolution. The hostility Frederick Calvert generated via these appointments made Harford's attempts to gain support in Maryland vastly difficult.

Baltimore's Lack of Personal Contact with Maryland.

Frederick Calvert never visited Maryland. This absence of their landlord had its effect on Maryland public opinion, making obvious the fact that he had little interest in his province. One might argue, on the other hand, that had Maryland leaders had the opportunity to know Calvert they might well have been repulsed and disgusted by the decadent Lord Baltimore. In both Pennsylvania and Virginia, however, such personal interest and presence did benefit heirs of those proprietors after the Revolution. In any case, Frederick Calvert did not come to Maryland.

At one point the languid sixth Baron's concern for his purse very nearly overcame his inertia. It has generally been believed that he never so much as considered such a visit, yet one of Secretary Calvert's letters from London to Governor Sharpe, dated July 3, 1765, tells us that the matter was under discussion.

Lord Baltimore, the Secretary wrote, was most dissatisfied with the way in which his Maryland business affairs were being taken care of and that Frederick Calvert was thinking of sending someone to look into the matter, ". . . or else, to visit the province himself, and this next spring; the latter he seems greatly inclined to do. . . ." The Secretary promised to advise Sharpe should this plan materialize (it did not).[36] The aborted journey reveals that Lord Baltimore was both concerned for his income and yet too indolent to attend to its source.

Calvert confined his interest in Marylanders to those officers serving his interests. He communicated with his men in Maryland in a tone of lordly paternalism, sending, for example, a full-length portrait of himself to Maryland in 1765. In a letter to Governor Sharpe, dated February 16, 1767, he commented that he was very happy at the harmony between himself and the upper house of the Assembly (the Council). These men, he confided to Sharpe, he regarded:

> More like the House of Peers in this country, as the middle part of Legislature, to prevent the Lower House with their democratic spirit from destroying the present happy Establishment, sanctified by experience and the Pattern of their Mother Country, whose Constitution and government is by all the world admired . . . I look upon the Upper House of the Assembly in Maryland as composed of the Wisest men of the Province. . . .

Frederick Calvert went on to express his recognition of the tension between the House of Delegates and the proprietary government by criticizing the Lower House and the unruly "Sons of Liberty."[37] (The Sons of Liberty was an organization formed throughout the colonies in the latter months of 1765 dedicated to forcing a repeal of the Stamp Act of 1765. This was a small but vociferous group in Maryland.)[38]

Even in his communications with his own men in Maryland, Lord Baltimore showed an interest only in obtaining a tame acquiescence to all his policies and to those of Parliament. This would allow the status quo to continue in Maryland, along with the stable conditions that caused well over £10,000 sterling a year to flow into the sixth Baron's purse.[39]

With good reason both the Proprietor's men and the anti-proprietary leaders believed that Lord Baltimore had not bothered to exert influence in England on members of Parliament in an effort to prevent the passage of the Stamp Act of 1765.[40]

Maryland men had long wanted to have an agent in London to represent their interests in that capital. Since Lord Baltimore had refused to allow this, they were forced to depend on him to bring Maryland interests to the notice of Parliament, and this duty he regularly neglected.

More and more in the 1760s and 1770s, the House of Delegates in the province found itself drawn into a position of opposition to both the proprietary government and to the British Parliament. As historian Scharf has remarked:

> . . . the idea of resisting by all lawful means all encroachments by that body (Parliament) upon their chartered privileges or their birthright of English freemen, grew stubbornly fixed in their minds. The restraining influences—personal affection for the proprietary, and the conviction that his welfare was identical with their own—were wanting; for in Baron Frederick they saw nothing but selfishness, rapacity, and indifference to their interests. . . .[41]

A Combination of Factors That Alienated Maryland Men From the Proprietor and Their Implications

Frederick Calvert managed to engender an ever-growing alienation between Maryland men and himself. He did this in several ways: by paying little attention to the business of the province and to the welfare of its inhabitants, and by demonstrating his carelessness for the safety of Marylanders in refusing to allow his lands in Maryland to be taxed to help provide funds for defense against French and Indian raiders. He sold off Calvert lands in Maryland in a way that revealed an obvious desire to invest neither time, money, nor interest in Maryland, showing a wish only to withdraw from the province, taking with him all the cash that he could raise. The unsuitable Church of England appointments which the Proprietor made, again demonstrated his rapacity and insensitivity to the welfare of the palatinate. He could have made, perhaps, important friendships in Maryland had he visited the province but he did not make the journey. In neglecting to represent Maryland by objecting to the Stamp Act of 1765, and by refusing to allow the province an agent in London, he again showed his indifference to the colony. All of these factors, plus his own regrettable reputation made him a man the provincials could hardly admire. With such a marked lack of loyalty demonstrated by the Proprietor to his American province, there was little reason for the provincials to be loyal to him.

There was, as well, the fact that Maryland men tended to think of the proprietary and Parliament as being linked, as indeed they were. This served more and more to cause the two governments to be considered common opponents and oppressors of the inhabitants of Maryland.

The estrangement between Maryland men and the Proprietor created, first, a climate in the 1770s conducive to allowing Maryland more easily to join with the other American colonies in rebelling against Britain, despite the provincials' conservative and legalistic cast of mind. Secondly, the Maryland inhabitants' disillusionment with their Proprietor placed great obstacles in the way of Henry Harford in his post-Revolutionary efforts to regain control of property that had belonged to the proprietary in Maryland.

[1] Will of Charles Calvert, fifth Lord Baltimore, Manuscripts Section, Maryland Historical Society, MS#174. Calvert Papers, microfilm roll 2, "Executor's Account of Charles, Lord Baltimore Estate," Manuscript Division, Maryland Historical Society, MS#480 and MS#481.
[2] Lois Carr and David Jordan, *Maryland's Revolution of Government: 1689–1692*, (Ithaca, N.Y.: Cornell University Press, 1974), p. 4; Matthew Page Andrews, *History of Maryland: Province and State* (Hatboro, Penna: Tradition Press, 1965, a facsimile reprint of the 1929 edition), p. 18; Ronald Hoffman, *A Spirit of Dissension* (Baltimore: Johns Hopkins University Press, 1973), pp. 46, 155–158.
[3] Charles Albro Barker, *The Background of the Revolution in Maryland* (New Haven: Yale University Press, 1940), pp. 118–122.
[4] Aubrey C. Land, "Provincial Maryland," *Maryland: A History, 1632–1974* (Baltimore: Maryland Historical Society, 1974), p. 46; Barker, pp. 155–157.
[5] Barker, p. 153.
[6] Ibid, p. 141.
[7] Will of Charles, fifth Lord Baltimore, MHS, MS#174.
[8] Calvert Papers, MHS, "Executor's Account . . . ," MS#480 and MS#481.
[9] Charles Browning, *An Appeal to the Citizens of Maryland* (Baltimore: n.p., 1821), p. 1.
[10] Richard J. Cox, "Notes on Maryland Historical Society Manuscript Collections: Some Personal Letters of Frederick Calvert, Last Lord Baltimore," *Maryland Historical Magazine,* 70:1 (Spring 1975), p. 103.
[11] *Archives of Maryland,* Vol. 31. Cecilius Calvert to Governor Horatio Sharpe, November 27, 1758, from London, p. 506.
[12] Lord Baltimore, Act (Estate Act of 1781), 21 George III, House of Lords, London, p. 30. Hereinafter, Estate Act of 1781.
[13] *English Consistory Reports, 1788–1821, Harford v. Morris,* pp. 792–797. Copies of this extract of the case are in the vertical files, MS Div., Maryland Historical Society, under the date of December 2, 1776., p. 792.
[14] *The Calvert Papers,* 3 vols. (Baltimore: Maryland Historical Society, 1889), II:216–220.
[15] *Gentleman's Magazine,* Vol. 41 (1771), p. 566; John G. Morris, *The Lords Baltimore* (Baltimore: Maryland Historical Society, 1874), pp. 54–58.
[16] Morris, pp. 53, 54.
[17] Ibid.
[18] *Gentleman's Magazine,* Vol. 38 (April, 1768), p. 187.
[19] Cox, p. 100.
[20] Ibid, pp. 98, 99.
[21] *Archives of Maryland,* Vol. 31, pp. 530–567.
[22] Land, p. 49.
[23] J. Thomas Scharf, *History of Maryland,* 3 vols., (Hatboro, Penna.: Tradition Press, 1967, facsimile reprint of the 1879 edition), II:45; Barker, p. 265.
[24] Sidney Charles Bolton, "The Anglican Church in Maryland Politics," (Master's thesis, University of Wisconsin, 1968), chapter 2.
[25] *Archives of Maryland,* Vol. 31, p. 564.
[26] Richard Walsh, "The Era of the Revolution," *Maryland: A History 1632–1974,* (Baltimore: Maryland Historical Society, 1974), pp. 68, 69.
[27] Barker, 223–230; Land, p. 45.
[28] Land, p. 47.
[29] *Archives of Maryland,* Vol. 31, pp. 530–567.
[30] Land, pp. 48, 49; Andrews, p. 253.
[31] Land, p. 49.
[32] Scharf, II:104.
[33] Scharf, II:45; Barker, p. 265.

[34]Browning, *An Appeal* . . . , pp. 78, 79; Scharf lists in his *History of Maryland,* Vol. II, pp. 104, 150, manors remaining undisposed of up to the time of the Declaration of Independence:

"Monocacy manor, and the reserves thereon as returned by the surveyor of Frederick county, 13,148 acres; Kent manor, Kent county, 3,018 acres; Gunpowder manor, Harford county, 5,603 acres; Queen Anne manor, Queen Anne's county, 4,322 acres; Nanticoke manor, Dorchester county, 4,777 acres; Woolsey manor, Dorchester county, 3,131 acres; Mill manor, Dochester county, 1,667 acres; Wicomico manor, Worcester county, 5,950 acres; Anne Arundel manor, Anne Arundel county, 301 acres; Chaptico manor, St. Mary's county, 6,110 acres; Beaver Dam manor, St. Mary's county, 7,680 acres; West St. Mary's and St. Mary's manors, St. Mary's county, 1,370 acres; Snow Hill, St. John, and St. Barnabas manors, Somerset county, 774 acres; Calverton manor, Charles county, 3,412 acres; Pangaiah manor, Charles county, 5,304 acres; Elk North and East manors, Cecil county, 3,976 acres. These last two manors were laid out for 6,000 acres each, and it is believed they were not less than that amount. Samuel Chase and John Churchman purchased two tracts of land in Cecil county, each 10,000 acres. My Lady's two manors and reserves, Baltimore county, 45,000 acres. My Lord's two manors and reserves, westward of Fort Cumberland, Alleghany county, 125,130 acres. The reserves within five miles of Annapolis."

[35]Bolton, Chapter 2.
[36]*Archives of Maryland,* Vol. 31, p. 564.
[37]Lady Matilda Ridout Edgar, *A Colonial Governor in Maryland* (London: Longmans, Green and Co., 1912), p. 228.
[38]Hoffman, pp. 38, 39.
[39]Barker, p. 143; Hoffman, p. 45.
[40]Walsh, pp. 68-69.
[41]Scharf, I:502.

CHAPTER III

THE SIXTH BARON ACTS TO REMOVE LEGAL OBSTACLES TO HARFORD'S ASSUMING THE PROPRIETORSHIP

It is curious that it was Henry Harford who gained the proprietorship of Maryland and the bulk of the Calvert fortune, rather than the legitimately-born descendants of the Calverts. Barring his way to the proprietorship was both the entail on Maryland and the explicit terms of the will of the fifth Baron of Baltimore. How, then, did Harford, Lord Baltimore's illegitimate child, gain possession of both the province and a fortune? Harford was able to do this, thanks to certain legal maneuvers carried out by his father, the placement of a well-instructed governor in Maryland by Lord Baltimore, and the way in which the sixth Baron wrote his will.

The Barring of the Entail on Maryland

While still only in his twenties, Frederick Calvert, caught in a tempestuous and childless marriage, decided to break the entail on Maryland. The birth of a legal heir seemed unlikely. He wanted the right to will the province, its prerogatives and incomes, to whomever he pleased.

First, he applied to Parliament for relief from the entail, but that body failed to honor his petition.[1] Next, he attempted to bar the entail by executing deeds of conveyance, on January 2, 1761.[2] Deeds of conveyances were legal expedients used to negate, to "break," entails. Property under the entail was first deeded to a "straw" person, that is, a person with no intention of actually owning the property. This person then deeded the property back to the original owner. Now the original owner held the property, not under an entail, but in fee simple and could will it to whomever he liked.

Obviously, Frederick Calvert was determined, as demonstrated by these legal actions, that neither of his sisters, Louisa or Caroline, should inherit the province. He lacked legal heirs, but the birth of his son, Henry Harford, on April 5, 1758, and the birth of a daughter, Frances Mary Harford, on November 28, 1759, gave him children. He resolved to leave Maryland's proprietorship to his son, and should that son die, then to his daughter.[3]

One might wonder why Calvert did not simply legitimatize his children and so remove all problems connected with leaving them the money-producing palatinate. The answer is that there was no method of doing this under eighteenth-century English law. Had Lord Baltimore decided to marry Hester Rhelan, after the death of his wife, even this would not have made the children born prior to the marriage legitimate. Nor was there as yet in England a legally recognized process of adoption. A way must be found, the sixth Baron decided, to completely bar the entail on Maryland.

Early in the spring of 1763 Lord Baltimore, to further legalize his plan to leave the province to Harford, directed Secretary Calvert to send deeds of conveyance to Maryland with instructions to Governor Sharpe to store and register them in Maryland, the "Deed on Record in the Office of the Council of State, there to remain Both to be produced on Emergency. . . ."[4] The "both" referred to the deed of conveyance and the letter of instruction from Lord Baltimore dated February 4, 1761, designating Harford as the next Proprietor.

The Secretary's letter of March 1, 1763, to Sharpe, read in part:

> ... By this opportunity I transmit a Deed of real Consequence Between Lord Baltimore and me and of and concerning the Province, as it may happen in right of Succession to the Province on Demise; with regard only to me in Case his Lordship died without Male Issue Legal Born.[5]

Secretary Calvert instructed Sharpe that should Frederick Calvert die without legal issue, his natural son, Henry Harford, was to be proclaimed Proprietor of Maryland. The deeds of conveyance, as described above, barred the entail and conveyed the province in fee simple to Harford. That the province was so devisable Secretary Calvert explained in the letter, saying:

> ... I am of opinion and confirmed by his Lawyer here whom I let see the late Lord's Charles Calvert, fifth Baron of Baltimore Marriage Articles, he says 'tis plain the Late Lord was only Tenant for Life, the present Frederick Calvert, sixth Baron of Baltimore in fee, makes the Late Lord's Land Legacy invalid.[6]

Still, not satisfied that even these measures would stand up to a determined legal suit over the proprietorship of Maryland, Lord Baltimore proceeded to suffer a "common recovery," which he registered in the provincial court of Maryland in 1767. A common recovery, according to Holdsworth, was a way that tenants in tail (under an entail) could evade the restriction. As Holdsworth explains:

> The expedients which were ultimately adopted to effect this purpose were the fictitious legal proceedings known as recoveries and fines ...
> ... X, a friend of A the tenant in tail, brought a writ for right in the court of Common Pleas claiming the land from A for an estate in fee simple. A voucher to warranty Y—a man of straw. Y admitted to the duty to warrant, asked to be allowed to talk the matter over out of court with X, and then departed in contempt of court. X therefore recovered the land from A for an estate in fee simple—which he at once conveyed to A; and A got judgement against Y ordering him to convey to A lands of equal value. This judgement Y was wholly unable to satisfy; but the courts regarded this as immaterial—they had done their best.[7]

The process was known as early as the fifteenth century. As time passed, all this elaborate pretence was not gone through. The steps in the fictitious action were merely enrolled on the records of the court, in this case, the courts of the Province of Maryland. Only this sort of recovery completely barred the estate tail (entail). The law, *De Donis Conditionalibus,* a 1285 statute creating the estate tail, remained in effect until abolished in 1833, at which time a tenant in tail of full age could simply bar the entail and turn his estate tail into an estate in fee simple.[8]

Lord Baltimore Planned Use of the Legal Factor of Seisin

Harford was to be assisted in gaining the proprietorship by the legal factor of *seisin.* This was an English legal practice of recognizing possession of land as a point of law, a practice persisting from medieval times. A person seized of the land in question, in possession, if "of the blood" of the original owners, was sometimes thereby entitled to possess the land legally. The term, "of the blood," was understood to mean that the person in question was descended from the owner or from common ancestors.

In actual practice, and this applied in Harford's legal contest over the proprietorship, males were given preference over females, in cases of contested inheritances "unless the lands had in fact descended from a female."[9] (The person who was to contest the proprietorship was Harford's aunt, Louisa Calvert Browning.)

Knowing of the legal point involved in *seisin,* Frederick Calvert made plans, as we have noted, for the governor of Maryland to seize the province in Harford's name. This action of seizure plus the preference for males over females in questions of inheritance were both to be important points in Harford's favor.

Anomalies in British Law

English law in late eighteenth-century England often stated one thing, but in practice did quite another. For example, the statutes plainly said that estates held in tail must go to the legitimate heir. In many cases these statues were circumvented by the legal expedients just described, which barred the entail, and also by simply willing the property to an illegitimate child. This practice served admirably if the will were not contested. A natural child might inherit under still another procedure, that of a private act of Parliament. In these cases settlements were worked out between the legal heirs and the person to whom the estate was devised. The exception was then made a law.

Theoretically, under English law illegitimate children had virtually no legal existence, nor was it possible to legally adopt a child. Yet in practice these children were recognized and given consideration.

All of these anomalies in British law were to work in Harford's favor.

Frederick Calvert's Will

Frederick Calvert wrote a will designed to insure Henry Harford's future. It was a truly machiavellian document with many features intended to buy off opposition to Harford's inheritance of Maryland's proprietorship, and one which provided liberally for all the Baron's children, former mistresses, and the executors of his will. It was couched in amazingly direct language for that day, a fact made the more surprising in that the will devised a complex fortune and the entire palatinate of Maryland. Had Calvert managed his business affairs, his personal life, and his province as cleverly as he managed to write his will, his career would probably have been a far more notable one.

The sixth Baron died in Naples, September 4, 1771. His will was found among his papers there, properly signed and witnessed. It was a fourteen-page document, written in English by Lord Baltimore himself. Each page was properly signed and the final sheet witnessed by three persons. The will bore no date, but in the body of the text there was a bequest to ". . . Charlotte Hope Daughter of a certain German woman Called Elizabeth Hope of the County of Munster in Germany now an Infant of the age of two Months more or Less and born at Hamburg . . ."[10] Since the child was born in 1770, the will was written either in that year or early in 1771.[11]

"I do hereby give Devise and Limit my said Province of Maryland and all other premises there unto belonging last mentioned to unto and to the use of a certain youth called or known by the Name of Henry Harford the Son of Hester Rhelan of the Kingdom of Ireland Born in Bond Street and now of the age of Nine Years or more and to the heirs Male of his Body lawfully to be begotten. . . ."[12] This was the bequest that was to be debated for ten years following Calvert's death.

Lord Baltimore wrote a will that was an open purchase of agreement of Calvert heirs who might oppose his wishes. He left each of his sisters and their husbands—Louisa and John Browning, and Caroline and Robert Eden—a sum of £10,000 only on the condition that the sisters and their husbands execute deeds of confirmation assenting to the conditions of Calvert's will. As a further condition, Lord Baltimore specifically prohibited institution of suits of law against those persons he designated as his principal heirs.[13]

Frederick Calvert purchased able executors to act for him in carrying out the terms of his will—Robert Eden, Hugh Hammersley, Robert Morris, and Peter Prevost—by leaving each, should he accept the trust and the executorship, £100 income a year for life, plus an outright cash gift of £1,500 to each executor.[14]

An item that did not appear in the will and was perhaps performed due to a private agreement between Lord Baltimore and Peter Prevost, was the fact that Prevost was to marry Hester Rhelan "Harford." The reason behind this marriage may have been Lord Baltimore's wish, Prevost's affection for the Irish lady, or a combination of affection for her and for her annual sum of £200 devised her by Frederick Calvert's will. In any event, the marriage did take place. To provide Hester Rhelan with the annual sum, £6,700 were set aside in investments.[15]

Lord Baltimore left legacies of £2,000 each to Sophia and Elizabeth Hales, his daughters by Elizabeth Hales. The mother was allowed a choice of an outright cash payment of £1,000, or an annual payment of £50 a year.[16]

Substantial amounts of cash, then, were to be paid to Lord Baltimore's sisters, to his executors, to his various children, and mistresses. The bulk of his estate, however, he left to Henry Harford with a most substantial settlement set aside for his daughter, Frances Mary Harford. Miss Harford was to be given £30,000 in cash to be invested for her by her father's executors. Other funds were made available, too, for Henry Harford and Frances Mary Harford, to provide for their maintenance and education. Frances Mary was placed in a young ladies' boarding school, located in England, by one of the guardians, Robert Morris. He sent her notes and cards there, and took her about to balls, places of amusement, and to dinners.[17]

Frederick Calvert had written a most effective document. He designed the will to buy off opposition to his plan to make his son the Proprietor of Maryland. True, Henry Harford faced obstacles to his acquisition of the proprietorship. There was the fact of his illegitimate birth; his being a minor when his father died; the provisions of his grandfather's will in which Charles Calvert willed the province to Louisa Calvert in the event that Frederick Calvert died without legal issue, and should Louisa not be able to inherit then to Caroline; and the lingering doubts as to the legality of barring the entail on Maryland. Yet Frederick Calvert's will, that of a nobleman in the late eighteenth century, was a powerful force in Harford's favor.

Status of the Calvert Fortune in 1771

What exactly did Henry Harford inherit from his father? The spendthrift sixth Baron had managed to spend enormous sums of money in his lifetime. Lord Baltimore had sold huge tracts of land in Maryland, had cashed in securities, had frittered away much of his annual income from Maryland, and had disposed of family lands in England. Even in death the heavy expenses continued, for the transport of the sixth Baron's body back to England and subsequent burial ceremonies were costly and elaborate.[18]

There was some delay before Lord Baltimore's will was found among his papers in Naples and could be forwarded to England.[19] When, at last, the terms of the will became known there, John Browning, husband to Louisa Calvert Browning, sought legal counsel and then took up the matter of the inheritance of the province of Maryland with the English courts.[20]

Browning's request that the proprietorship be awarded to his wife by reason of the will left by her father, Charles Calvert, the fifth Baron, was impeded by the fact that his wife was not able to speak or act for herself. She had been mentally ill for some years.[21] The Brownings did have a son, however, and since the fifth Baron was his grandfather and the boy was of legitimate birth, the Browning attorneys hoped this would lend support to their case against Harford. By 1780 a commission was set up and sent to assess Louisa Browning's mental state. The commission members found that she had lucid intervals, but that these did not occur frequently enough to enable her to govern herself or her manors. Sir Cecil Wray, Baronet, and Louisa Browning's husband were appointed her guardians. John Browning continued his efforts to obtain either the proprietorship or, in lieu of that, other recompense for his wife and their son.[22]

Of the great fortune left by Charles Calvert to Frederick Calvert there remained a most valuable portion of that estate, the province of Maryland with its annual income to the Proprietor of over 10,000 pounds a year, plus approximately a quarter of a million acres of unsold land that belonged to the Proprietor. In England there remained no real estate, for, after his trial for rape, Lord Baltimore resolved to sell off every inch of land he had in England and leave the country.[23] By April 1768 most of the estates had been sold, including the family homes near Epsom.[24]

Family estates in Ireland had been placed out of the immediate reach of Frederick Calvert by the terms of his father's will, as we have seen. A court order enforced the terms of that will regarding those estates. The same held true of the Calvert town house in London.[25] One may be certain that the sixth Baron pledged away future expectations regarding these properties, since neither is shown in the formal accounting of his estate made after his death.[26]

Considerable difficulty was experienced by the executors of Frederick Calvert's estate in determining just where his personal fortune left off and where the finances of the province of Maryland began. Years went by before the accounting of the estate was completed. As finally determined, it was found that despite Calvert's frantic spending and waste a considerable and complex fortune remained.

For example, the land left unsold in Maryland represented a total value of £327,441, according to an evaluation placed on it in 1785 by Henry Harford with the aid of the executors of the estate. He was to revise this estimate later to £447,000.[27] In any case, the Maryland lands alone of the Calvert estate represented an enormous amount of money and it was the proprietorship of Maryland that was in litigation.

Even without the possession of Maryland and its incomes, however, Henry Harford became legally possessed of a great fortune. After the satisfaction of outright cash legacies and debts amounting to well over £35,500, there remained deposits and investments held in trust by the executors worth approximately £145,400.[28] Of this amount about two-thirds reverted to Henry Harford immediately and the remainder upon the demise of the recipients of various annual legacies. If Harford could assume and keep the proprietorship of Maryland, as well as this wealth from his father's personal estate, he would then be enormously rich.

In Harford's favor in his efforts to obtain the proprietorship of Maryland was his father's will, and a nobleman's will was a powerful document at the time. The great fortune Harford had inherited also would aid him in making it possible for him to employ attorneys to carry on legal defenses. Further, Frederick Calvert had brought into play for his son the machinations of the legal profession, as we have seen, to bar the entail on Maryland.

Opposed to Harford was the legal suit instituted by the Brownings. The right to the proprietorship remained in question as the suit wended its way through the ponderous machinery of the courts of England. With the outbreak of the American Revolution the Lord Chancellor refused to hear the Browning-Harford case further until the outcome of the conflict was determined. Even if the English should lose the American revolution, however, there would still be good reason to continue the court battle, albeit on different terms, because there yet remained the matter of revenues collected from Maryland since the death of Frederick Calvert in 1771. There was also a very good chance that after the Revolution, land and other property might be salvaged by an ex-Proprietor.

The question as to whether Harford (with his illegitimate birth and his lack of a title) could make legal claim to the province, remained open at this point.

[1] Charles Browning, *An Appeal to the Citizens of Maryland* (Baltimore: n.p., 1821), p. 1. "Frederick, Lord Baltimore, on his marriage with Lady Diana Egerton, the 9th of March, 1753, made his marriage settlement, subjected expressly to the trust for Lady Baltimore's jointure, and finding he had no way of barring the entail made an application to the British Parliament for that purpose, but failed . . ."
[2] Browning, p. 1.
[3] Frederick Calvert Will, Public Record Office, London, Ref. Prob. 8/165. See Appendix A.
[4] *Archives of Maryland,* Vol. 31, p. 537. The deed is described as being: "Inrolled in the Court of Chancery on the Back," as of 4 February 1761.
[5] Ibid., pp. 537, 538.
[6] Ibid.
[7] Sir William Holdsworth, *An Historical Introduction to the Land Law* (Oxford: Oxford University Press, 1935), pp. 55-60.
[8] Ibid.
[9] Ibid.
[10] Frederick Calvert Will, Appendix A.
[11] Ibid.
[12] Ibid.
[13] Ibid.
[14] Ibid.
[15] Ibid.
[16] Ibid.
[17] Frederick Calvert Will, Appendix A. The terms of both Frederick Calvert's will and that of his father, Charles Calvert, fifth Lord Baltimore, bring up the interesting point that the Proprietor of Maryland might very well have been a woman at this point. Since Frederick Calvert died without a legitimate child, the province was, by the terms of Charles Calvert's will, supposed to have gone to Louisa Calvert (Mrs. John Browning), the sixth Baron's sister. Under that same will should Louisa not be able to serve, then the province was to go to her younger sister, Caroline Calvert (Mrs. Robert Eden).

These two ladies were not the only females in line for the proprietorship of Maryland; there remained another, Frances Mary Harford. Under the terms of the sixth Baron's will, should Henry Harford die or be unable to assume the proprietorship, then it was to devolve upon Frances Mary Harford, his sister.

As it happened, however, Maryland was never under the direction of a female Proprietor. Henry Harford bought off the claims of both Louisa and Caroline and, further, he lived to inherit the province and to obtain the proprietorship, thus preventing his sister, Frances Mary, from being named Proprietor of Maryland.

[18] *Gentleman's Magazine,* Vol. 41 (December, 1771), p. 566, mentions the formalities attendant upon the sixth Lord Baltimore's funeral; another account of the funeral is given by W. Dorling and J. Hearns, in their book, *History of Epsom,* (London: n.p., 1825), p. 22. The account says that the interment took place, "in Epsom Church with much funeral pomp; the cavalcade extending from the church to the eastern extremity of Epsom."

It is geographically quite possible that Henry Harford attended his father's funeral, for his school at Richmond was only about ten miles distant from Epsom.
[19] This information derived from documents relating to the filing of Frederick Calvert's will for probate. These documents associated with the will are located in the Public Record Office, Chancery Lane, London, ref. Prob. 8/165.
[20] Browning, p. 5.

[21]Ibid. John Browning had been secretary to the fifth Baron, Charles Calvert. Browning married Louisa Calvert, eldest daughter of Charles Calvert. She was reported to have been "in a low and melancholy way" prior to her marriage, and her health failed before the birth of the Browning's only son, Charles. He was born in July, 1765. Louisa was placed in the care of the Reverend John Willis in Lincolnshire, the same Willis called in to treat King George III in 1788. Willis and his son were interested in the care of the insane although they were not physicians. Both were esteemed for their work.

[22]Charles Browning, *The Granting of Lands in Maryland* (Baltimore: For the Proprietor, 1825), p. 7.

[23]*Gentleman's Magazine,* Vol. 38, (April, 1768), p. 180.

[24]Gordon Home, *Epsom, Its History and Surroundings* (Epsom, n.p., 1901; republished York, England: S. R. Publishers, Ltd., 1971), p. 81; Calvert Papers, microfilm roll 2, "Executor's Account of Charles, Lord Baltimore Estate," MS Div., Maryland Historical Society, MS#480 and MS#481.

[25]Ibid.

[26]Estate Act of 1781, Record Office, House of Lords, London, p. 37.

[27]Memorial of Henry Harford and related proceedings, a broadside dated January 6, 1786, published by the Maryland House of Delegates, MS Div., vertical files, "Harford, Jan. 6, 1786," Maryland Historical Society. See Appendix B.

[28]Estate Act of 1781, pp. 37, 39.

CHAPTER IV

GOVERNOR EDEN IN MARYLAND

To understand the entire scope of Frederick Calvert's maneuvering to gain the province of Maryland for his son, we must look back to the year 1768. At that time, before the sixth Baron left England, he chose Robert Eden to replace Horatio Sharpe as the governor of Maryland. Baltimore charged Eden with the duty of furthering the claims of Henry Harford as sixth Proprietor of the province in the event of Lord Baltimore's death. The new governor was further directed by Frederick Calvert to maintain a status quo in the province, a condition that had been most profitable to the Proprietor in the past. This meant that Eden had to find ways to continue to raise money from Maryland and yet, at the same time, concede enough to the demands of the inhabitants to prevent an increase in anti-proprietary sentiments. Robert Eden had both familial and financial reasons for accepting the assignment, for he was married to Frederick Calvert's younger sister, Caroline, and he was deeply in debt.

Eden Begins His Assignment

Eden's opportunities to further Lord Baltimore's designs were bolstered by his family connections. He was not only married to a sister of the Proprietor, but he was the son of Sir Robert Eden as well. He was also young, personable, educated, and a former member of the prestigious Coldstream Guards.[1]

Governor Horatio Sharpe accepted the appointment of a new governor gracefully, his loss of office somewhat softened by messages of appreciation for his services from the Maryland gentry.[2] To the booming of a formal cannon salute, Robert Eden and his family arrived in Annapolis in June, 1769.[3] Ostensibly he was assigned the task of carrying on provincial administration, a difficult enough assignment at this particular time, but he bore as well the secret instructions regarding the succession given him by Lord Baltimore.

Eden was generally popular with the high-spirited Maryland gentry. At Government House he extended lavish hospitality and took an active interest in the society of Maryland. He often traveled about the province and was frequently on hand for the horseraces that were so well liked in Maryland.

Even though glamorous, handsome, and hospitable, the governor had his critics because his style of living offended some of the more conservative Marylanders.[4] "The governor had the reputation of being a lady's man—any lady's man—and his parties were notorious. On one occasion he threw so boisterous a drunken frolic that his wife miscarried in the ballroom. . . ."[5] Also, historian Ronald Hoffman notes:

> Eden had a penchant for lavish spending, and was mired in debt. Boucher (Jonathan Boucher, an Anglican clergyman) wrote of Eden that 'he had been in the Army, and had contracted such habits of expenses and dissipation as were fatal to his fortunes, and at length to his life . . . With an income of three or four thousand pounds a year he was always in debt.'[6]

Issues Faced by Eden

To be in a position to help Henry Harford assume the proprietorship, and to continue financial returns from Maryland to the proprietary, Eden wanted to maintain order. He would need all the support he could muster if he were to be able to carry out Lord Baltimore's instructions. When issues arose Eden had to face them by giving just enough ground to satisfy

Marylanders, yet not yield excessive financial benefits to them at the Proprietor's expense.

Soon after Eden's arrival in Annapolis, the matter arose concerning the renewal of an act to inspect tobacco and regulate the quality of exported tobacco. The lower house allowed the law to expire in November of 1769. Delegates wanted no new law put into effect unless inspection fees given officials were reinstated at either the original level or at a lower level. The members of the upper house objected. These men held most of those well-paying posts in the proprietary government which were involved in tobacco inspection. It was in their interest to obtain higher fees. Due to this deadlock, public service by proprietary officials could not legally be carried on after October 22, 1770. When an official, William Stewart, the clerk of the land office, accepted fees after the expiration of the law, he was ordered before the lower house and arrested. Robert Eden promptly prorogued the assembly and released him. The governor then reconvened the assembly but little was accomplished. A month later, Eden again prorogued the assembly and on November 26th he announced the reestablishment of the fee schedule by proclamation, which in effect continued the fees of the expired inspection act.[7]

The governor then called for a new election before the assembly of 1771, but the new assembly proved to be just as unmanageable as had the previous one. Markets for Maryland tobacco began to suffer, for due to lack of proper inspection the quality of the tobacco offered for sale declined. Only this economic pressure finally pushed the delegates into a compromise with the proprietary government in the fall session of 1773. At the November–December session a tobacco inspection measure passed both houses of the Assembly with no set fee schedule attached.[8] With regard to the effects of economic conditions on political affairs, a mature political body began to emerge in the lower house of the assembly, as historian Ronald Hoffman notes ". . . the growth of a popular political movement in

(Photograph courtesy the Maryland Historical Society)
Sir Robert Eden, Governor of Maryland.

50

Maryland came at a time when the colony's economy was undergoing a serious decline."[9]

Another issue that had caused criticism of the proprietary was met and partially solved by Eden when, late in 1773, he signed a tax bill reducing the salaries of the clergy. The payment for the support of these men had long been a point of disagreement between the proprietary and the people in Maryland. Eden's action eased tensions to some degree.[10]

Even though no final agreement had been reached between the governor and the lower house of the assembly regarding the matter of officers' fees, the province was quiet. The resolution of issues was simply postponed as similar ones had so often been in the past. The governor, it seemed, was successful in maintaining the proprietary government and continued to collect money for the Proprietor. He had not allowed the Proprietor's income to be reduced and made only enough concessions to the lower house to quiet them.

Eden Proclaims Harford as Proprietor

True to his instructions, and as soon as he learned of the death of Lord Baltimore, Eden set about securing Maryland for Henry Harford. Following the sixth Baron's demise there was considerable delay in finding the will and having it sent to England. A copy eventually was sent to London and processed through the probate courts there. Once this was done the instructions contained in the will had to be copied, letters had to be written, and the necessary legal documents had to be gathered before the formal acknowledgement of the next proprietor could be sent to Maryland.

Frederick Calvert's executors acted with decision and the proper announcements were dispatched to the province. The long sea voyage delayed matters another few weeks, but in June, 1773, Governor Eden formally announced to the assembly that Frederick,

Lord Baltimore was dead and his son, Henry Harford, was the new Proprietor of Maryland.[11] The records reveal that the assembly made no objection to this and the transition of the proprietary from Frederick Calvert to Henry Harford slipped smoothly down the throats of the assembly members. By means of this proclamation, the carrying on of the business of the province in Harford's name, and the acceptance of his proprietorship, the legal factor of *seisen* was accomplished for Harford as planned by Lord Baltimore many years before.

To further bind Maryland to Harford, Eden set about the formation of a new county to bear the name, "Harford," in honor of the new proprietor. This legislation passed the assembly before the end of 1773. To further emphasize the legitimate nature of the Calvert family connection with Harford and with Eden's government, the governor eased through that same year the naming of a county in honor of his wife, Caroline Calvert Eden, i.e., Caroline County.[12]

In the name of the new proprietor, a letter dated March 2, 1773, sent by the guardians of Henry Harford (Frederick Calvert's executors), instructed Eden to continue governing Maryland, to appoint men to office, and to collect revenues in exactly the same way as had been done under the proprietorship of Frederick Calvert.[13] Eden's continuance as Governor, too, went unopposed by the Assembly. The letter of instruction was a most impressive document bearing as it did the signatures, not only of the familiar names associated with past proprietary government but that of the Dean of Canterbury as well. Minors of the nobility were placed under the guardianship of the state and also under the protection of appointed executors. Marylanders did not question the continuation of Eden in office nor the fact that Henry Harford was proclaimed their next Proprietor.

Yet Eden, heading an administration rooted in a paternalistic system of government that was already outmoded in England, was to be unable to control or repress the growing political maturity of Maryland leaders.

An example of political awareness and maturity among the Maryland gentry is evident in the newspaper debate that arose in the pages of the *Maryland Gazette* early in 1773 between Daniel Dulany (the younger) and Charles Carroll of Carrollton. Dulany attempted to justify the fee proclamation issued by Governor Eden regarding tobacco inspection fees to be paid to provincial officials. Carroll objected, saying that Maryland's governor and upper house relied upon "prerogative power," an old-fashioned concept.[14]

The debate swelled and ranged far afield into constitutional questions. The ultimate question, and one not carried to its logical conclusion by either party, emerged as that concerning where the ultimate power of government lay—in a king and parliament or in the people themselves.[15] The Antilon-First Citizen debate, as it came to be called, indicated the legalistic turn of mind of Maryland's elite. It revealed political sophistication and political maturity missing from earlier periods of tension between the inhabitants of Maryland and the proprietary government.[16]

The Maryland gentry began to resist both proprietary and English imperial governmental pressures. Out-of-door politics began to replace the old agreements between members of the elite. Maryland members of the gentry both in and out of government began to play on the power inherent in the electorate.[17]

The Imperial Policy of Parliament

Though the proprietary government in Maryland was largely autonomous it was also inescapably linked with the government of Britain. Lord Baltimore and later his son might rule Maryland, yet both were loyal subjects of the Crown. As a result, Maryland men more and more often in the 1770s began to think of the proprietary and the English Parliament as joint opponents of the inhabitants of the province.

Adding to the anti-proprietary sentiment in Maryland and increasing political tensions was the imperial policy embarked upon by the British Parliament. Following the end of the war with France, England began a much-needed reorganization of the government of her expanded empire. An over-all plan and method was required to govern the far lands of the Empire to shape them to the needs of Britain and to provide funds for their defense. In 1763 a new ministry headed by George Grenville undertook this task. Historian Richard Walsh asserts that it was this policy which revived the anti-proprietary movement, refreshed the long struggle for local rights in Maryland, and opened the way for revolution in Maryland.[18]

Some of the measures, such as that issued by Proclamation of the King in Council, October 7, 1763, forbidding settlement across the mountains to the west, did not arouse much reaction in Maryland. People simply continued to cross the set line and move west.[19] Nor did the measures, designed to prevent a continuance of American smuggling, create much more than irritation at paper work and delay in Maryland. After all, Maryland had her cash crop, the "golden leaf." More irksome was the curtailment of paper money, especially in the months following 1763 when the colony's paper money ran out. Necessity forced further emissions under legislation worked out in 1766 and 1773.

It was the final measure of the Grenville ministry that created common cause for all and brought colonial unity: the passage of the Stamp Act.[20]

The Stamp Act was designed to provide funds for the protection of American borders. Such legislation was a common expedient for fund-raising in England, yet the Act set off a furore in the colonies. Slowly, and then with more enthusiasm, Marylanders voiced opposition to the Act and refused to use the stamps on the official papers required in many business transactions. Eventually American resistance forced the repeal of the Stamp Act. Maryland political leaders along with other American colonial leaders tasted power and success.

In Maryland even the proprietor's men objected to the Stamp Act.[21] Both the then Governor Horatio Sharpe and Attorney General Daniel Dulany wrote letters that expressed their view that the Proprietor might have exerted himself to prevent the passage of the Act and that Parliament, though having the power to rule the province, did not have an absolute power to tax it. Under English law, Dulany noted, those taxed must be represented and Maryland had no agent to represent her in England.[22]

Eden Unable to Save Maryland for the Proprietor

In the 1760s the Stamp Act had occasioned considerable out-of-door political activity in Maryland, yet it was the news of the Boston Port Act of 1774 that accelerated change and caused active resistance to be directed at both the Crown and the proprietary. Antiproprietary forces were revitalized which had an anti-imperial, anti-Parliamentary focus. Rapidly schooled by their resistance to the Stamp Act and incensed by the development in Boston, Marylanders soon learned to cooperate with other American colonies. There was a great reluctance to break with England but there was no resisting the tide of revolution that swept England's Atlantic seaboard colonies.[23]

"On June 22, 1774, a first provincial convention was held at Annapolis. Maryland had enthusiastically made the cause of Boston her own," as historian Barker notes.[24] Maryland leaders, both in and out of the House of Delegates, could see in the trend toward revolution a threat to their own class. It was imperative for their own sakes that they continue to lead Maryland politics and lead it in a property-conscious, conservative direction.[25] Though still proclaiming the hope that the differences between the colonies and England could be patched up, the Maryland Convention made preparations for a possible armed conflict.[26] More and more the extra-legal Maryland Provincial Convention took over the governing of the province.[27] By December, 1775, the Convention was meeting in an organized and orderly manner and arranging to raise money and men to resist England.[28] The Convention resisted a demand by the Continental Congress to arrest Governor Eden, rather choosing in an orderly procedure to decide that "Governor Eden's usefulness was ended, . . . he was courteously but formally and finally notified that he was at liberty to depart, which he did by boarding the warship *Fowey,* June 23, 1776. Thus from Maryland passed the power of the British Empire."[29]

The leaders of this American revolutionary movement in Maryland were much the same men aligned with the anti-proprietary movement. They may well have learned their techniques of usurpation of a legal government from the agents of the late Lord Baltimore who had taken Maryland for Henry Harford. The executors of the late lord, and Governor Eden, as we have seen, seized the proprietorship for Harford by having local officials on the scene effect that changeover, and by having familiar local authorities carry along the business of government unchanged and the populance with them. Similarly in 1775 and 1776, committees filled with faces familiar in the Maryland lower house of the Assembly seized lines of communication and the reins of government, purporting to speak for the people. The public was slow in both cases to realize that these familiar men were actually forming an extra-legal government.[30]

Eden did his best to oppose the dissolving away of his power. He attempted to form a gentlemanly militia but without much success, and he used every legal means at his disposition. Yet Eden was no Dunmore. He remained in Annapolis attending social events and keeping up the pretense that he still governed the province. The June Convention at last formally resolved to disobey the Governor.[31] After an elaborate farewell ball in Annapolis Eden left to return to England.[32] He had not been able to prevent Maryland from being swept up in the American Revolution.

Still, the fact remained that Eden had succeeded in proclaiming Henry Harford as Proprietor and had held Maryland in the name of the young Proprietor. This was later to enhance Harford's legal claim on the proprietorship in English court battles. If Harford could manage to become fully recognized as legal Proprietor, there were three possible situations promising future wealth related to his proprietorship of Maryland. First, should Britain quell the insurgents the Proprietor might return to power. Secondly, should the province be lost, there was the possibility of the Proprietor's being compensated for losses in Maryland by the British government. Finally, even though the Americans were victorious they might vouchsafe an ex-Proprietor the return of his manor lands and other recompense for his losses.

All in all, Eden had made a creditable showing in attempting to carry out Frederick Calvert's instructions. Forces that the sixth Baron could not have foreseen, and ones too large for Eden to manage, caused the collapse of proprietary government in Maryland. Eden at least had improved Harford's claim on the proprietorship.

---

[1]Bernard C. Steiner, *Life and Administration of Sir Robert Eden* (Baltimore: Johns Hopkins Press, 1898), pp. 81, 82.
[2]*Archives of Maryland,* Vol. 62, p. 4.
[3]*Maryland Gazette,* June 8, 1769.
[4]Steiner, p. 82.
[5]Ibid.
[6]Ronald Hoffman, *A Spirit of Dissension* (Baltimore: Johns Hopkins University Press, 1973), p. 123.
[7]James Haw, "Maryland Politics on the Eve of the Revolution: The Provincial Controversy, 1770–1773," *Maryland Historical Magazine,* Vol. 65 (Summer 1970), p. 127; Hoffman, p. 121.
[8]Ibid.
[9]Hoffman, p. 124.
[10]Ibid, p. 120.

[11]*Archives of Maryland,* Proceedings of the Council of Maryland, April 15, 1761–September 24, 1770. Willian Hand Browne, ed. (Baltimore: Maryland Historical Society, 1912), pp. 501–503; Matthew Page Andrews, *History of Maryland: Province and State* (New York: Doubleday, Doran & Co., 1929, later reprinted in facsimile by Tradition Press of Hatboro, Penna., 1965), p. 292.
[12]*Archives of Maryland,* Vol. 64, pp. 59–72, 115–118, 143, 198–201.
[13]Ibid.
[14]Charles Albro Barker, *The Background of the Revolution in Maryland* (New Haven: Yale University Press, 1940), pp. 353–355.
[15]*Maryland and the Empire, 1773: The Antilon—First Citizen Letters,* introduction and ed., Peter S. Onuf, (Baltimore: Johns Hopkins University Press, 1973), pp. 44–46.
[16]Hoffman, p. 103.
[17]Barker, pp. 355–356.
[18]Richard Walsh, "The Era of the Revolution," *Maryland: A History, 1632–1974* (Baltimore: Maryland Historical Society, 1974), p. 56.
[19]Walsh, p. 57.
[20]Walsh, pp. 59–60; Hoffman, pp. 50–58.
[21]Walsh, p. 60; Hoffman, pp. 30, 31.
[22]Ibid.
[23]Hoffman, pp. 181, 187, 195, 223–224; J. Thomas Scharf, *History of Maryland,* 3 vols., (Hatboro, Penna.: Tradition Press, 1967, facsimile reprint of the 1879 edition), II:161; Haw, pp. 128–129; Walsh, pp. 78, 80.
[24]Barker, p. 370.
[25]Hoffman, p. 125.
[26]Andrews, pp. 306–308.
[27]Walsh, p. 80; Hoffman, pp. 142–152; Scharf, II:183–186; Barker, pp. 370–373.
[28]Andrews, p. 311.
[29]Ibid, p. 317.
[30]David Ammerman, "Annapolis and the First Continental Congress: A Note on the Committee System in Revolutionary America," *Maryland Historical Magazine,* Vol. 66, No. 2 (Summer 1971), pp. 179–180.
[31]Scharf, II:218.
[32]Ibid.

CHAPTER V

HENRY HARFORD: HIS ENGLISH BACKGROUND

Made rich by his father's will, Henry Harford inherited, as well, good reason to expect a great deal more wealth if he could legalize his claim to the proprietorship of Maryland in the English courts, and if he could then salvage either land or recompense from Maryland after the American Revolution. His education was to be an asset to him in both of these endeavors.

Harford's English Background and Education

There is but scant information about Henry Harford's early years, and little more on the years in which he acquired his excellent education. We do know that he was raised as the tacitly acknowledged son of Lord Baltimore and was given the education of a gentleman at Eton and Oxford.

Harford was born April 5, 1758, in a Bond Street residence in London.[1] His mother was Hester Rhelan from Ireland who used the alias, "Mrs. Harford." Henry Harford was no doubt still in London when his sister, Frances Mary Harford, was born there on November 28, 1759.[2] The liaison between Harford's father and mother seems to have lasted another year or so according to letters dated 1762 and 1764, exchanged between Cecilius Calvert, Secretary of the Province of Maryland, and Lord Baltimore. The Secretary, based in England, reported to the sixth Baron that he paid various amounts to Mrs. Harford and that she and the children were well.[3] Later, while Lord Baltimore enjoyed his travels and his mistresses on the Continent and in England, his son began his

St. Martin's Parish Church, Epsom

(Courtesy the Vicar of St. Martin's Parish Church)
Here several members of the Calvert Family are buried.

education. Before the age of nine Henry Harford was sent to be schooled under the supervision of the Reverend Dr. Loxton at Richmond School. The school was situated near the former Calvert estates at Epsom and not far from his mother's residence at Mortlake, another London suburb.[4] At the age of fourteen he was ready to enter Eton College.

Henry Harford, Etonian

The years that Harford spent at Eton (1772–1775), after leaving Richmond School, were significant to his development.[5] At the beautiful old school he learned the history of England and steeped himself in English tradition. Eton was a stronghold of ancient custom and tradition. Several American youths attended Eton and later found it possible to reject loyalty to Britain learned there, but Harford took Eton's lessons in loyalty to heart. He and the other students at Eton admired King George III, who often came to the school and frequently strolled the fields nearby, stopping to chat with Eton boys. The English populace held their family-loving, hard-working king in great esteem.[6] King George took more interest in the Eton boys and the college than had any British sovereign since the time of Henry VI (who founded Eton in 1442).[7]

In no manner, then, did Harford's Eton years prepare him to reject his loyalty to his king and his country. Nor did his training there cause Harford to consider throwing in his lot with a group of rebellious English colonists, strangers three thousand miles away in Maryland.

Harford was aware of affairs outside his school, for he was called upon to sign papers relating to the province of Maryland and the court suit being waged against his claim to the proprietorship by John Browning. Harford was at Eton while the case progressed. As noted above, the case was eventually tabled by the Lord Chancellor to await the outcome of the Revolu-

(Photograph courtesy the Windsor and Eton Society)

Aerial view of Windsor and Eton. Windsor Castle with its gardens and parks lies in the foreground. Just across the Thames is Eton College and the town of Eton.

tion. Harford was kept informed of the progress of the litigation.

Harford experienced anxiety on behalf of his sister in 1772, while he was at Eton. In the spring of that year she either eloped or was kidnapped by one of her guardians, Robert Morris.[8] Morris carried the thirteen-year-old heiress off to the Continent and married her not once but twice. Harford heard of the elopement and of the pursuit of the pair by the other guardians of the Harford children. Frances Mary was eventually returned to England. Morris was disqualified to continue as one of the guardians and executors, and lost, as well, a cash bequest from Lord Baltimore's estate.[9]

Harford's Oxford Years

The month before Governor Eden left Maryland (Eden was forced to depart in June, 1776), Harford matriculated at Oxford University. He could have chosen to abandon further study upon leaving Eton, as his father had done, but Harford obviously enjoyed academic life enough to continue it. He took advantage of his opportunity to obtain an education to prepare himself to cope with his future responsibilities. Thus, in 1776 he began his university studies at Exeter College, Oxford University.[10]

When Eden reached England he no doubt visited Harford and attempted to explain the rebellion in Maryland to the young Proprietor. The matter may well have been beyond Harford's conservative nature to understand and he may have only fully expected and hoped that the English lion might place a firm paw on the uproarious colonials.

Despite uncertainties pertaining to his inheritance of the proprietorship of Maryland, and to the state of the province itself, Harford continued his studies at Oxford, taking his degree shortly before he came of age in the spring of 1779.[11]

(Author's 1974 photographs)

From Turl Street, Oxford, one may open a door and step into a quadrangle around which Exeter College, Oxford University, is located. Students live in the building shown through the archway. To the left is the College Chapel and to the right (not shown) is the great Dining Hall which fills a side of the enclosed grassy area.

A Brief Political Foray

In the year after he left Oxford, Harford turned his attention toward politics to run with a partner for a seat in Parliament for Lyme Regis, a town in southeastern England. The election ended in a "double return" (a tie) on September 9, 1780. Upon the matter being referred to the House of Commons his opponent, whose family owned a great deal of property in the district, was awarded the seat.[12] Though Harford had made a most creditable showing in his first attempt to obtain political office, the experience seems to have soured him for he did not seek office again.

He settled down, instead, in London to await the end of the American Revolution and to lead the life of a well-to-do English gentleman of means.[13] Harford spent his days attending dinners and other social events, and sat for his portrait.[14] These activities, however, took only a part of his time, for many more of his hours were occupied in sitting with his attorneys.

Harford's Proprietorship Legalized

There was a great deal at stake. Harford, Sir Robert Eden, and John Browning, spent much time making offers and counter-offers to each other and consulting with their respective attorneys. A formal document, Articles of Agreement, dated June 15, 1780, eventually emerged from their deliberations.

The three men next applied to Parliament to approve the agreement and make it law. Accordingly, the Estate Act of 1781 was drawn up.[15] This was concerned with the agreement between the three parties and was one of those private acts of Parliament used to settle cases that would otherwise outlast the participants.

The Act, engrossed on one hundred pages of parchment, first related the legal history of the ownership of Maryland, together with mention of the various marriage settlements and wills that had affected the ownership of the proprietary and the province over the years.

Frederick Calvert's will had been a thorny issue for the various attorneys, the document revealed, for it had been difficult for the courts to ascertain just what part of Frederick Calvert's remaining funds at his death were a part of his personal estate, and what part should be considered as part of the proprietorship of Maryland. John Browning at first contended that both Maryland and the funds received from the province since Lord Baltimore's death in 1771, plus incomes that might result in the future following a British suppression of the revolutionaries, belonged legally to his wife and her heir (their son, Charles Browning). In the agreement contained in the Estate Act of 1781 Browning relinquished this claim. In return Browning required payment as well as the original £10,000 willed to Louisa Calvert Browning by Frederick Calvert.

The agreement made between Henry Harford, Sir Robert Eden, and the John Brownings numbered eighteen items. In brief, the agreement provided for the payment of £22,000 to John Browning and his wife; £17,500 to the Edens of which £2,500 were to be withheld in payment of a like sum borrowed by Eden while in Maryland; and the remainder of a capital sum of £43,000 that might be left after payment of these amounts to Browning and Eden was to be paid to Harford. Further sums totaling over £17,000 were also due Harford. Each of the three parties to the agreement was to have an additional £10,000 upon Harford's being reinstated as Proprietor of Maryland. Most important was the clear title, given by the Estate Act of 1781, to Harford as the legal proprietor of Maryland.

Thus the terms of Lord Baltimore's will with only minor exceptions were fully carried out. The Estate Act of 1781 passed Parliament and with it the Articles of Agreement dated June 15, 1780.[16] Henry Harford's claim to the proprietorship of Maryland was now an entirely sound and legal one.[17]

By the fall of 1781 Harford's hope of being reinstated in Maryland by the British government vanished with the surrender of Lord Cornwallis at Yorktown, Virginia, on October 18, 1781. Still, the work involved in getting the Estate Act of 1781 passed was not wasted, for now the Court of Chancery was able to turn over to Harford, after deduction and payment of the amounts agreed upon in the Act, substantial amounts of cash and securities.[18]

Harford's fight for the proprietorship ended in financial reward. He hoped, however, that his proprietorship would render him still more financial gain, either from Maryland or from the government of Britain.

At this point, then, Harford was by no means penniless, yet he wanted even more. He waited only long enough to hear that the Paris Peace Conference was nearing an end, with an agreement between the United States and Britain, before leaving England for Maryland. Harford had more than enough money to live on for the remainder of his days, yet the way in which he was to hurry to Maryland indicates that he did not feel himself rich enough while great additional wealth lay to the west to be had for the asking. He believed that the unsold manor lands and reserve lands in Maryland belonged to him and that he should be compensated for their loss. He had reason for his expectations, for in both Pennsylvania and Virginia the heirs to the proprietary families had been compensated to a considerable extent.

[1]Will of Frederick Calvert (Appendix A); Burial Register, Parish of Bray, Record Office, Reading, England, file number D/P23/1/11.
[2]*English Consistory Report, 1788–1821* (London: n.p., n.d.), p. 792. Maryland Historical Society, MS Div., vertical files.
[3]Cecilius Calvert to Frederick, Lord Baltimore, from London. *Calvert Papers,* Vol. II (Baltimore: Maryland Historical Society, 1889) pp. 216–220.
[4]Ibid; Frederick Calvert mentions this fact in his will. See Appendix A.
[5]*Eton College Register: 1753–1790,* ed. Richard Arthur Austen-Leigh, (Eton: Spottiswoode, Ballantyne, & Co., Ltd., 1921), unpaginated, alphabetical entries. Harford entry reads simply: "Harford, 1772–1775, (Manby)."
[6]John Brooke, *King George III* (New York: McGraw-Hill Book Co., 1972), pp. 316, 317, 322.
[7]Brooke, p. 287.
[8]*English Consistory Report: 1788–1821*, p. 792; Letter of Daniel (3d) Dulany, Jr. to Walter Dulany, from London. MS. Div., Dulany Papers, filed under date, "1792."

[9] Estate Act of 1781, Record Office, House of Lords, London, p. 5; *English Consistory Report: 1788–1821*, pp. 792–797.

[10] Joseph Foster, *Alumni Oxonienses: The Members of the University of Oxford, 1715–1886* (Oxford: Parker & Co., 1887), p. 607. The entry reads:

> HARFORD, Henry, s. Frederick, of Westminster, baron, EXETER COLL., Matric. 4 May 1776, aged 18; created M.A. 10 March 1779, unduly elected M. P. Lyme Regis 1780, died Dec., 1805.

The date of Harford's death is an error. Harford died in 1834. The age mentioned in the *Oxonienses* entry affirms that Harford was born in 1758, not in 1760 as has been commonly cited to date.

[11] Ibid.

[12] "Henry Harford, Etonian," *Etoniana*, Vol. 109 (December, 1950), p. 136.

[13] Appointments Book, George Romney, as reported in *Romney* by T. H. Ward and W. Roberts (London, n.p., 1904) Vol. II, p. 71. Sittings are recorded for February 8, 15, 22, 29, and for March 7, 15, 1780; December, 3, 10, 14, 21, 1781; July 6, 10, and on November 4, and 9 of 1782; November 10, and 14, 1783. Also, "Notes and Queries, Portrait of Miss Harford," *Maryland Historical Magazine,* Vol. 35, No. 1, p. 87.

[14] Ibid.

[15] It is to be regretted that the Estate Act of 1781 has escaped mention in Maryland histories. Historians might well have benefitted from its full history of the ownership of Maryland; from an accounting of the estate of Frederick Calvert, sixth Lord Baltimore; and the precise details of the transfer of all claims on the proprietorship of Maryland from the sixth, Lord Baltimore's sisters, Louisa and Caroline, the legal heirs under the will of the fifth Lord Baltimore, to the sixth Baron's son, Henry Harford, Esquire.

The document was located by the writer after a first clue as to its existence contained in Charles Browning's book, *An Appeal to the Citizens of Maryland* (Baltimore: n.p., 1821), pp. 8, 9. Some settlement had been made, it seemed from this mention, between the legal heirs and Henry Harford. A further clue emerged during a search of the catalog of the Bodleian Library at Oxford University in a reference to Harford to be found in *An Analytical Table of the Private Statutes Passed, 1727–1812,* compiled by George Bramwell. Unfortunately the library staff was unable to find the volume among their six million books. The writer had better luck at the Law Library, Library of Congress. Once obtained, however, the book gave only a bare listing, indicating that a private act had indeed been passed as a statute by Parliament in 1781. This clue was enough, however, to enable the writer to dispatch a request for a copy of the Act from the Record Office, House of Lords, London. A microfilm copy of the 100-page statute, handwritten on parchment, was sent to the writer in the summer of 1975.

[16] Estate Act of 1781, p. 99.

[17] Ibid.

[18] Ibid, pp. 30, 39, 77.

CHAPTER VI

TWO PRECEDENTS: PROPRIETARY HEIRS IN PENNSYLVANIA AND VIRGINIA

If Maryland would treat Harford as well as Pennsylvania had treated the Penns, his chances of recovering his American lands and revenues were good.

The Pennsylvania Precedent

Following the Revolution John Penn of Stoke, principal heir to the proprietors of Pennsylvania, assessed the value of the estate appropriated by Pennsylvania at £1,536,545. This included the value of 21,592,128 acres of land, arrears in current quitrent payments (over four million acres had been sold by the proprietary prior to the American Revolution), value of unsold lands, plus the value of the quitrent rights, capitalized at twelve years' purchase. Most of the sum was made up of the value inherent in the unsold lands. John Penn of Stoke and the other heirs of Pennsylvania's proprietary family petitioned the Pennsylvania assembly for redress of this loss.[1]

The legislature of Pennsylvania, acting in answer to the petition, passed by November 27, 1779, "An Act for vesting the estates of the late Proprietaries of Pennsylvania in the Commonwealth." The act took away all rights of the proprietary to Pennsylvania soil, *yet excepted the private lands and the proprietary tenths, or manors.* Quitrents were cut off, and yet *£130,000 were to be paid,* one year after the war should cease, "to the widow and relict of the said Thomas Penn" or her heirs. The payments were not to be more than £20,000 in any one year nor less than £15,000 a year.[2] Thus, while the Penns did lose giant tracts of land, the family still had a comfortable 553,784 acres in Pennsylvania which they were permitted to keep. Also, the Penns were to be paid £130,000.

It seems virtually impossible that Harford failed to hear of the restitution awarded the heirs to the Pennsylvania proprietary, yet he does not allude to this fact in his appeal to the Maryland General Assembly, a curious omission. He may have believed the point so well known and taken that it needed no restatement. Knowledge of the Penn family's being paid by the Pennsylvania legislature must almost certainly have been one of the reasons he was willing to come to Maryland in the first place, for it seemed by the precedent set in Pennsylvania that the Maryland legislature likewise might award the heir to their proprietary family similar recompense.

When comparing the claims of the proprietary heirs for recompense for losses in America, one notes that more unsold land remained in Pennsylvania at the outbreak of the Revolution due to the fact that Pennsylvania was four and one-half times the size of Maryland. The Maryland colony had been in existence fifty years longer, and so had opportunity to sell off land that much longer. Still, enough land that could be claimed by the proprietary heirs remained in Maryland to offer a tempting target for Henry Harford's attentions.

The Virginia Precedent

Lands in America inherited by the heirs of Thomas, Lord Fairfax, proprietor of the "Northern Neck" of Virginia, amounted to well over 200,000 acres. The Virginia situation after the Revolution differed from that of the Pennsylvania one in that the Penns received cash compensation for their losses and were allowed to keep certain lands, whereas in Virginia the Fairfax heirs were allowed to retain only manor lands and town lots that formerly had been held by Lord Fairfax and were paid no sums for revenues lost. In both Pennsylvania and Virginia, however, the proprietary heirs were permitted to retain land ownership.

As in the case of Pennsylvania, in Virginia there was a history of long personal contact with the proprietary family. Lord Fairfax of Leeds Castle, England, an amiable bachelor, visited Virginia about 1739 and decided to spend the rest of his life there. He settled in the Northern Neck region, an area now called northern Virginia, to live at Greenway Court Manor, and at a mansion and estate known as Belvoir.[3] Before 1747 Lord Fairfax arranged to buy out other members of his family who held interests in the proprietary of the Northern Neck portion of Virginia and became sole proprietor of that part of the colony. At one time, early in the 18th century, he owned an estimated one-quarter of the land in Virginia, around six million acres.[4]

Lord Fairfax proved to be a capable, kindly, and generous landlord in Virginia. He was loved and admired by George Washington whom he had helped in Washington's youth. Washington's Mount Vernon estate was near Fairfax's mansion, Belvoir.[5] Josiah Dickinson in his work, *The Fairfax Proprietary,* has noted that Lord Fairfax showed such disinterest in the British ascendancy and was so generally beloved and respected that during the American Revolution he met with neither insult nor molestation from either side in the conflict. He was allowed to continue to cultivate his Virginia acres undisturbed.[6] "So popular was the English lord that when the Revolution broke out, this resident peer was voted all the privileges of Virginia citizens. When the Commonwealth abolished feudal land tenures in 1777, Fairfax's huge holdings were specifically exempted. No attempts were made to interfere with his collection of his rents," notes Virginia historian, Marshall W. Fishwick.[7]

The legislature of Virginia was obliged to work out answers to problems posed by resident Loyalists and those posed by absentee land owners, specifically owners who were British citizens. A sweeping law on land tenure was passed in 1775, abolishing reservations for royal mines, the payment of quitrents, and specifying that all lands were now to be held in common with those granted by the Commonwealth of Virginia.[8]

Yet even this law did not affect Lord Fairfax, for he held his land as a private owner. He had made it a practice to grant land to himself in the same way he granted it to others, giving himself the same status as that enjoyed by other grantees. Further, his manors were granted first to a nephew and then granted back, a legal device that emphasized the individual nature of his land ownership. This strategem helped his manor lands to pass into the hands of his heirs.[9] Further, Lord Fairfax, on lands to which he had given title to others, collected quitrents by virtue of an act of the Assembly.

It is said that when Lord Fairfax heard of the surrender of Lord Cornwallis, he commented, "It is time for me to die." He did, in fact, die in 1781, at nearly ninety years of age.[10] Lord Fairfax was buried at the church he had caused to be built in Winchester, Virginia. In his will, dated November 8, 1777, he gave his Virginia manors of Leeds and Gooney Run to a nephew, the Reverend Denny Martin of County Kent, England, on the condition that Martin take the name of Fairfax, which that gentleman did.[11]

Reverend Denny Martin Fairfax's hopes of inheriting giant tracts of unoccupied Fairfax lands would seem to have been crushed by an act of the Virginia Assembly passed in 1779 which had added provisions against the holding of property by British subjects, at least those who lived outside the United States after April 19, 1775.[12] Denny Martin Fairfax persisted, however, by coming to Virginia in 1786 to attempt to gain ownership of all grants made by the Virginia government in the Northern Neck area! He did not succeed, for the last grant honored to the Fairfax family was dated April 3, 1780, when Lord Fairfax was still living. After that date Virginia took over the granting of unoccupied lands.[13]

All was by no means lost to the Fairfax heir, however, for he was allowed possession of the manors of Leeds and Gooney Run willed to him by Lord Fairfax. These tracts contained 160,382 acres of land. He was awarded, too, the South Branch Manor lands, another extensive holding. Further, another nephew of the old Proprietor, Thomas Bryan Martin, was allowed to inherit the manor of Greenway Court with 10,000 acres attached to it.[14]

The heirs of a proprietor in Virginia, then, lost unalloted land in Virginia, and were not compensated for the loss of quitrent incomes, yet they were vouchsafed undisturbed ownership of the thousands of acres of manor lands the old Proprietor willed them.

In the Virginia case there were two items that differed from the situation in Maryland. As in Pennsylvania there was a pre-Revolutionary relationship with members of the proprietary family that led to a cordial post-Revolutionary climate whereby heirs were able to claim American lands. In Virginia, there was the added factor that Lord Fairfax had taken the precaution of making the titles to his lands legally unassailable.

In view of the precedent set in Virginia wherein the Fairfax heir, Martin, had lived in England during the Revolution it would seem that Henry Harford might logically expect to be granted at least the land held in Calvert manors and some recompense for lands and incomes seized by the government of Maryland.

[1]Howard M. Jenkins, "The Family of William Penn," *Pennsylvania Magazine of History and Biography*, Vol. 21, No. 4, 1897, pp. 425, 426.
[2]*Minutes of the Supreme Executive Council of Pennsylvania*, Vol. 16 (Harrisburg: State of Pennsylvania, 1853), p. 5. See, Jenkins, p. 426. See, Arthur Pounds, *The Penns of Pennsylvania and England* (New York: The Macmillan Co., 1932), p. 306.
[3]Josiah Look Dickinson, *The Fairfax Proprietary* (Front Royal, Va.: Warren Press, 1959), p. 126.
[4]Moncure Daniel Conway, *Barons of the Potomack and the Rappahannock* (New York: Grolier Club, 1892), p. 215.
[5]Dickinson, p. 126.
[6]Marshall W. Fishwick, *Gentlemen of Virginia* (New York Dodd, Mead & Co., 1961), p. 262. See Dickinson, pp. 130–131.
[7]Dickinson, p. 126.
[8]*Revised Code of Virginia*, 1819, Vol. 2, p. 375.
[9]Dickinson, p. 23.
[10]Conway, p. 250.

[11] Frederick County Will Book, Frederick County, Virginia, Book 4, p. 583.
[12] Dickinson, p. 17.
[13] Ibid; Fauquier County, Virginia, Record of Land Causes, Book 2, p. 297; Frederick County, Virginia, Will Book 4, p. 583.
[14] Frederick County, Virginia, Will Book 4, p. 583.

(Author's 1976 photograph)

The Maryland Inn, Annapolis.

CHAPTER VII

HENRY HARFORD'S MARYLAND SOJOURN

To understand the situation into which Harford planned to plunge during the summer of 1783, it will be useful to see how Loyalists in general were treated in Maryland, for this was to have a definite bearing on the success of Harford's mission.

Treatment Accorded Loyalists in Maryland

During the Revolution, Maryland members of the new state government debated the question of proper treatment to accord Loyalist Maryland residents and absentee owners of Maryland property who were loyal to Britain. The question was complicated by the many degrees of support given the Crown by Maryland's inhabitants. Some actively resisted the revolutionary movement, joining British Loyalist regiments. Others carried out guerilla-like operations, a choice popular with Eastern Shore Loyalists. Still others fled to British-held American areas or to Britain. A sizeable number, however, simply stayed in Maryland, refusing to lend support to the Revolution yet not hampering the efforts of American patriots. Many made no clear commitment either way.[1]

To determine the status of Loyalists in their midst, the Maryland revolutionary leaders passed various laws in 1777 and 1778. These attempted to obtain clear declarations of support for the revolutionary government from the inhabitants of Maryland. Thanks to the constraint exerted by the Maryland Senate upon the more radical House of Delegates, a certain leeway was allowed Loyalists. Even so, the Security Act of December 1777 was a severe one. It required absentee owners of property in Maryland to

(Author's 1976 photograph)

Shown here is a view of Charles Carroll of Carrollton's Annapolis home as it appears today. It overlooks Spa Creek.

return by September 1, 1779. The date set allowed time for the content of the act to become known in England. Upon their return absentees had a month to take an oath of allegiance before the imposition of triple taxes and other penalties. (This option was open to Henry Harford but his loyalty to his king and country made such an action inconceivable.) Those refusing to return and take the oath were to be declared traitors by the Maryland courts and their property seized.[2] "As finally resolved," Richard Overfield states, "confiscation in Maryland applied only to British property, and absentees were the only Loyalists considered British subjects."[3]

During the December 1779 session of the Maryland General Assembly, the legislature passed a bill through the lower house authorizing confiscation of British property. Senator Charles Carroll of Carrollton objected, claiming that land speculators would quickly buy up the land since travel during the winter in Maryland was difficult. If passed in the winter season, with property placed immediately upon the market it would, said Carroll, "turn into a private job what might have been intended for public benefit." He opposed confiscation, too, because he saw in the action a violation of respect for private property and believed this would be hazardous to the social and political future of Maryland.[4] Then, too, Maryland families with property in England, such as the Carrolls, might well expect England to retaliate in that country by confiscating the personal property of Americans there. Still, by June of 1780 Carroll yielded and agreed to confiscation. The summer gave all a chance to travel to the land sales. As he had predicted, however, many speculators rushed to buy up huge tracts of land.[5] Much of this land had been owned by the Proprietor.

By 1780, then, property owned by British subjects was seized. In the following year after the defeat of Lord Cornwallis, the hopes of those Britons who had expected the return of the old order were dashed.

As late as the summer of 1781, Harford himself held such hopes, for those were expressed in several of the articles of the Estate Act of 1781.[6]

Harford's Maryland Journey

On hearing that the negotiations of the peace treaty between the United States and Britain were coming to a close, Harford left London for Maryland. The Browning and Eden claims were settled. Harford's mother and sister were living comfortably in London, and all in all Harford had set his personal and business affairs in order.

The former Proprietor had every reason to expect at least some success in America. He planned to apply to the Maryland legislature for recompense for 116,642 acres of manor and reserved land, plus consideration for 125,120 acres of reserved lands to the west of Cumberland. These two land claims totaled 241,762 acres. Harford planned to remind the General Assembly that Maryland had realized £116,000 from the sale of a part of these confiscated lands. He also hoped to be compensated for the loss of his quitrents due prior to 1774, an important sum since the annual income from quitrents was estimated by the former Proprietor at £8,518 valued at twenty years' purchase. The total value of the claim that Harford planned to present to the Maryland legislature added up to £327,441. (Later, in Britain, Harford was to set this figure of his total losses at £447,000.)[7]

Sir Robert Eden accompanied young Harford to assist in the negotiations with the Maryland legislature. The two men left England on June 7, 1783, aboard the ship *Harford*.[8] Nathaniel Richardson, captain of the vessel, acquainted them with recent events in Maryland. Eden spoke of his rollicking days with the jovial members of the provincial gentry. The men discussed the possibility of violence awaiting them in Annapolis; the bitterness of the recent fighting probably still existed, for active hostilities had only just ended.

Upon their arrival in Maryland's capital city their worst fears seemed about to be realized when rough-spoken men ordered Captain Richardson to strike his British flag. They were rescued from the rough attentions of the crowd, however, by a letter from Benjamin Stoddert in Council, Annapolis, who wrote to Richardson assuring him that the Anne Arundel County magistrates had been instructed to restrain the people from interfering with ships of British registry and other foreign vessels.[9]

With Harford's arrival in Maryland came the news that peace negotiations had been completed in Paris. The terms included an agreement between Britain and the United States that Loyalists were not to be harmed and that debts contracted prior to the war were to be paid. Among the terms of the treaty was one that British negotiators had fought to make stronger but without success, concerning property owned by British subjects which had been confiscated during the conflict. This had had to be left ambiguously worded with only the recommendation that the United States consider restoring such property, for the American negotiators refused to give a firm commitment in this matter. In practice, the individual states were to decide the matter.[10]

News of the peace treaty agreement and of Harford's arrival may well have caused the members of the Maryland legislature to groan at the realization that they now had to face up to scores of Loyalist claims, including that of the ex-Proprietor, who was to make the largest claim of all.[11]

Dr. Upton Scott offered Eden and Harford the use of his Annapolis townhouse. Scott was a prominent man in Maryland, a Loyalist who had been allowed to live quietly on his wife's Severn River plantation. While living in Scott's house Eden and Harford heard the news that the treaty of peace had been signed September 3, 1783.[12]

Harford had brought from England deeds to lands, unsold warrants for land, and other documents that would reinforce his claims to tracts and parcels of land. Eden and Harford computed the amounts due the proprietary before the Revolution in unpaid quitrents. The value to be set on land was easily found for the land had been sold after its seizure and these transactions had been registered in the land offices in Maryland. Once these tasks were done, the pair from England filled their days as well as they could, for it promised to be a long time before they would be heard by the legislature.

The Maryland lawmakers were besieged with urgent matters to be attended to: armies were only now being disbanded; ships were being decommissioned from combat status; and pleas for recompense of every nature were pouring into the General Assembly. Money was an ever-present problem for the Maryland government, yet funds had to be found to pay officials, to make required restitutions, and to operate the various state services. We are struck, upon reading the journals of the legislature at this point in Maryland's history, by the fact that there seemed to be no screening of matters presented for solution to the Assembly. Matters involving a few pounds took up members' time, while at the same time the legislators were obliged to concern themselves over the need for devising and revising new governments at both the state and national level. The legislators somehow coped with it all. While the assembly labored, Harford, Eden, and their attorneys wrote and re-wrote the memorial they planned to present to the General Assembly. Then they waited.

Some of the men's hours were occupied with social events. Business, too, occupied Sir Robert, who spent some of his time in January of 1784 issuing and signing patents for the sale of land claimed by Harford.[13] This last occupation, however, speedily came to the notice of the legislature, which body quickly ordered Eden to desist, and this he was obliged to do.[14]

Spring and summer passed and then early in September, 1784, Eden, who had not been entirely well for some time, died at Scott's house at the age of forty-three.[15] Harford was left to wrestle with his problems in Maryland without the guidance and support of the ex-governor. The last Proprietor continued to work on his appeal with the aid of attorney John Clapham, a prominent Loyalist who had returned to Maryland from England at about the same time as had Eden and Harford.[16] Another year passed.

A number of people in Annapolis sympathized with the request of the former proprietor for recompense for his losses. The Treaty of Paris had "earnestly recommended" that American properties be restored to Britons.[17] Harford had reason to hope for success when late in November of 1785, a motion was made in the House of Delegates to consider his case.

Immediately Harford presented his carefully-worded memorial. He asked that the members of the legislature consider that Maryland had originally been settled by the proprietary family, his ancestors, at considerable risk and expense. Further, "Your memorialist respectfully represents, that he was a minor at the commencement of the late war, and placed during his infancy under the guardianship of the Chancellor of Great Britain, which prevented his leaving the kingdom." Harford went on to say that legal suits against him had ended only in July of 1782.[18]

Harford attached to the memorial a list of quitrents due and a list of properties to which he laid claim and requested a total sum from Maryland of £327,441.[19] The former proprietor filled his memorial with conciliatory phrases and expressed the hope that "his most sanguine hopes would be realized."

There is no specific mention in Harford's memorial of the precedents established in Pennsylvania and in Virginia with respect to those states' treatment of proprietary family members. This is a puzzling omission and it appears that Harford missed making a telling point by failing to mention these precedents. He

(Author's 1976 photograph)

Dr. Upton Scott's house in Annapolis.

possibly believed that they were too well known to restate. The opening paragraph of his memorial did refer to the "benevolent interposition, which have dignified the acts of former assemblies."

The legislature seemed very much inclined to take Harford's claims seriously. By Friday, December 2, 1785, the House of Delegates, after hearing Harford's attorney present information on the ex-proprietor's behalf, made the motion that a message be prepared to be sent to the Senate proposing a conference on the subject of the Henry Harford memorial. Samuel Chase, John Hall, and Charles Carroll of Carrollton were named to a committee and charged with writing the message. The very next day Mr. Carroll delivered a proposed letter to the Speaker of the House.

In brief the message expressed the wish that the Senate would assist the House in the matter of the Harford's request for restitution of his Maryland lands and incomes. The letter advised that the House had heard counsel on behalf of Mr. Harford, "late proprietary of this State," soliciting compensation for his confiscated property.

"The case of Mr. Harford", the letter stated, "is attended with such very particular circumstances, as merit, in our opinion, the peculiar attention of the general assembly, and involve such difficulties, as require the united wisdom of both branches of this government to decide."[20]

The House letter asserted that the law that allowed the confiscation of British property in Maryland was completely just, but noted also that few laws apply to every case. In the eyes of the world, the letter went on, it is important to discover how a new nation and its new states will comport themselves. Maryland must acquire a national character associated with justice, humanity, and benevolence.

The message concluded:*

---
*Italics added.

Actuated by these principles, this house have retained the memorial of Mr. Harford; and we propose a conference with your honours on the subject matter thereof.

We wish that the cause and calamities of the late war could be buried in perpetual oblivion; and *are willing to make a compromise with Mr. Harford,* as far as the present very distressed situation of our public affairs will permit. We are involved, in consequence of the late war, in an enormous and very heavy debt, foreign and domestic; and our creditors are very urgent and pressing for payment. *Our wishes far exceed our abilities;* and we must limit our humanity and beneficence by our necessities.

If your honours agree to the conference, *this house will afterwards determine what sum of money our finances will permit to be given to Mr. Harford, and the time and mode of payment.*[21]

The House heard the proposed message December 6th and only eleven members of the body voted for it, while forty-four voted against it. The committee then retired to draft another message. Two prominent men of Maryland, Charles Carroll of Carrollton and Samuel Chase, supported Harford's right to compensation. Peregrine Letherbury and Joseph Dashiell, less prominent but still important men, also favored his application.[22]

Harford, his hopes raised by the letter read to the House, then depressed by its rejection by the lower house, did not have long to wait for a revised letter to be offered. Two days after the first message had been rejected, Carroll was back with another, less specific message for the Senate:

May it please Your Honours,

This house have heard counsel at its bar on the memorial of Mr. Harford, late proprietary of this state, in which he solicits a compensation or retribution from this government for his confiscated property. We esteem the case of Mr. Harford very important, and of such nature as to require the united wisdom of both branches of the legislature to decide properly thereon, and do therefore propose a conference with your honours on the subject matter of the said memorial. Should the senate accede to the proposed conference, we will nominate some of our members to meet such of your house as you may please to appoint for the above purpose.[23]

When the House heard this proposed letter read, thirty men swung over to the affirmative; forty-one votes were now for sending the message to the Senate, and fourteen were against the action. Such prominent Maryland names as Goldsborough, Bowie, Stone, and Beall, were found on the list of those opposing the message.

Harford waited for two anxious weeks for an answer to the House message. The Senate then replied to the House in a message dated December 19, 1785. The letter clarified not only Harford's claim but as well, those of other British subjects claiming special recompense from Maryland.

In brief, the Senate message stated that Harford could not rightfully ask of the State of Maryland relief for his losses occasioned by the action of the legislature in passing laws to confiscate British-owned property in Maryland. Adequate time had been allowed by the legislation for news of the proposed confiscation of property to reach England, in order to allow Britons who wished to come to Maryland, to claim their property at that time. Harford, the Senate letter continued, had chosen to remain attached to the British government, had remained in Britain during the whole war, and ought now to seek recompense from Britain. He had had ample time to come to Maryland and claim his property and to make an oath of loyalty to the revolutionary government:[24]

> The memorialist came of age in the spring of 1779, full twelve months after the measure had been warmly and generally agitated in this state, and must have been known in England . . .
> This state of facts leaves not the smallest room to doubt that the memorialist, both from interest and inclination, continued a British subject, and devoted to his native country, which, although free, endeavored by lavishing its blood and treasure, to deprive us of our freedom. We cannot

(Author's 1976 photograph)
St. Anne's Church, Church Circle, Annapolis, where Sir Robert Eden was interred.

discover a single circumstance in the case of the memorialist, to distinguish him from other British subjects.[25]

Likewise, the Senate sternly rejected the former proprietor's claim for quitrents past the date of Maryland's declaration of independence from Britain. Debts incurred and due to Harford previous to this date were apparently allowed by this statement. The Senate blandly assured the House that it would always be happy to confer with that body, but that in this instance it would be a waste of time.[26] The message ended with a bald Senate resolution that the "memorial and application of the said Henry Harford, Esquire, be rejected."[27]

House members heard the message from the Senate with its accompanying resolution, and adjourned for the Christmas and New Year holidays without further action on the matter.[28] This holiday season must have held little cheer for Harford, allowing him only an overabundance of time in which to contemplate to what a sorry state the great Calvert name and fortune had fallen in Maryland. There was little reason to hope that the House would oppose the Senate in the matter.

When the legislature reconvened on January, 1786, Harford's case again came before the House. House members heard the entire message read again on January 6th, and a vote was called for. The result was overwhelmingly against the former proprietor. Forty-nine members of the House voted not to consider the Harford appeal further, seven doggedly voted to review the matter. Among the seven Harford supporters remained the names of Carroll, Chase, and Letherbury.[29] So the matter was closed and Henry Harford was denied all recompense for his losses in Maryland.

There is a curious absence of Harford's name in the newspapers of Maryland during the time of his visit. These gossipy journals, usually so quick to report every move of members of the gentry, totally ignored

Harford after only two early mentions in 1783. It seems that pressure must have been brought to bear on the Maryland editors by powerful men in Maryland for such a total absence of news to have occurred. This indicates that powerful opposition and hostility existed toward Harford. No item noting his departure is to be found in the *Maryland Gazette,* for example, though there is little doubt that Harford did depart wearily enough for England, early in 1786.

Harford left agents behind him in Maryland to collect the few debts allowed him by the laws of Maryland, sums due prior to the Declaration of Independence in Maryland.[30] These payments of relatively small amounts continued until the year 1818.[31]

Why Harford Failed in Maryland

Harford came to America in 1783 with every right to expect at least some compensation for his losses in Maryland because of the examples set by the state legislatures in Virginia and Pennsylvania toward the heirs of their proprietary families. Yet Maryland's ex-proprietor left the state two years later without a pound of payment, save for those few debts contracted to him prior to the Declaration of Independence.

To summarize, it appears that the reasons for his lack of success were: his illegitimacy, his minority at the time he became Proprietor, the fact that he was not the legal heir to the province, his refusal to consider coming to Maryland when he came of age to join the rebels, his own mild character, the loss of Eden's assistance, and most harmful to his chances of all—the hostile climate left for him by his father's poor management of the province of Maryland. Calvert's disgraceful life style had done nothing to create loyalty in Maryland. Also, hostility remained, directed at English citizens in general, due to the recent fighting of the Revolution.

The heirs to the Pennsylvania and Virginia proprietary property in America fared better because they were legitimately born and were unquestionably the legal heirs of the proprietaries. Harford's being a minor gave him scant opportunity to come to Maryland to live and create friendships and loyalties, whereas both the Penns and Lord Fairfax had a long and cordial personal relationship in Pennsylvania and Virginia with the inhabitants of those former provinces.

Harford's education and background made it impossible for him to consider leaving his king and his country to join the rebels when he came of age. Yet, neither the Penn nor Fairfax heirs joined the rebellion against England. Members of each family, in the Virginia case Lord Fairfax himself, did stay in America during the war, however, on a neutral basis.

The personality of Henry Harford apparently was not forceful or charismatic enough to rally support.

All these factors eventually dealt a death blow to Harford's hopes of regaining a part of the Calvert fortune from Maryland. He could now only turn his back on his American failure and sail eastward toward his home, family, and friends in England.

[1] Richard A. Overfield, "The Patriot Dilemma: The Treatment of Passive Loyalists and Neutrals in Revolutionary Maryland," *Maryland Historical Magazine*, Vol. 79, No. 2 (Summer, 1973), p. 140.
[2] Ibid, p. 147.
[3] Ibid, p. 150.
[4] Ronald Hoffman, *A Spirit of Dissension* (Baltimore: Johns Hopkins University Press, 1973), pp. 258, 259.
[5] Ibid, pp. 260, 268. Still, a summer sale offered a more equal opportunity to the public than had the proposed winter sale.
[6] By 1781 "certain Articles of Agreement," were made between Henry Harford and his two Calvert aunts, legal heirs to the Calvert family palatinate. This was done by means of one of those private acts of Parliament that allowed certain cases to be settled, rather than to drag on indefinitely. George Bramwell, *An Analytical Table of the Private Statutes Passed, 1727–1782* (London: n.p., 1837), unpaginated, Harford entry. LC JN 688B8. Edward Jenks, *The Book of English Law* (Athens, Ohio: Ohio University Press, 1967), pp. 260–262. Also, Charles Browning, *An Appeal to the Citizens of Maryland* (Baltimore: n.p., 1821), pp. 8, 9.
[7] J. Thomas Scharf, *History of Maryland*, 3 vols (Hatboro, Penna.: Tradition Press, 1967, a facsimile reprint of the 1879 edition), II:392–395; also Henry Harford Memorial, Appendix B, p. 2.
[8] *Maryland Gazette,* August 14, 1783, noted: "On Monday last arrived here the ship *Harford,* capt. N. Richardson, from London. She left England the 7th of June, and brings London prints to the fifth, but they contain nothing new. In this ship came several passengers, among whom are the late proprietor and governor of Maryland."

[9]*Archives of Maryland,* Vol. 48, pp. 446, 447.
[10]Mary Beth Norton, *The British Americans: The Loyalist Exiles in England, 1774–1789* (Boston: Little, Brown, 1972), pp. 178–180.
[11]*Maryland Gazette,* August 14, 1783: "Yesterday the brig *Peace and Plenty,* captain Bradstreet, arrived in this port from England. Captain Bradstreet informs, that he understood the definitive treaty was signed a few days before he sailed." Also Scharf, II:496.
[12]Ibid.
[13]*Archives of Maryland,* Vol. 47, preface, p. 447.
[14]*Archives of Maryland,* Vol. 48 pp. 506, 508, 509, 517, 518.
[15]Lady Matilda Ridout Edgar, *A Colonial Governor in Maryland* (London: Longmans, Green and Co., 1912), p. 277. An Annapolis lady writes: "Sir Robert Eden seems in bad health. He no longer flirts. . . . They are very agreeable neighbours to us. . . . They live in Doctor Scott's House. The Doctor himself is in a state of ill health."
[16]Scharf, II:502.
[17]Norton, pp. 178–180.
[18]Memorial of Henry Harford, Appendix, B.
[19]Ibid.
[20]Ibid.
[21]Ibid. Emphasis added.
[22]Ibid.
[23]Ibid.
[24]Ibid.
[25]Ibid. Note the comment made in the Memorial with reference to Henry Harford's age which confirms his birth in 1758.
[26]Memorial of Henry Harford, Appendix B.
[27]Ibid.
[28]Ibid.
[29]Ibid.
[30]*Maryland Gazette,* March 2, 1786:

Annapolis, Feb. 15, 1786.
The agent for the late PROPRIETARY of this state having returned, many of the farmers of quit-rents, and others in receipt of his then revenue, in arrears—to avoid expense and trouble, those concerned are requested to make immediate payment to
JOHN and JONAS CLAPMAN
Attornies for Henry Harford, Esquire.

[31]Account book of Jonas Clapham for May 21, 1785, to Jan. 21, 1718. Scharf Papers, MS Div., Maryland Historical Society.

CHAPTER VIII

HARFORD APPEALS TO THE BRITISH GOVERNMENT

In Britain, Harford was vastly more successful in obtaining recompense for the loss of his Maryland lands and incomes. When the British Parliament had passed the Estate Act of 1781, Harford was made, without any reservation, Proprietor of Maryland. This gave him firm legal grounds to expect equal treatment with others claiming compensation for losses from the British government, sustained as the result of the American Revolution. Aided by his own persistent efforts and his considerable wealth, Harford managed to extract thousands of pounds from the British treasury.

Harford's First Appeals to Britain

Parliament passed a Compensation Act in July of 1783. This resulted in a five-man board being set up as a commission to judge claims filed by ". . . all such persons who have suffered in their rights, properties and professions, during the late unhappy dissensions in America, in consequence of their loyalty to his majesty and attachment to the British government."[1] The commissioners set to work, reading claims presented to them, and by 1785 payments began.[2]

Henry Harford received about £90,000. This was computed upon a figure of £447,000, which Harford claimed was the value of his losses in Maryland. Further sums of £10,000 each were paid to two other claimants, one sum to Sir Robert Eden and his wife Dame Caroline, and the second sum to John Browning and his wife Louisa.[3]

Ironically, Maryland did have to make some compensation to her former proprietor, albeit an involuntary payment. The Bank of England held stock, in

Maryland's name, purchased before the American Revolution and valued at £29,000.[4] Years of litigation over possession of this stock followed the American Revolution. The case was finally settled and much of the stock was returned to Maryland, but only after the deduction of 10,000 pounds paid to Henry Harford and after the discharge of several other claims.[5]

Harford's Later Appeals to the Government of Britain

Five Loyalist claimants, Henry Harford, John Tyndale Warre, William Cuninghame, Henry Glassford, and John Nutt Davisson, claimed under the various treaties made between Britain and the United States regarding the collection of debts contracted prior to the American Revolution in both America and in Britain, the sum of two and one-half million pounds. The king, however, agreed to accept in cancellation of all these claims against Americans £600,000. As the claimants expressed it:

> It thus appears, That by the Convention of 1802, His Majesty was pleased, *in consideration of 600,000 pounds to cancel and annul the 6th Article of the Treaty of 1794,* whereby America would have been bound to pay to the Petitioners, 1,420,000 pounds (this amount derived from action of Parliamentary, House of Commons Committee appointed to parcel out the 600,000 pounds, who found that the claimants should receive 1,420,000 pounds); and by the same Convention, His Majesty's Government was pleased, on the other hand, to stipulate, that Great Britain should, nevertheless, pay to American Citizens, the *full amount of their demands under the 7th Article;* and these demands have been discharged by Great Britain, to the extent of 1,369,448 pounds. . . .[6]
>
> The Petitioners have, therefore, applied to Parliament, for Compensation, on account of the heavy loss they have sustained, by the above Convention—having as yet received only 659,493 pounds, instead of 1,420,000 pounds, to which they have been found justly entitled . . .
>
> The Claimants commenced this statement, by asserting,—that their Claim is *not* for a Loss occasioned by War.—And it

should be known, that besides the Loss now claimed, *arising solely in time of Peace,* and occasioned by America's violation of the Treaty of Peace, they have actually sustained Losses, to the amount of several millions, by the American War, for which they do not ask any Compensation whatever.[7]

The case of the British American Claimants, quoted above, began years before. In January of 1802, armed with the knowledge that the British American claimants would agree to settle with the Americans for £2,500,000, the king's agents agreed to accept a payment "from America," as the United States was often termed, of £600,000 in complete settlement of the British claims. The claimants were not consulted and soon objected to this state of affairs. They were to be paid by a committee, appointed in April 1803 by Act of Parliament, their various shares of the £600,000. The committee, however, came up with a total due the claimants of £1,420,000! Finally, £659,493 were paid out to the claimants.

The "American claimants," that is, Britons claiming more compensation for debts in America cancelled out by the British government, petitioned Commons on January 22, 1812, where the matter went into committee, emerging in March 1, 1813. The five claimants then wrote a letter to the Earl of Liverpool, dated May 8, 1813, advising him that their case was to be submitted before the House of Commons on May 13th, and asking for the support of the Prince Regent's Government.[8] The case duly came before Commons and on May 20, 1813, a motion was made "that the petitioners have established such a case as forms an equitable ground for Parliamentary relief."[9] The motion was defeated in the Commons, however, and no further action was taken.[10]

How much did Harford realize out of these various petitions to Parliament? He was originally adjudicated £43,401 by the commission appointed in April 1803 to apportion out the £600,000 from the United States.

All in all, though the commission's total rose to £1,420,000—only £659,493 were dispersed. Since £659,493 is a little less than 47% of £1,420,000, we may estimate Harford's share as being paid at 47% of £43,401, or approximately £20,398. This was paid to Harford after the committee eventually made its report in May 1811.

Summary of Reparations

In negotiations lasting from 1786 until 1813 the persistent Harford gained £90,000 from the British government for losses incurred by his loyalty to that government during the American Revolution; £10,000 indirectly from Maryland through the action of the British government in deducting that amount before returning Maryland's Bank of England stocks; and an estimated £20,398 from the British government and the government of the United States to compensate him for losses due to uncollectable debts in the United States. Thus, Harford garnered from the British government the munificent total of £120,398.

---

[1]Mary Beth Norton, *The British Americans: The Loyalist Exiles in England, 1774–1789* (Boston: Little, Brown, 1972), pp. 192; J. Thomas Scharf, *History of Maryland*, 3 vols., (Hatboro, Penna.: Tradition Press, 1967, facsimile reprint of the 1879 edition), II:392–393.
[2]Norton, p. 192; Scharf, II:394, 397.
[3]Scharf, II:394.
[4]Scharf, II:504.
[5]Scharf, II:504, 505, 506.
[6]Case of the British American Claimants, MS Room, British Museum, London, document #38252.F.352, and document #38252.F.353. See Appendix C.
[7]Ibid.
[8]Ibid.
[9]Letter, H. S. Cobb, Deputy Clerk of the Records, Record Office, House of Lords, London, to Vera Rollo, Lanham, Maryland, July 24, 1975. See Appendix C.
[10]Ibid.

CHAPTER IX

FRANCES MARY HARFORD

Henry Harford had a sister, Frances Mary Harford, whom we mentioned earlier in this narrative. Her father was Frederick Calvert and her mother Hester Rhelan. She was born, a year and eight months after the birth of her brother, on November 28, 1759.[1]

Twelve years of age when her father died, she became by his will the heir to an outright cash gift of £30,000. The will also provided that she was to be Proprietor of Maryland should her brother be unable to assume the proprietorship. Upon Lord Baltimore's death, Frances Mary Harford and her brother were placed under the care of the executors of his will: Robert Eden, Hugh Hammersley, Robert Morris, and Peter Prevost.

Robert Morris took special interest in the young heiress. He placed her in an English boarding school, visited her frequently, and wrote notes to her. He was apt to descend upon her at school, or when she was visiting friends, to carry her off to balls, public gardens, and all sorts of outings.[2] This courtship was enough to turn the head of any young girl.

It appeared that another delightful outing was in prospect one day in May, 1772, when Morris drove her away once more in his carriage from the home of a Mrs. La Touche. Yet the journey soon resolved into more than an afternoon's jaunt. Morris insisted that his ward accompany him to France. In Bologne, she began to have second thoughts about a romantic elopement, being only thirteen years old. Quite naturally she began to weep and to wish that she were home again. She begged Morris to take her back to England, whereupon he terrified the girl by saying that he would kill himself if she did not stay with him. Where now, she must have wondered, was the smiling gallant who had taken her to dinners and balls so protectively? At any rate she went with him. They arrived in France on May 16th and on the 21st of May, 1772, they arrived at Ypres where they were married by a chaplain in the Dutch garrison before two witnesses and other persons.[3]

News of the abduction of Frances Mary Harford reached Maryland, as the following letter from Daniel (3d) Dulany, Jr. in London, written to Walter Dulany in Maryland, reveals:

London June 13, 1772

. . . before this reaches you, you will have heard of the most villainous Breach of trust of R. Morris, in running away with his ward, Mifs. Harford. Whether he's actually married to her or not is uncertain, but it is very confidently reported that he is. The young Lady I understand is between thirteen and fourteen . . .[4]

The pair stayed a night in Ypres and then moved on. Doubtless Morris was uneasy, for it was certain that the other guardians of his child bride would soon have agents hot on his heels. True enough, the other three executors of Lord Baltimore's will were sending men hither and yon in an attempt to find their young ward. So it was that Morris took his wife to Lisle, then into Holland, and later to Hamburg and "other places."

Just to be certain that there was no question as to whether or not he were well and truly married to his ward, Morris caused still another marriage ceremony to be held on January 3, 1773, at Ahrensburgh, by virtue of a license from the king of Denmark, granted December 5, 1772. The marriage took place at a private house in the presence of four witnesses. Since the bride was above twelve years of age, the legal age of consent in England at the time, Morris had reason to believe that having been married once in a church and once by private marriage via a special license, the legality of the event could withstand any scrutiny and challenge.[5]

(Courtesy the Frick Collection, New York)

Frances Mary Harford. This portrait was painted by George Romney.

Now Robert Morris himself wrote to England and let his location be known. Agents sent by Lord Baltimore's executors then pursued the pair and, by means not made clear, took possession of Frances Mary and brought her back to England. A long legal suit was begun in the courts to have the marriage annulled.

Attorneys arguing for Miss Harford contended that she was taken away without the consent of either her mother or of her guardians, married abroad, and, further, was not legally married because Morris provided foreign authorities with false information as to his place of residence and the age of his bride. Frances Mary, the attorneys argued, was taken by force and caused to marry Morris through fear of what he would do.[6]

Combating these statements, lawyers for Robert Morris argued that Frances Mary was above the legal age of consent and voluntarily took part in the elopement and marriages. They stated that foreign marriages had long been recognized as legal and gave several precedents to bolster this assertion.

Having heard the pleas of both sides, the judge ruled (December 2, 1776) that Frances Mary had no grounds for annulment and that the marriages appeared to be legal.[7] Morris must have exulted, for he believed himself to be gaining control over his young wife's fortune. Yet he could not seem to get his hands on her money. He was displaced as her guardian, as executor of Lord Baltimore's will, and so lost the substantial amount willed him by Lord Baltimore.

So matters stood for several years. Frances Mary, a wealthy young woman, lived in London. She and her brother must often have discussed their future. Maryland loomed large in their minds, for once England succeeded in suppressing the American rebels, the Harfords fully expected to gain great wealth and status from the proprietorship of that province.

Between 1780 and 1783 Frances Mary sat for portrait artist George Romney. Her portraits reveal a pretty young woman with a gentle, appealing expression. She had light brown hair, brown eyes, and a complexion of English perfection.[7] According to the number of sittings recorded by Romney, several portraits must have been painted, yet only two, one at the Frick Galleries in New York, and another belonging to the estate of Frederick McCann, New York, have been discovered. Romney also painted a portrait, or several, of Henry Harford but these have not yet been identified.[8]

The lovely young Englishwoman, in spite of her illegitimate birth, held a high position in English society. She was the recognized daughter of the sixth Baron of Baltimore and was officially allowed to use his family crest, "with suitable alterations."[9] She was wealthy and sister to the affluent Henry Harford, Proprietor of Maryland. Once plucked from the arms of Robert Morris, she lived in London probably with her mother, Mrs. Hester Rhelan Harford Prevost.

In time she attracted a young officer of the prestigious Coldstream Guards, William Frederick Wyndham, the youngest brother of George, third Earl of Egremont. Young Wyndham's interest in her, it appears, caused the courts to take a less adamant stance, for upon reapplication to the High Court of Delegates for the annulment of her marriage to Morris, the case was at last settled, and in May, 1784, at twenty-five years of age, Frances Mary was free to marry. As *Gentleman's Magazine,* May, 1784, editorialized:

> This day the great cause that has been so long depending, and has furnished an ample harvest to the doctors, proctors, etc., of the civil law, in which Mifs. Harford was complainant, and Mr. Morris defendant was finally determined, and judgement given. That both *pretended* marriages were void: That Mifs. Harford, falsely in the libel called Morris, was at full liberty to marry again; and that Mr. Morris was at full liberty to marry again.[10]

At the time her court case was concluded, her brother was in America. With the assistance of a battery of legal advisors a long marriage settlement was negotiated without his on-the-scene assistance.*

Since her husband-to-be was of such a distinguished family and since she had by this time £36,000 in her own right to bring to the marriage, the marriage settlement was an involved document. It spelled out the nature of the various trusts to be established for children that might arrive as a result of the marriage. The exchange and disposition of various amounts were agreed upon by both parties.[11]

On the heels of her being granted an annulment in May, Frances Mary married the Hon. William Frederick Wyndham on July 21st, by special license.[12]

The man she married had much to offer her. When he was born, April 6, 1763, his father was the Secretary of State, second Earl of Egremont, and his mother, Lady of the Queen's Bedchamber. King George and Queen Charlotte had personally stood as sponsors when William Frederick was christened by no less a personage than the Bishop of Bristol.

After a childhood spent under the supervision of a number of tutors and at exclusive schools, young William Frederick obtained a commission in the Coldstream Guards. He resigned this commission to marry Frances Mary in 1784.[13]

The couple lived unemployed at Bignor, near Petworth, the Wyndham family estate, and spent much of their time abroad. When at Petworth, Frances Mary no doubt listened to the family horror story with which the very existence of her husband was linked. The story goes: Miss Florence Wadham married John Wyndham in 1558. The following year the young woman became ill and fell into such a deep coma that she was believed to be dead. With suitable ceremony she was interred in the family vault. The night of the funeral, carrying a lantern, the sexton who knew she was wearing three valuable rings, went to rob the cof-

---

*It was from this document, incidentally, that we discovered that he was definitely in America at this time.

(Author's 1974 photograph)

Petworth House backs against the village of Petworth. As one circles and passes through an iron gate the grand, and rather forbidding front of the mansion is revealed. Frances Mary Harford, after her marriage to William Frederick Wyndham, may have strolled to the hilltop shown here. From here she could view the mansion, the ornamental lake, and the fields surrounding the luxurious seat of the Earls of Egremont.

fin. To get at one ring he cut at one of her fingers and sprang away terrified when blood poured from the slash and the body moved. Horror stricken, he fled, leaving his lantern.

His would-be victim, poor Florence Wyndham, then picked up the lantern and made her way a half mile through the night to her home. Arriving dressed in her burial garments, nursing her bloodied hand, she beat upon the door, faint with relief at having regained her doorstep. But her family was afraid to open the door and refused to let her in for some time. At length, they were convinced that she was no ghost.

Some time afterwards she bore a son, her only child, from whom almost all the later family were descended. Except for the birth of this son the male line would have ended, although distant cousins, immigrants to America, did exist.[14]

Frances Mary lived at Bignor and probably visited Petworth House nearby. It seems possible, too, that Henry Harford may have viewed the mansion at times during his sister's marriage to William Frederick Wyndham. An interesting place, the manor of Petworth was old when the Normans invaded England in 1066. Via marriage it descended to Elizabeth Percy, along with a mansion containing a great library and a collection of paintings. In 1682 she married the Earl of Somerset, who set about rebuilding Petworth House on a quite impressive scale with her money. He transformed the mansion from a fortified house with medieval undercrofts into a grand, symmetrical building of French design.

The Wyndhams became Earls of Egremont and heirs to Petworth House in 1750, again as the result of family links and marriages. At the time Frances Mary married in 1784, Petworth House was owned by the third Earl of Egremont (1751–1837), a remarkable man albeit quite an eccentric one. He was a most hospitable person, entertaining in particular many artists and literary figures of the day. He chose to play but little part in political life, preferring to spend most of his time at Petworth. He used his huge income to indulge in his passion for farming, friends, and art. He shared his palatial home with Elisabeth Iliffe, a daughter of the librarian of Westminster Abbey. Her portrait, which hangs in Petworth House today, shows her expression one of mingled kindliness and patience. George O'Brien Wyndham, the third Earl, did not marry her until 1801, and so their six children, born prior to this date, were not legally able to inherit the title. His earldom passed to a nephew, as we shall presently see.[15]

Frances Mary while visiting Petworth House saw there the elaborate series of reception rooms, the marvelous carved curtains of wood in the chapel, the ceilings and walls adorned with rosy maidens and cherubs. Quite possibly, too, she may have been present at some of Lord Egremont's annual feasts for his tenants and workers.

With ample wealth and high social status assured her by her marriage, all should now have been well with Frances Mary. Her illegitimate birth, her youthful elopement, the long legal battle to annul her marriage to Morris, were all behind her now. Certainly she and her husband were happy over the birth of the first child, George Francis, on October 30th, 1785.

Her husband was pleased, too, by his appointment as envoy extraordinary to the Court of Florence in 1794.[16] By this time three daughters had been born to the Wyndhams, Frances, Laura, and Julia. Yet for all the promise of the marriage, it proved to be a tempestuous and unhappy one. According to a Wyndham family history, "Frances Mary was a frail human craft having neither rudder or anchor. She was miserable at Bignor and not less so in Florence."[17]

Another boy was born, in Florence in 1794, and named William. The child soon died, however, casting Frances Mary into a deep depression.

Motherhood did not quench Frances Mary's romantic nature for William Frederick was obliged to fight a duel over a slur cast upon his wife's name while they lived in Italy.[18] Next his rebellious wife contracted an alliance with a man described by a Wyndham ancestor as the "erratic Lord Wycombe." The family chronicler continued: "William, however, was non-suited in the action he brought against his supplanter, while his wife was reduced by her new consort to a state bordering on mental derangement."[19]

Frances Mary, beset by both husband and lover, chose to live apart from them both and set up a domicile in Florence.

"Wyndham," officially George Francis Wyndham, son of Frances Mary and William Frederick, entered the Royal Navy in 1799 at the age of fourteen. Eight years later he married. In 1837, since his uncle (George O'Brien Wyndham, third Earl) had no legitimate children, Wyndham inherited the title and became the fourth Earl of Egremont. With the title came large incomes and the estate Orchard Wyndham along with other estates in Somerset and Devon. He and his wife had no children, therefore, upon his death in 1845 at the age of sixty, the title lapsed.

Although his uncle had had to allow the title and certain estates to be inherited by Wyndham, a great deal of the third Earl's wealth went to his children, mentioned earlier. This family was granted a title and descendants of the third Earl live at Petworth House today.

Frances Mary meanwhile lived on in Italy, probably for the most part in Florence. There her life was a dim but recognizeable likeness to that of her father. Surrounded by persons attracted by her wealth; she enjoyed the beauty and ease of life in Italy.

That lady died in Florence, March 18, 1822, leaving a short will devising £15,000 to her daughter, Mrs. Laura Wyndham Boultbee. Small sums were left to her retainers. Silver plate, gold plate, ". . . a very few diamonds, . . .", carriages, and personal effects were mentioned in the will.[20] So a most adventurous life closed.

Frances Mary Harford had eventually come to live a life of ease, fully independent of husband or protector, no small feat in her day. She married worth £36,000 in her own name, and as we have seen, she married very well. In her lifetime, too, she attracted the love of several men. She seems to have survived the adventurous life she led with much of her fortune intact, for she died with a substantial estate worth approximately £20,000.[21]

Was she lonely in a foreign land surrounded by her paid companion, her servants and a religious advisor? Or did she live in Italy fully independent and quite content? Should letters written to her brother in England come to light one day, then we may know the answers to these questions.

Her husband went on after their separation to carry out many important and adventurous assignments for his government in Europe. He served his country well through several evacuations, wars and rebellions that occurred during this unsettled period. He formed an alliance with the widow of a Polish nobleman, the Comtesse de Spyterki, Julia Konstancia de Smorzewska. When news of Frances Mary's death reached him, he then married the comtesse.[22]

So it was that the lady who might have been Proprietor of Maryland died, survived by her former husband, her children, and by her brother, Henry Harford.

---

[1]*English Consistory Report: 1788–1821* (London: n.p., n.d.), p. 792. Maryland Historical Society vertical files, Manuscript Division.
[2]Ibid, p. 793.
[3]Ibid.
[4]Letter of Daniel (3d) Dulany, Jr. to Walter Dulany, from London to Annapolis. MS. Div., Dulany Papers, filed under "1792."
[5]*English Consistory Report: 1788–1821*, p. 792.
[6]Ibid, pp. 792–794.
[7]Ibid, p. 797.
[8]T. H. Ward and W. Roberts, *Romney,* London, np, 1904, II, p. 71.
[9]"Portrait of Miss Harford," *Maryland Historical Magazine,* Vol. 35, No. 1, p. 87.
[10]*Gentleman's Magazine,* Vol. LIV, (May, 1784), p. 383.
[11]Marriage Agreement between Frances Mary Harford and William Frederick Wyndham, Petworth House Archives, file 3027.
[12]*Gentleman's Magazine,* Vol. LIV (July, 1784), p. 556; *Gentleman's Magazine,* Vol. XCVIII (April, 1828), pp. 363–364.

[13]Hugh Archibald Wyndham, *A Family History: 1688–1837. The Wyndhams of Somerset, Sussex and Wiltshire,* London: Oxford University Press, 1950, p. 226.
[14]W. A. Barron, "A Famous Sussex Family," *Sussex County Magazine,* XXIV, No. 9 (September, 1950), pp. 392–393.
[15]Information gathered from visit to Petworth House, England. Also: *The Life and Letters of George Wyndham,* London: Hutchinson & Co., 1925, Vol. I, pp. 1–38.
[16]*Gentleman's Magazine,* LXIV (March, 1794), p. 286.
[17]H. A. Wyndham, p. 227.
[18]Ibid, pp. 227, 263.
[19]*Life and Letters of George Wyndham,* p. 10.
[20]Will of Frances Mary Harford, Appendix F. This will located in the Petworth House Archives by Mrs. Patricia Gill, County Archivist, courtesy the present Lord Egremont and acknowledgments to the West Sussex Record Office, File No. Petworth House Archives, 3027, and 1608.
[21]Ibid.
[22]H. A. Wyndham, p. 227; also *Dictionary of National Biography,* London: Smith, Elder and Company, 1889, pp. 240–243.

CHAPTER X

HENRY HARFORD'S LIFE IN ENGLAND: 1785-1834

Henry Harford was a well-educated, wealthy man in his thirties in the 1790s. In spite of his illegitimate birth he held a high social standing, in London society. He lived at this time in a luxurious New Cavendish Street home in London, and planned to marry Louisa, daughter of Peter Pigou, Esquire, of Berners Street. The marriage took place in London in June, 1792.[1]

Marriage settlements were made only when there was wealth involved. It was this sort of document that Henry Harford and the representatives of Miss Pigou wrote and signed in the presence of witnesses prior to their marriage. The financial standing of possible children to be born of this union was carefully delineated in the settlement.[2]

As it happened, the Harford's first child was a boy, born October, 1793, and christened with pride and joy, "Henry Harford." Sadly, this infant son did not survive. In 1794 another child, Louisa Anne, was born. Two years later another daughter, Frances, arrived. This choice of name indicates, incidentally, that Harford was on good terms with his sister in 1796. Frances Mary Harford by this time had left her husband and was living in Italy.* Yet another daughter was born in 1797, and named Frederica Louisa Elizabeth, in honor of her grandfather and her mother.[3]

There followed a period of about five years in which the Harfords had no children indicating that Louisa Pigou Harford may well have suffered a long period of ill health. Indeed, following the birth of her last child,

---

*This continuing affection between Henry Harford and his sister indicates that many letters must have been written between them. None have been found, however, to date.

the long-awaited heir, Frederick Paul, born in 1802, Louisa died at Exmouth, near Exeter. This small town was favored as a resort by persons suffering from respiratory diseases. She was buried in the Exeter Cathedral.[4]

Henry Harford returned from the elaborate funeral to live with his three young daughters and infant son in London.

Three years later Harford decided to marry again. With this marriage he linked his name to that of the wealthy and socially prominent family of Sir Nelson Ryecroft, Baronet of Farnham, Surrey, by marrying Sir Nelson's sister, Esther. The marriage took place on June 5, 1806, Harford's second June wedding.[5]

A period of calm in Henry Harford's life followed, if one can so term the arrival of five more children. To the four children in the household at the time of the marriage, Henry and Esther Harford added two boys and three girls. The children arrived in fairly close sequence: George Harford born May 9, 1807; Charlotte Penelope born June 30, 1808 (but did not survive her father); Esther Harford, born February 23, 1810; Charles, born March 1, 1811; and finally, Emily, born February 4, 1814.[6]

Harford could well afford his brood of children, for he was a very wealthy man. Further, both his wives brought him comfortable doweries.[7]

To provide a more spacious, healthful environment for his family, in 1807 Harford purchased a country home, "Down Place," located about four miles outside the towns of Windsor and Eton.[8] He bought considerable acreage with the home and obtained other parcels of land nearby, as well.[9] Down Place was a pleasant country seat for the Harfords, located as it was by the Thames River and having broad fields about it. Nearby were several outbuildings to shelter carriages and horses and to provide space for various activities outside the main house. Roman ruins were located on the site where Harford's children may have dug hop-

(Photograph courtesy Florence M. and Pamela V. Harford)

Thames side of Down Place, near Windsor, the country home of Henry Harford and of three generations of the Harford family that followed him.

ing they would find coins or skulls. Harford retained his New Cavendish Street home in London.[10]

All through the years Henry Harford stayed on good terms with his stepfather Peter Prevost, for when that gentleman died, his will contained a small bequest for Henry Harford.[11]

Prevost left Harford's mother, Hester Rhelan Harford Prevost, 500 guineas and all their household belongings. Another bequest, a small one, was left to Elizabeth Rhelan, his wife's sister.[12] The will suggests warm family ties between Peter Prevost, his wife and her sister, and Henry Harford.

Prevost had had during his lifetime his £100 a year from Lord Baltimore's estate, and Hester's £200 a year from that same estate. Apparently the pair had lived on these incomes and had managed to accumulate little capital.[13]

Henry Harford's mother survived her husband by about twenty-three years, dying early in 1812 while living near Bath, England. Her short will bequeathed, ". . . all the goods, chattles, personal Estate and Effects which I may be possessed of unto Henry Harford of New Cavendish Street, park and place, Son and Esquire . . ." Simply, Hester Rhelan Prevost noted that her son was to be her executor and to have all that she owned.[14] Her daughter, Frances Mary, is not mentioned; whether from an estrangement between them or because the daughter was well enough provided for, we cannot know. The simple language and the brevity of this will indicates that Harford's mother died possessed of no complex properties or extensive wealth. Her death did cause Harford to receive a large sum of money, however, for he then came into possession of the £6,800 capital sum which had provided her annual income.[15]

Henry Harford's Will: A Revealing Document

Maryland's sixth and last Proprietor died at Down

Place, December 8, 1834.* He was buried in the churchyard of the Church of St. Michael, parish church of Bray, a small village not far from his country home.[16]

During his lifetime Henry Harford had inherited over 100,000 pounds from his father, and had realized over 120,000 pounds reparations for losses of Maryland lands and incomes. A great deal of this money must have been transferred to his son during Harford's lifetime, as was the custom, via marriage settlement. Large settlements, too, were no doubt made to his other children. In his will, dated July 16, 1829, he provided his wife with an outright and immediate cash gift of £1,000. She was also to receive, her personal jewels, plate up to 1,200 ounces, carriages, wines, spirits, and all household effects and furnishings. She was provided with a home at Down Place. In his will he at first provided her with an annual legacy of 500 pounds a year, but in a codicil dated June 1, 1833, this was revoked.[17] The reason is not given. It could have been that she neither wanted nor needed the income, Harford's business affairs could have suffered a decline, or he may have become annoyed with his wife. The principal sum of the Calvert fortune, then, by no means came to Esther Ryecroft Harford.

The four children resulting from Henry Harford's first marriage inherited a capital sum of £10,000. This was due to a legacy left them by Frederick and Jemima Pigou, their maternal grandparents. Again indicating that Frederick Paul Harford had adequate funds, Harford directed that this £10,000, "shall go in equal one-thirds" to Frederica Elizabeth Harford (Mrs. Robert Thomas John Glyn)*, to Louisa Ann Harford, and to Frances Harford the sum was not to be paid to them, but rather held for them and they were to receive only the interest.

---

*John Penn of Stoke, former proprietor of Pennsylvania, also died in the year 1834. Both proprietors died in the same year, something of a coincidence.

*Descendents of the Glyns live in England today.

(Illustrations courtesy the Vicar of Bray)
The Church of St. Michael at Bray in 1760 from an old drawing.

(Illustrations courtesy the Vicar of Bray)
The village of Bray, from an old print.

Due to a marriage settlement with Esther Rycroft, dated 4 June 1806, Harford noted that he had been holding a £7,000 trust in 3% annuities for the children of his second marriage. These securities were to be turned over to the four surviving children born to Harford and his wife Esther, in four equal amounts. All of the bequests to his minor children carried the condition that the child must be twenty-one years of age in order to inherit the money. An exception was made in the case of the females, who were allowed to receive their inheritance upon the date of their marriage, even though this took place prior to their twenty-first birthday.

Frederick Paul Harford, the oldest son, inherited a major fortune, though the will is not specific as to the details. A marriage settlement had settled a considerable amount on him, as a phrase in his mother's will indicated later,[18] while in his father's will he is simply devised the residue of the estate after certain bequests are satisfied. Frederick Paul was to inherit Down Place, though his mother was entitled to live out her life there.

Henry Harford left to his other children:

Louisa Ann	£4,000	
Frances	£2,000	
Frederica Elizabeth (Mrs. Glyn)	£2,000	(As promised in her marriage settlement, dated June 29, 1829.)
George	£5,000	
Charles	£5,000	
Esther	£3,000	
Emily	£3,000	

These were the major sums left to the heirs of the man who had been Proprietor of Maryland. Though substantial sums, the Calvert fortune passed down to Henry Harford was greatly reduced by the time of Harford's death.

Lesser sums were left, as well, £500 to George William Killett Potter, one of Harford's executors, as payment for execution of the trusts described in the will. Three servants were to have a year's wages, *if* they were still in Harford's service at the time of his death. Also, there is a person named in Harford's will whose name will tantalize historians of the Calvert family. Harford left to Henrietta Emily Calvert, Spinster, a bequest of £100 per year.

From the amounts left by Harford, it is difficult to see more than a comfortable life style and financial position. Gone were the days of bequests and trusts of tens of thousands of pounds, dowries of £30,000. The effects of the loss of Maryland to the former proprietary family are obvious. Where had the great wealth gone that Harford inherited? Gone in legal suits to obtain more wealth, gone in years of luxurious living, gone in providing for eight children? So it would seem, for his total estate was valued at only £60,000.

Esther Rycroft Harford: Her Legacies

Nearly twenty years after the death of Henry Harford, his wife Esther died at Down Place, May 17, 1853, at the age of 78.[19] Her children were all grown, her duties as a mother faithfully carried out.

Esther Harford's will shows that she had relatively little wealth in her own name, in itself a comment on the customs of the times with regard to the transmission of wealth and to the status of women. Her will documented her love for her own children and her stepchildren, as well. Various bits of jewelry were left to all the Harford children, and to Frederick Paul, as the head of the family, "all the family diamonds consisting of necklace, earrings, and sprig."[20]

Esther Harford made several small cash bequests to her step-children, as well as to her own children. The largest sum she had at her command, £800, she left to her son George.

The total value of the estate, aside from her jewelry, was about £1,000.[21] This is a modest estate for a woman of position:

Where had the tens of thousands of pounds gone? We can speculate that Harford's legal expenses had been heavy in the long litigation involved in his securing the proprietorship. Much money no doubt was turned over to his children in various settlements while he lived. Raising eight children and educating them, too, must have occasioned considerable expense. Also, Harford and his family lived well. They maintained two luxurious homes. There were dozens of servants and other workers to be paid. All in all, since Frederick, Lord Baltimore, died in 1771, Henry Harford had managed his affairs well enough to provide a luxurious life style for himself, and later for his dependents, for sixty-three years. Further, he left his family very comfortably off. It was no mean achievement.

[1] *Etoniana*, Vol. 109 (December, 1950), p. 136.
[2] Harford family pedigree, College of Arms, London. The information regarding Henry Harford's children was copied from a parchment pedigree in the possession of the Misses Harford, great-great-granddaughters of Henry Harford at their home in Buckinghamshire, England, in the summer of 1974, by the writer.
[3] Ibid.
[4] *Gentleman's Magazine*, Vol. 73 (November, 1803); J. W. Hewett, *A Complete Monumentarium of the Cathedral Church of St. Peter, Exeter* (Exeter: Exeter Diocesan Architectural Society, 1849), p. 24.
[5] *Gentleman's Magazine*, Vol. 76 (June, 1806), p. 582.
[6] Harford family pedigree; also Harford family Bible in the possession of the Misses Florence M. and Pamela V. Harford, Buckinghamshire, England. The writer copied entries from the fly leaf of this large old Bible. The names written there begin with Frederick, Lord Baltimore. Louisa Calvert's name is jaggedly cut out as though in anger, and the Harford names follow.
[7] Will of Henry Harford, Appendix D.
[8] Charles Kerry, *The History and Antiquities of the Hundred of Bray* (London: n.p., 1861), p. 132.
[9] Extract from the Bray Inclosure Award Map of 1817. Bershire Record Office, Shire Hall, Reading, England.
[10] Ibid; also *Burke's Genealogy and Heraldic History of the Landed Gentry*, 1937 edition, p. 1055.
[11] Will of Peter Prevost, Public Record Office, London. Probate Div., Ref. Prob.11/1176/page 109.
[12] Ibid.
[13] Ibid.
[14] Will of Hester Rhelan Harford Prevost, Public Record Office, London. Probate Div., Ref. Prob.11/1530/page 91.
[15] Will of Frederick Calvert, Appendix A; also Estate Act of 1781, p. 56.

[16] Burial Register of Parish of Bray, Burials 1813-1837. D/P23/1/11. "Henry Harford, Esq., Down Place, [buried] Dec. 16, 1834, age 77." Ceremony performed by W. Levette, Vicar; also, *Gentleman's Magazine,* Vol. 3, New Series, (Jan.-June, 1835), p. 218. "Obituary: Berks.—Dec. 8, Aged 75, Henry Harford, esq., of Downplace."

Note the disparity in birth date assumption. The old lie told by Frederick Calvert that Harford was born in 1760 persisted for over seventy years.

Henry Harford is sometimes described as, "Sir Henry Harford," and his will is recorded in that manner in the Public Record Office, London. In a letter, however, from the Society of Genealogists, dated 28 October 1974, to Vera F. Rollo, and signed by the Secretary of that Society, C. M. Mackay, this was found to be a courtesy title only:

London 10.28.74

It seems fairly clear that Henry HARFORD was styled, 'Esquire' always and there is no foundation for the idea that he was 'Sir Henry.' He is not mentioned in Shaw's *Knights of England* and was certainly not created a baronet. The addition of the title must have been a flight of fancy on the part of someone else.

/s/ C. M. Mackay, Secretary

[17] Will of Henry Harford, Appendix D.
[18] Will of Esther Harford, Public Record Office, London. Probate Div., ref. Prob. 11/2174.
[19] Burial Register of Parish of Bray. Burials: Jan. 1850-Oct. 1860. #252 entry in register, page 32: "Esther Harford, Down Place, [buried] May 24, 1853, age 78." Ceremony performed by I. Edw'd Austen Leigh.
[20] Will of Esther Harford. The will was dated 9 March 1849, and proved 16 June 1853.
[21] Ibid.

CHAPTER XI

THE DESCENDANTS OF THE CALVERTS

Charles Browning, named for his grandfather the fifth Baron of Baltimore, was born to Louisa Calvert Browning and John Browning, July 29, 1765 at Hackethorn in Lincolnshire. The Brownings had come to this location to be near a clergyman, the Reverend John Willis, who was known for his treatment of mental disorders. The reason for this was that both before and after her marriage Louisa Browning was "in a low and melancholy way."[1] She dropped deeper into her depressions, and mentally withdrew following the birth of her son, having only a few lucid intervals from that time until her death. Her "physician," the Reverend Willis, seemed to have no success in mitigating her illness. (Nor was he to benefit King George III later when called upon to treat what appeared to be insanity afflicting the king.)[2]

When his uncle, Frederick, Lord Baltimore died in 1771, Charles Browning was only six years old. His father salvaged what he could from the prolonged litigation over the proprietorship of Maryland. Eventually he obtained about £25,000 from the Calvert estate. John Browning died in 1792, leaving his wife in the care of their son.

Only after Charles was grown and married, in the year 1795, did he learn that he, not Henry Harford, might be regarded as the legal heir to the province of Maryland. For some time he did not have the leisure to investigate the matter, being sent to Scotland for six years with the Cambridgeshire Fencible Cavalry. A part of this time was spent on special duty in Ireland. At length, however, his regiment was disbanded and Charles Browning returned to England.[3]

Children were born to the Brownings with an almost annual regularity and numbered six by 1804. Having only a small income, and this growing family, Browning "began to turn my attention to try to increase my income, which I began to do by doing the duties of an officer in the Temple, of which my mother was then entitled to one sixth. I also bought a situation under the appointment of the Dean and Chapter of Westminster, of High Baliff of Westminster. I sold the latter to advantage in 1806, and the form I gave up, being much in town . . ."[4]

Through talks with a friend, Robert Smith, about America and about Maryland in particular, Browning began to believe that there was considerable substance to his claim to the former province and its miles of Calvert family lands. Obtaining a copy of his grandfather's will, Browning grew even more certain that he was indeed, the heir in law to money that Maryland owed the Calvert descendants.[5]

Oddly enough, for the Browings and Harfords had opposed one another, Charles Browning even applied to Henry Harford for assistance in gathering documentation to support his claim. Harford replied that all his papers had been left with the commissioners in England, who had sat upon the claims commission some thirty years before. Though delayed by the illnesses of both his wife and his mother, Browning set sail for Maryland, October 1, 1819.[6]

Once there, it took him many months to obtain a hearing. While he waited he gathered together a great deal of material relating to land ownership practices in Maryland under the Calverts. In 1820 Browning presented his case to the General Assembly and received a polite hearing. This, however, was all that he received.

Browning stayed in Maryland for years, writing in 1821 his *Appeal to the Citizens of Maryland,* and in 1825 his *Granting of Lands in Maryland.* The General Assembly eventually politely heard him again, but gave him no encouragement to continue to press for the sums he believed the state owed him.[7]

Browning later left America to live in France. From that country he wrote a series of bitter letters regarding the treatment he had been given in Maryland. He believed himself robbed of his legal inheritance of many miles of American land.

Maryland had substantially contributed to his livelihood, however, for his father had realized some thousands of pounds by relinquishing claims upon the proprietorship to Henry Harford by way of the Estate Act of 1781.

Four generations of the Harford family followed Maryland's last Proprietor. In the three generations that came immediately after Henry Harford, the Harford line produced but one son a generation. In each of these three generations the son joined the British military service and attained a respectable rank.

Frederick Paul Harford

Frederick Paul Harford, Henry Harford's eldest son, served in the Scots Fusilier Guards. He retired with the rank of Captain. His wife was the second daughter of Reverend R. Fitzwilliam Halifax. The couple lived at Down Place and had a son and two daughters.

Captain Harford served the county of Berkshire as a Justice of the Peace and Deputy Lieutenant of the county. He died by his own hand on February 21, 1860, at the age of 58 and was buried in the churchyard of the parish church, St. Michael's and All Angels, at Bray.

His wife, Elizabeth Louisa Harford, seven years his junior, lived on for another sixteen years. She died at 66 years of age and was buried beside her husband.[8]

Frederick Henry Harford

The Proprietor's grandson, Frederick Henry Harford, like his father, also chose to live much of the time

GEORGE CALVERT = Ann Mynne
　　　　　　　　　= Joan

CECIL CALVERT = Anne Arundell

CHARLES (I) CALVERT = Mary Darnell
　　　　　　　　　　　= Jane Sewall
　　　　　　　　　　　= Mary Thorpe
　　　　　　　　　　　= Margaret Charleton

BENEDICT LEONARD CALVERT = Charlotte Lee

CHARLES (II) CALVERT = Mary Janssen

Louisa Calvert = John Browning　　　　Caroline Calvert = Robert Eden
　　　|　　　　　　　　　　　　　　　　　　　|
　Charles Browning　　　　　　　　　　　　Issue

FREDERICK CALVERT = Diana Egerton
　　　　　　　　　　　|
　　　　　　　　　No Issue

with Hester Rhelan

HENRY HARFORD = (first) Louisa Pigou　　Frances Mary Harford = William
　　　　　　　　　　　　　　　　　　　　　　　　　　　　　　　　　　　Frederick
　　　Issue: Henry, b. Oct. 12, 1793　　　　　　　　　　　　　　　　　Wyndham
　　　　　　　d. young
　　　　　　Louisa Anne, b. Dec. 29, 1794
　　　　　　Frances, b. Jan. 22, 1796　　　　　　　　　George Francis
　　　　　　Frederica Louisa Elizabeth　　　　　　　　(4th Earl of Egremont)
　　　　　　　b. Mar. 3, 1797
FREDERICK PAUL HARFORD, b. April 29, 1802 or 1803　　Frances
　　　　　　　　　　　　　　　　　　　　　　　　　　　　Laura
　　　　　　　　　　　　　　　　　　　　　　　　　　　　Julia
　　= (secondly) Esther Ryecroft　　　　　　　　　　　　William (d. an infant)
　　　Issue: George, b. May 9, 1807
　　　　　　Charlotte Penelope, b. June 30, 1808
　　　　　　　d. young
　　　　　　Esther, b. Feb. 23, 1810
　　　　　　Charles, b. March 1, 1811
　　　　　　Emily, b. Feb. 4, 1814

= Louisa Elizabeth Bourke

　　　Edith　　　　　Marion

FREDERICK HENRY HARFORD = Florence Helen Isabel Parsons

　　　Violet Evelyn Harford = 12th Earl of Stair
FREDERICK REGINALD HARFORD = Maude Isabel Lardelli

　　Florence Marianne Harford　　Pamela Violet Harford

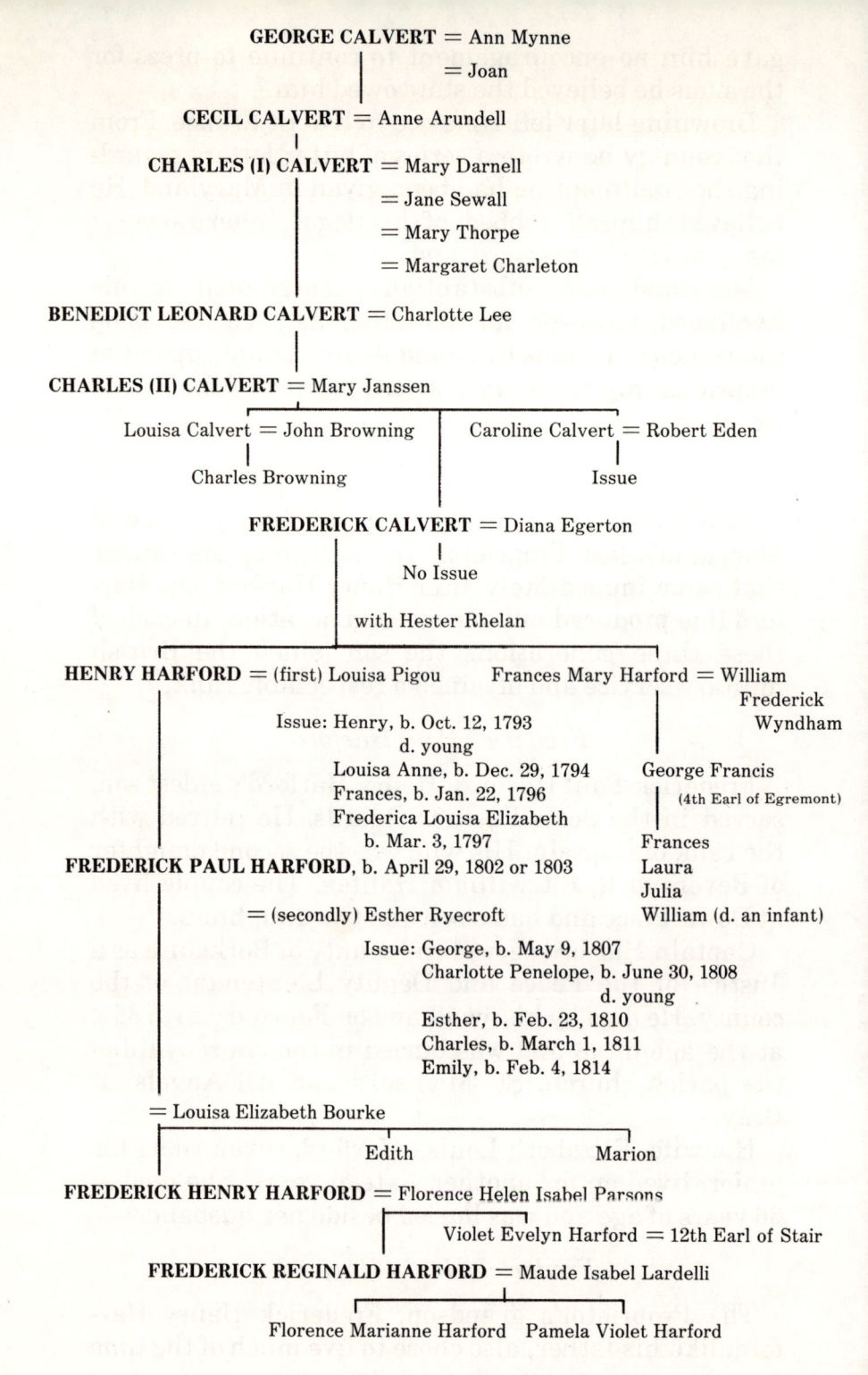

LINE OF DESCENT, PROPRIETARY FAMILY

at Down Place. He also served in the military, being for some years an officer in the Scots Fusilier Guards. He retired from the Guards with the rank of Colonel.

Colonel Harford married Florence Helen Isabel, youngest daughter of the Honorable Lawrence Parsons. Once again a Harford marriage produced a son and a daughter. The daughter, Violet Evelyn Harford, married the twelfth Earl of Stair on October 20, 1904.[9] This marriage indicates that the Harford family had maintained their high social status.

The Proprietor's grandson came into contact with an agent from Maryland in the 1880s. The meetings at this time were the only instances during the past two hundred years, prior to this study, that there was such contact between Harfords and Marylanders. The meeting of Frederick Henry Harford and representatives of the Maryland Historical Society came about due to a casual note made by writer and researcher Colonel A. W. McDonald. McDonald had been sent to London in March of 1860 to seek papers relating to the original legal boundary lines of Virginia.

In his report Colonel McDonald mentioned the fact that he had sought an unnamed "representative of the Calvert family," and found the man in prison for debt at Queens Bench Prison. The poor man had been there for twelve years and prior to that had served another eight years in Fleet prison. The man told McDonald that he had not seen the original charter to Maryland among the other family papers and believed it lost. The identity of this man has not been ascertained.

Somehow Colonel McDonald's remark about seeing this prisoner and his remark about "other family papers," and further, a sighting by the colonel of a chest in the British Museum marked "Calvert Papers," came to the eyes of members of the Maryland Historical Society. Colonel McDonald's report stirred the interest of the Society members but the Civil War intervened at this point. It was not until the mid-1880s that the matter came up again. A letter was written to the British Museum by representatives of the Maryland Historical Society to inquire about the chest of Calvert papers. The Museum replied that no such chest could be located and that it must have been there temporarily pending possible purchase by the Museum.

The Society then contacted Henry Harford's grandson, Colonel Frederick Henry Harford, at Down Place near Windsor. He had some family papers, Colonel Harford admitted, stored in a chest housed in his orangery there. The Society managed to have the papers rescued from their damp resting place and held in the offices of Colonel Harford's attorney in London.

Next the Society chose Mr. Mendes Cohen as chairman of a committee to determine the authenticity of the papers and the possibility of acquiring them. His work was greatly assisted by a monetary grant made by Mr. T. Harrison Garrett to aid the project. The Society was relieved to have gotten the chest into safekeeping when, to the anquish of committee members, they heard that still another chest of papers had been casually buried in a field adjoining Down Place! Correspondence with London revealed that these papers had been buried to get them out of the way. This was too much for the Society, something must be done quickly, members resolved. Mr. Garrett, interested in the project, spared the Society his employee, J. W. M. Lee, who was also Librarian to the Society, to go to England to see about retrieving the historic papers. The fact that priceless Maryland documents were being scattered about in damp English country houses and even fields seemed an extreme example of British eccentricity to Society members.

The acquisition of early papers relating to Maryland was made more important due to the fact that early in Maryland's history, in 1643, the records of the first ten years of settlement at St. Mary's City and records of the first meetings of the Maryland Assembly had been lost when Richard Ingle swooped down upon the small capital and took control. Due to the destruction of these records substantial gaps existed in the record of the first settlement of the Calvert colony.

Once in London, Mr. Lee immediately contacted Colonel Harford's attorneys and examined the papers they held. It took him but little time to realize that he had found a most valuable assortment of early papers relating to the settlement of Maryland. Now he yearned to recover, as well, the buried chest and with that in mind journeyed to Windsor by train, taking that opportunity to view Windsor Castle on the way. He then traveled by hired carriage to Down Place. There he was entertained by Colonel Harford and the colonel's wife but was disappointed to learn that no trace of the buried chest of papers could be found. The gardener who had buried it was no longer in Colonel Harford's employ and it seemed the papers were lost.

In spite of not being able to secure the second chest, the Society members were happy to be able to ship at least one collection of papers to Maryland. In June of 1888 the precious documents were safely secured in the vaults of the Maryland Historical Society in Baltimore. Later, as members of the Society examined the papers they were delighted to find that they had purchased around a thousand documents in all! Some of these dated back to 1633, the year prior to the founding of St. Mary's City. Selections from these papers were later published, following a formal presentation of the collection to the Society in December 1888.[10]

Jubilant as the Marylanders were over this great gain, there remained the tantalizing, painful thought of the lost chest of papers. In pursuit of this lost historical treasure, Mr. Julian LeRoy White set off for England in July of 1889. A member of the Maryland Historical Society, he was determined to attempt the discovery of the second chest. He visited Colonel Harford at Down Place. Mr. White, further, managed to locate the old gardener who was reported to have buried the missing chest. Colonel Harford's former servant was brought to Down Place and asked to point out the spot where the chest was buried. Then, with a gang of laborers hired for the purpose, White set about digging up the Colonel's garden. The men dug on and all about the spot indicated, without the least success. In his letter to the Society, White stated that *nothing* had been found at all, and pointed out that this was in itself most unlikely. An old chest would have left some trace and, also, old parchments are not easily rotted. Therefore, Mr. White seemed to feel that there was a possibility that the chest of papers had never been buried at all, but had been disposed of by the gardener. Naturally the old servant did not admit to this.[11]

So the story seemed to end in the empty English earth of Colonel Harford's garden. And yet, only about five years later, more Calvert papers were to be heard of, via a most unlikely train of circumstances.

A man in Lincoln, Nebraska wrote to the Maryland Historical Society early in 1894, asking if that society would be interested in some very early papers relating to the settlement of Maryland! Mr. Cohen still headed the committee for the recovery of Calvert papers. One can imagine Mr. Cohen's face as he held the letter from Nebraska in his hands. Certainly his expression must have revealed excitement, puzzlement, and doubt.

Further correspondence revealed that a Mr. John Roland Phillips of Lincoln, Nebraska, had in fact inherited what seemed to be authentic documents relating to early Maryland. (Oddly, the papers had originally come into Mr. Phillips' hands at just about the time negotiations were going on in England to recover the chest of papers from Colonel Harford, for it was with the death of Phillip's father, in 1887, that the papers came to John Phillips.)

It seemed that the senior Phillips had served in England in several military campaigns, had indeed, written a book on his experiences in England. It may well have been that during this time he obtained the papers. His son could not shed light on how his father had acquired them.[12]

Examining them, Society members determined that these were extremely valuable papers of a very early date, again as early as 1633.[13] Were these the papers missing from Colonel Harford's garden? To date this question has not been answered but it does seem possible. In any case, the Society gladly purchased the papers from Mr. Phillips and again published selections for the use of those interested in Maryland history.

The affair of the Calvert Papers gave us a brief look at the life of Henry Harford's descendant, Colonel Frederick Henry Harford. He was found to be a genial man who kindly entertained the representatives of the Maryland Historical Society who had traveled to Down Place to seek him out. He and his wife lived in considerable style by the Thames at Down Place. Many servants were employed to maintain the old Harford home and to serve the family.

Interest in the Harfords then apparently lapsed for another hundred years until this study began in the 1970s.

Colonel Harford died at the age of 85, on August 12, 1926 and his son inherited Down Place.

Frederick Reginald Harford

The great-grandson of Maryland's last Proprietor, in the family tradition joined the Scots Guards. He married a member of the gentry of Europe, Maude Isabel, the elder daughter of T. F. Lardelli of the Malt House, Hurley, Berkshire. Frederick Reginald Harford retired from the Guards with the rank of major.[14]

In 1932, Frederick Reginald Harford broke the long residence of Harfords at Down Place and sold the old mansion with its remaining 39½ acres of land. He moved his wife and two daughters to a more modern and luxurious home, "Broadfield," in Buckinghamshire.[15]

Today the great-great-granddaughters of Maryland's last Proprietor, Florence M. and Pamela V. Harford, live near Broadfield in a modern home surrounded by a large and pleasant English garden. Neither lady has rested on her family laurels, though their background is well represented in the pages of *Debret's*, preferring to carry on the family tradition of service to England. During World War II both were active in the war effort.[16]

From the time of Henry Harford to the present day his direct descendants have maintained their social status and financial standing. This was due in part to the Calvert family fortune and in part to their own considerable abilities.

---

[1] Charles Browning, *An Appeal to the Citizens of Maryland* (Baltimore: n.p., 1821), p. 5.

[2] John Brooke, *King George III* (New York: McGraw-Hill Book Co., 1972), p. 371; also Browning, pp. 5-8.

[3] Browning, pp. 5-8.

[4] Ibid, p. 10.

[5] Ibid, p. 12.

[6] Ibid, p. 11.

[7] Copies of both of Browning's books may be found in the library of the Maryland Historical Society, and in the Library of Congress.

[8] Death Certificate, Frederick Paul Harford. Personal papers of the Misses Harford, Buckinghamshire, England. Cause of death is given as suicide while temporarily insane. Gravestone in churchyard of the parish church at Bray. See Appendix H.

[9] *Burke's Genealogy and Heraldic History of the Landed Gentry*, 1937 edition, p. 1055.

[10] *The Calvert Papers*, Vol. I, Fund Publication 28, 1889; Vol. II, Fund Publication 34, 1894; Vol. III, Fund Publication 35, 1899 (Baltimore: Maryland Historical Society), prefaces. The story of the acquisition of the Calvert Papers is told in the prefaces of the three volumes of items selected for publication from the Calvert Papers collection.

[11] *The Calvert Papers*, Vols. II, and III, prefaces.

[12] Manuscripts Div., Maryland Historical Society, Calvert Papers, vertical file, To Maryland Historical Society, Baltimore, from John Roland Phillips, of Lincoln, Nebraska, Oct. 9, 1889.

[13] Ibid.

[14] *Burke's*, p. 1055.

[15] Ibid.

[16] Ibid.

(Author's photograph)

Florence M. Harford and Pamela V. Harford, the great-great-granddaughters of Maryland's last Proprietor in the garden of their Buckinghamshire home, in the summer of 1974.

Epilogue

In this examination of the life of Henry Harford we have found answers to some of the questions we asked. Harford did become the legally recognized Proprietor of Maryland. He was not, as hitherto believed, simply foisted upon Maryland entirely by his father's circumvention of British law, but rather gained a clear title by adding his own efforts, in 1780 and 1781, to the machinations of his late father. The legal heirs did unquestionably relinquish all claim to the proprietorship, as evidenced by the Estate Act of 1781, an important new source of information regarding the transfer of Maryland's proprietorship. Charles Browning's claims in the early nineteenth century mentioned some sort of agreement but it was not made clear to us that it was such an entirely legal and solid relinquishment. Harford's carrying forward the battle for legal possession of the proprietorship gives us a different picture of him than that furnished by previous mentions of his life in the literature. Henry Harford was no mere puppet whose strings were operated first by his father and later by his father's executors; rather Harford himself displayed considerable resolution and ability in gaining his ends.

Studying the proprietorship during the closing years of English colonial rule in Maryland, we have found that, though several factors were involved, one of the most important reasons for Harford's lack of success in Maryland following the Revolution lay in the climate of hostility engendered by the proprietorship of Harford's father, the dissolute Frederick Calvert. Prior to this study, Harford's rebuff in the light of precedents set in nearby Virginia and Pennsylvania seemed inexplicable. Even though it ended in failure, we learned that Harford exhibited both courage and tenacity in his Maryland journey in search of reparations.

Giving us yet another insight into Harford's character is the way in which he, on a scale far larger than previously known, gained thousands of pounds of compensation from the government of Great Britain. Again, in these able and persistent claims Harford's abilities are revealed. And here again, documentation found in the course of this study has helped fill gaps in the record.

An analysis of the money gained by Harford from his father's estate and from the government of Britain has been shown above as amounting to about £190,400. Harford's will revealed that he died worth only £60,000. His estate was diminished due to amounts disbursed prior to his death, for the most part in settlements made in favor of his eldest son and seven other children. Then, too, Henry Harford lived well in England for nearly fifty years following his American journey, and maintained two large and luxurious residences.

As for Harford the man, the study has been less successful than expected because of the lack of personal letters and journals. It was hoped that a body of these would come to light but this has not yet occurred. From the documentation that has been found, however, we have learned a great deal about the last Proprietor of Maryland. We now see that he possessed character, intelligence, and strength of purpose as evidenced by his completion of his education at Eton and Oxford in a reasonable time. His acquisition of a full and legal right to the proprietorship of Maryland also revealed ability and determination. He demonstrated staying power again in his dogged pursuit of recompense, both in Maryland and in England.

Enough evidence has come to light in the course of this examination of the life of Henry Harford to show him a man of conservative investment habits, and a patriarch who made full and careful provision for his family. Very much a devoted family man, he married twice, and fathered five children in each marriage. Of his ten children, eight survived him. All eight were well provided for in his will and via various marriage settlements.

Harford had considerable social standing, we have seen, for his standing as the natural son of a nobleman, his life style, and his marriages to women high on the social scale all give evidence of this. Unofficially he was known as "Sir Henry Harford," and his will is so registered in London, though no official record of knighthood is extant. Harford's sister, Frances Mary, shared in this social standing. Once retrieved from her teen-age elopement, she was later granted an annulment and made a brilliant second marriage.

New light has been thrown on the relations between Maryland revolutionaries, the proprietorship, and Loyalists, prior to, during, and following the American Revolution, by this study of Harford's life. We understand a little more of that important and complex period of Maryland's history. Further, we have corrected errors, ranging from Harford's date of birth to his date of death (1758–1834), which have entered into the scant record previously available on his life and times. The discovery of new documentation has allowed us to fill in the gaps in the literature with regard to Maryland's last Proprietor, a man amazingly neglected by historians. Finally, we have shown Harford to be more of a man than previous mention of him would have led us to believe, a man of considerable character and ability in his own right.

APPENDIX A

WILL OF
FREDERICK CALVERT

SIXTH LORD BALTIMORE

Public Record Office, London. Reference:

Prob. 8/165.

The following is a transcription of manuscript copies of the will of FREDERICK, LORD BALTIMORE. The document itself is not dated but bears internal evidence of having been written three months following the birth of Lord Baltimore's natural daughter, Charlotte Hope, who was born in 1770.

THE LAST WILL AND TESTAMENT of me FREDERICK LORD Baltimore, Lord Proprietary of the province of Maryland and Avalon in America WHEREAS by Indenture of Lease and Release bearing date respectively the thirtieth and thirty first days of January in the year of our Lord one thousand seven hundred and sixty one The Release being Tripartate and made between me the said Frederick Lord Baltimore of the ffirst part Shobet Don Esquire of the Second part and the Hon Sir Thomas Dormer and Dr. Gregory Marrjor* of the Third and Fourth part I have in Pursuance of certain Indentures of covenant made on my Intermarriage with the Right Hon'ble Lady Diane Egerton afterwards Lady Baltimore my late wife deceased and of such other rights as are vested in me as well under the settlements of my late ffather and grandfather made on their respective Marriages as otherways Settled and assured my said Province of Maryland with all and every the Dependency privileges loyaltys Rights [illegible word] and appurtenances there unto belonging to the use of my Self for Life with remainder to Trustees to preserve the contingent Thereunto the remainder to my ffirst and other sons in tail Male thereunto to the said Caecilius Calvert my title for Life with remainder to his ffirst and other sons in tail Male and in Default of such issue to the use of such person and persons and for such Estate or Estates as I the said Frederick Lord Baltimore should from time to time and at all times hereafter by any Deed or Instrument in writing with or without a power of Restoration to be sealed and De-

---

*These were names, rather illegibly given, of the "straw men" involved in Frederick, Lord Baltimore's legal maneuvers to bar the entail on Maryland.

livered by me in the presence of two or more creditable witnesses or by my Last will and Testament in writing or by any Instrument in writing purporting to be my Last Will and Testament to be signed by me in presence of and attested by two or more Credible Witnesses direct or appoint in which said Indenture of Release or settlement there is confirmed or a certain power and authority whereby I am Enabled by any Deed to be by me Signed and Published in the presence of and attested by three or more Credible Witnesses to Charge all or any part of said province or Territory of Maryland and other the premises therein mentioned with the payment of any sum or sums of Money not Exceeding in the whole the principal Sum of Twenty Thousand pounds Sterling for the portion of my Daughters' or younger sons or for such other uses [indecipherable word] and purposes and with such interest for the lands and to be paid in at such kinds and under such conditions and instructions and Limitations over as in and by Deed or Will should be mentioned directed or appointed with full power to me to make any Devise of the said province and other the premises by way of Mortgage for any term not Exceeded three hundred years without Impeachments of Waste redeemable on payment of the Money to be thereby charged by virtue of such power with Interest From I Do by this my last and only will and Testament which I mean should be observed by me Signed and published in the presence of and attested to as witnesses ratify and Confirm and Establish the said recited Indentures of Lease and Release or Settlement and all the Limitations therein mentioned AND I Do hereby by Will Devise Declare and Desire that the several Estates therein Specified Shall be held and Enjoyed according to the purport true intent and meaning of said Indentures of Settlement and according to such further purport and to such further Intent and meaning as I shall and now Do by this my last and only Will mention Express and Declare Concerning the same that is to say in pursuance of the said vested

Power and Authority whereby I am enabled to Charge the Said Province and other the premisses [sic] in the said Settlement Comprised or any Part thereof with any Sum not Exceeding the principal Sum of Twenty Thousand pounds Sterl. and of all other powers and Authorities Enabling me in that behalf I do hereby accordingly by this my last and only Will Charge the said Province and other the said premisses [sic] and every part thereof with the payment of the full and principal Sum of Twenty Thousand pounds Sterl. Lawful [sic] Money of Great Britain which I Direct to be levied and raised immediately after my Decease and to be paid to and received by the Trustees and Executors of this my Last and only Will and to be by them paid Over and Applied and Disposed of to such persons and in such manner as I have herein after Directed or Shall by any Codicills [sic] be added to this my Last Will Direct Concerning the same and for the better Raising and Securing the said Sum of Twenty Thousand Pounds and the Interest to Arrive Due thereon which I will to be at the Rate of ffive pounds by the hundred by the year I Do hereby Grant and Devise unto Robert Eden Hugh Hammersley Esquire, Robert Morris Barrister, of Lincolns Inn and Peter Prevost Esquires and the survivor of them and to the Executors Administrators and assigns of such Survivor all that my said Territory of Maryland and other the premisses [sic] comprised in said Indentures of Settlement to hold unto them the said Robert Eden, Hugh Hammersley, Robert Morris and Peter Prevost and the Survivors of them and the Executors and Adm'trs of said Survivors for the full term of three hundred years to commence and take Effect from the Day of my Decease without Impeachment of Waste which term nevertheless I mean shall be the Demandable on full payment of said sum of Twenty Thousand pounds with the Interest thereof at a Day therein to be named by the person or persons who for the time being shall be entitled to the ffreehold or Inheritance of the premisses [sic] so Devised and Subject to and Charged and Chargeable with the said principal Sum of Twenty Thousand pounds and Interest from and after the termination of the said Term of three hundred years and of the several rides and Estates already limited of the said premisses [sic] by the said Indenture of release or settlement and from the failure of [two unclear words] of my Uncle Cecilius Calvert I DO hereby in further pursuance of the powers and Authorities in me Vested by the said Indenture of Release or Settlement and of all other Persons and Authoritys [sic] enabling me in that behalf Give Devise and Direct my said province and territory of Maryland and all other the premisses [sic] in the said Settlement Comprised and other my lands and [indecipherable word] whatsoever situated and being in America to the use of such persons and for such Estates and Subject to and Chargeable with the payment of such yearly Sums of Money as herein after mentioned that is to say I Give and bequeath unto Each of them the said Robert Eden, Hugh Hammersley, Robert Morris and Peter Prevost Esqr my Executors herein after named who shall prove this my last and only will and take upon them the administration thereof the yearly sum of one hundred pounds Lawful [sic] Money of Great Britain over and above all Deductions whatever be Arising out of the said province only and during possession thereon by those as herein directed and payable to him so proving my will and taking upon him the Execution thereof During the term of his natural life by equal half yearly payments the ffirst payment to be made at the End of Six Months after my decease over and above all other provisions made for my said Executors or any of them by this my will and I do hereby give Devise and Limit my said Province of Maryland and all other premises [sic] there unto belonging last mentioned to unto and to the use of a certain youth called or known by the Name of Henry Harford the Son of Hester Rhelan of the Kingdom of Ireland Born in Bond Street and now of the age of Nine years or more and to the heirs Male of his Body lawfully to be begotten and in the Default of such Issue to the heirs Male Lawfully begotten on the Body of a certain ffemale called Ffrances Mary Harford daughter of the said Hester Rhelan and born in Bond Street aforesaid and now of the age of eight years or more and to the heirs of the said Ffrances Mary Harford and if there shall be failure of Issue of the said Ffrances Mary Harford then to the use of the Honorable Mrs. Eden my youngest Sister to her and her heirs and assigns for ever, and as touching the said principal sum of ten thousand pounds part thereof to my eldest Sister Louisa Browning and to her husband. And the Sum of Ten Thousand pounds other part thereof to my youngest Sister the Honorable Caroline Eden and her husband to be paid to them respectively within six months after my decease with Interest of five per Cent till paid provided always and my Will and meaning is that the respective Sums of Ten Thousand pounds so given to my Sisters and their Husbands are given upon this Express Condition that they and each of them Shall and do before they or either of them shall receive the said Sums or either of them or any other benefit by virtue of this my last and only Will or of the said described Settlement by Sufficient Deed or Deeds in Law to be by them Duly Executed at the request and at the costs and Charges of my Executors herein after named ratify and confirm the said described Settlement and the further Dispositions made by this my will of the said province and other the premisses [sic] and all and every the limitations uses trusts Conditions Matters and Things in the said Settlement and in this my will contained and Expressed concerning the same or in case my said Sisters or their husbands or either of them shall refuse or neglect to Execute such Deeds of Confirmation as aforesaid within twelve Months after my Decease or shall after my Decease Institute Prosecute or promote a Suit whatsoever in Law of equity whereby or otherwise to Attempt to set aside disappoint frustrate or avoid the Effect of Said Settlement or any Disposition made by me of said Province or of any other my Estates real or personal or any part thereof or in any manner Molest or Disturb any person or persons to whom any Estate Or Interest is limited by Said Settlement or in this my Will or the Executors' of this my Will in the use Exercise Enjoyment and application of all my Estates real and personal or any part thereof in any manner whatsoever Then and in such Case my Mind and Will is that the said Gifts and bequests of the said respective Sum of Ten Thousand pounds as to such of my sisters or their husbands who shall so refuse or neglect as aforesaid shall be and are hereby declared void and Null and of none Effect to all Intents and purposes and as touching further the said Legacies of Ten Thousand pounds to Each of my Sisters and their husbands making together the principal Sum of Twenty Thousand pounds in case the said sums should not become payable according to the terms and Conditions of my Will I do hereby will and Direct that the said Sums not become payable shall go and be received and be claimed by my Executors' as part of my personal Estate to be applyed [sic] to the purpose and according to the directions of this my Last and only will touching my personal Estate AND I DO hereby Authorize and Empower my said Executors and Trustees in case the person or persons to whom I have Devised and Given my said Province and other the premisses [sic] shall then be a Minor or Minors under the age of Twenty one years to fill up and appoint to all places and offices Civil and Military within my said province and to Exercise all Arts of Government and ownership as well as are which they shall think Expedient for the better ordering and administration of the said province and the Government and the affairs thereof I Direct all my Just Debts to be paid as soon as convenient may be after my Decease I GIVE and bequeath to Ffrances Mary Harford the Sum of Thirty Thousand pounds I GIVE and bequeath to Sophia Hales an Infant so called and to Elizabeth

Hales her sister and Infant so called the daughters of Elizabeth Dawson of the County of Lincoln Spinster the Sum of Two Thousand Pounds to each of them the said Infants respectively [sic] to be paid when they come of Age of Twenty one years I GIVE and bequeath to Charlotte Hope Daughter of a certain German woman Called Elizabeth Hope of the County of Munster in Germany now an Infant of the age of two Months more or Less and born at Hamburg the Sum of two thousand pounds I GIVE and bequeath to Robert Eden, Hugh Hammersley, Robert Morris and Peter Prevost whom I do hereby appoint and constitute my Executors of this my Will that is to say to such of them who shall prove this my will — and take upon him or them the Execution thereof I do give and bequeath the Sum of ffifteen hundred pounds over and above the annuities Secured to them in this my will to be paid out of my personal Estate upon their so proving my will with Interest till payd [sic] of ffive per Cent per annum and in Case any one of these Executors shall dye [sic] before me or refuse to prove this my Will for the space of six months after my Decease then that the Legacys [sic] given to the Executor or Executors so Dying or refusing or neglecting to prove this my said and only Will shall be Divided equally amongst the other Executors of this my will who shall prove the Same as aforesaid over and above all other provisions made for him or them respectively — AND I DO hereby Give and bequeath all the rest and residue of my personal Estate Moneys and Annuities whatsoever and all my Goods and Chattels and Effects which I will shall be turned [unclear word] as soon as may be after my Decease and the produce thereof not before Disposed of unto my Said Executors and the Survivors of them IN TRUST to place out the same upon government or other Securities at their Discretion and so from time to time in like manner to place out the Dividends and Interest which shall Accrue due thereon and in case the said Henry Harford shall live to attain the age of twenty one years but not otherways Then UPON

FURTHER TRUST from and after this said Henry Harford shall have attained his age of Twenty one years to pay and Transfer all my said residuary personal Estate with the Intermediate Interest and Profits thereof and the Securitys [sic] on which the same shall be invested unto the said Henry Harford to his own absolute Use and Disposal and in Case the said Henry Harford shall happen to Depart this Life before he shall have attained the said Age of Twenty one years or after having attained that age before he shall have disposed of the same THEN UPON TRUST to pay and Transfer the same unto his sister Ffrances Mary Harford to her own absolute use and in case the said Ffrances Mary Harford before She attains the age of Twenty one years or has disposed of the same THEN to my youngest Sister the Hon'ble Caroline Eden and her husband to their absolute use and Disposal and I do hereby further Will that in case the said Ffrances Mary Harford or any other of the Legatees herein mentioned shall Depart this Life without having Disposed of their respective Legacys [sic] and Sums of Money to them Left then shall revert to my Residuary Estate all such Legacys [sic] Surplus [indecipherable word] and profits Interests and Dividends and I make it my earnest request to my Executors that they will Superintend and take upon them the Care of the persons and fortunes of the said Henry and Frances Mary Harford and that they will to their utmost Support the Disposition made in the said recited Settlement AND this my Will of my Estates Real and personal and I will that my said Executors and Trustees Shall be at full Liberty to retain and shall be amply reimbursed all such Costs and Charges as shall attend the Execution of the Trusts in them reposed and that they shall not be answerable for the Arrs [arrears] Receipts and Defaults of other or others of them but each of them for his own proper Arrs [arrears] receipt and Default only and LASTLY I DO hereby revoke and rescind all former and other wills at any time herein-before by me made and do declare this only to be my Last Will and Testament written in my own hand writing In Witness whereof I have hereunto set my hand and Seal and Signed every Leaf ffourteen in Number This ffourth of March - - - - - in the year of our Lord one thousand Seven hundred

I GIVE and bequeath the Sum of One Thousand pounds to Elizabeth Hales Mother of the herein mentioned Infants and two hundred pounds annum for Life to Hester Rhelan Mother of Henry and Ffrances Harford

Lord Baltimore /s/s/ [Witnessed by three witnesses] [An added few lines finish the will]
If Elizabeth Hales chooses rather an Annuity I direct my Executors to give her instead of one Thousand pounds ffifty pounds per Annum for her Life but I Direct her two children herein mentioned to be paid to each of them only two Thousand pounds each and no more and for this I have solid Reasons having been ill used by her (according to Custom) Shamefully and Irrisistably During our acquaintance.

[END]
[The will was found among Frederick Calvert's papers and letters after his death, written on fourteen sheets of paper, written by Lord Baltimore himself in English. Each page was properly signed and the final sheet witnessed by three witnesses. Pages of depositions follow as the will is sent for, but requested in copy so that the original document might not be lost. The copy was sent to London.]

APPENDIX B

MEMORIAL OF
HENRY HARFORD

Text of the Henry Harford Memorial
and Proceedings thereon.

Published by order of the
House of Delegates
General Assembly of Maryland
January 6, 1786.

Ref.: "Henry Harford, Memorial." MS Division, Vertical Files, Maryland Historical Society.

By the HOUSE OF DELEGATES,

January 6, 1786.

ORDERED, That the memorial of Henry Harford, Esq; and all the proceedings thereon, be published in the Maryland Gazette and Baltimore Journal, and that the printer strike two hundred copies of the said proceedings for the use of the general assembly.

By order,
W. HARWOOD, Clk.

To the honourable the GENERAL ASSEMBLY of MARYLAND, the MEMORIAL of HENRY HARFORD, late proprietor.

AN appeal to the dictates of equity and the feelings of humanity is, with peculiar propriety, addressed to the representatives of a free state; and the many instances of benevolent interposition, which have dignified the acts of former assemblies since the revolution, evince, that the genuine principles of liberty are equally averse from unmerited severity and indiscriminate punishment. Emboldened by this consideration, your memorialist hopes, that his fallen fortunes will not be thought unworthy attention, nor a reasonable compensation be deemed incompatible with private justice, or public good.

The difficulties, expence, and dangers incurred by his ancestors, in originally peopling a country, whose inhabitants now rejoice in the smiles of freedom, forbid to him to expect that their exertions will terminate in the ruin of a descendant, whose conduct has never been inimical to the American cause.

Your memorialist respectfully represents, that he was a minor at the commencement of the late war, and placed during his infancy under the guardianship of the chancellor of Great-Britain, which prevented his leaving the kingdom. That during his minority suits were instituted against him by Sir Robert Eden and Mr. Browning, who intermarried with the daughters of Charles lord Baltimore, to recover the government and revenues of Maryland; and which suits were not terminated until the month of July, 1782.

His situation and embarrassments, must therefore forcibly plead against every rigorous-exposition to his prejudice.

Permit him therefore further to observe, that the objects of this address is not to question the policy of any governmental measures, nor to create uneasiness in the state, but solely with a view to obtain such retribution for his wreck of property, as the justice, generosity, and magnanimity of the general assembly, and the peculiar circumstances of your memorialist, may prompt them to make: An investigation of which, he flatters himself, will manifest the propriety of his being relieved from a law of policy, framed only for the guilty; and he humbly hopes this investigation may be permitted by counsel at the bar, or in such other manner as shall be thought expedient.

Should the result of this application be different from his expectations, your memorialist shall still feel an anxious solicitude for the prosperity and happiness of America, and incessantly wish, that the citizens of Maryland may be gratified in their most sanguine hopes of felicity from the late revolution: But at the same time he cannot yield to the mortifying reflection, that the assembly of Maryland, so distinguished for their benevolence and rectitude, will place him in a situation that might probably make any other person regret an event which has filled the hearts of America with the most lively joy.

HENRY HARFORD.

A State of part of the Loss sustained by HENRY HARFORD, Esq; late proprietor of Maryland.

			Sterling.
The annual amount of his quit-rents for 177, being the last accounts settled,		8518 6 2	
Manor rents paid to the agent for ditto,	322 11 6		
Ditto, due from the steward in Baltimore county	162 5 10		
		474 17 4	
Amount from the 29th of September 1773 to 29th September 1774		8993 3 6	
Arrears on £.8993 3 6, from the 29th of September 1774 to the 29th of September 1784, is 10 years,	89931 15 0		
Deduct for payments acknowledged by the agent on account of 1775,	809 13 4		89122 1 8
Annual amount of quit-rents £.8518 6 2, valued at 20 years purchase,			170366 3 4
		Carried over	259488 5 0

MANORS

Manors and Reserved Lands, viz.

Brought over 2594388 5

	Acres.		
Monocacy manor and the reserve thereon, as returned by the surveyor,	13148 at 3 *of*	19072	0 0
Gunpowder ditto,	5003 at 1 *of*	2801	10 0
Kent ditto,	3018 at 2 *of*	3018	0 0
Queen-Anne's ditto,	4322 at 2 *of*	4322	0 0
Nanticoke ditto,	4775 at 1 8*f*	4297	10 0
Calverton ditto,	3412 at 15*f*	2559	0 0
Anne-Arundel ditto,	301 at 2 *of*	301	0 0
Woolley ditto,	3131 at 7*f*6	1174	2 6
Chaptico ditto,	6110 at 12*f*	3666	0 0
Padgaiah ditto,	1101 at 1 *of*	550	10 0
Mill ditto,	1667 at 8*f*	666	16 0
Snow-hill, St. John's, and St. Barbaras,	774 at 9*f*	398	3 0
West St. Mary's ditto,	1370 at 6*f*	411	0 0
Zachaiah ditto,	5304 at 1 *of*	2652	0 0
Beaverdam ditto,	7680 at 6*f*	2304	0 0
Wiccomico ditto,	5950 at 5*f*	1487	0 0
East and North-east ditto, laid out for 6000 acres, each, Rent charge,	3976 at 9*f*	1784	4 0
Reserve in Baltimore county (barren land) supposed to contain	45000 at 1*f*6	3375	0 0
Four reserves to the westward of Fort Cumberland, containing	125130 at 2*f*	12513	0 0

67952 15 6

£327441 0 6

Part of the above manors, valued in this schedule at about £.42,000 sterling, have been sold by the state's commissioners for upwards of £.116,000 current money. Exclusive of the above, Mr. Harford has also lost the usual caution on all vacant lands, the composition on certificates returned by surveyors, and the royalties.

MONDAY, November 21, 1785.

ON motion, ORDERED, That the memorial of Henry Harford, Esq; referred from the last to the present session, be taken into consideration on Friday the second day of December next, and that he be heard by counsel if required.

FRIDAY, December 2, 1785

The house took into consideration, the order of the day respecting the memorial of Henry Harford, Esq; and after hearing counsel on behalf of the memorialist, the following motion was made, That a message be prepared to the senate to propose a conference on the subject matter of the memorial of the said Henry Harford, Esq; ORDERED, That Mr. Chase, Mr. Hall, and Mr. Carroll, be a committee to prepare the said message.

SATURDAY, December 3, 1785.

Mr. Carroll, from the committee brings in and delivers to Mr. Speaker the following message:

BY THE HOUSE OF DELEGATES, DECEMBER 3, 1785.

MAY IT PLEASE YOUR HONOURS,

THIS house have heard counsel at its bar on the memorial of Mr. Harford, late proprietary of this state, in which he solicits a compensation or retribution from this government, for his confiscated property.

We are fully convinced of the justice, policy, and necessity of the law passed during the late war, which confiscated British property, and that on the principle of retaliation alone, the legislature that made the act, were justified by the laws and practice of all civilized nations.

From the limited wisdom of man, but very few general laws can provide for all cases that may happen, and circumstances will often arise which the legislature would have excepted from the general rule, if they could have been foreseen. A power therefore is always reserved in the legislative body, to make exceptions and provisions for particular cases, as they may occur.

The case of Mr. Harford is attended with such very particular circumstances, as merit, in our opinion, the peculiar attention of the general assembly, and involve such difficulties, as require the united wisdom of both branches of this government to decide.

As this state hath taken rank among the nations of the world, and in its political capacity must be considered as a moral person, under the obligations of justice, humanity, and benevolence, and we now have a national character to acquire and establish, this house, with anxious solicitude wish, that the government may be made known and esteemed by the powers of Europe for its sacred and inviolable regard to justice and humanity, public faith and national honour; and we wish, as far as in our power, to act with liberality and generosity.

Actuated by these principles, this house have retained the memorial of Mr. Harford; and we propose a conference with your honours of the subject matter thereof.

We wish that the cause and calamities of the late war could be buried in perpetual oblivion; and are willing to make a compromise with Mr. Harford, as far as the present very distressed situation of our public affairs will permit. We are involved, in consequence of the late war, in an enormous and very heavy debt, foreign and domestic; and our creditors are very urgent and pressing for payment. Our wishes far exceed our abilities; and we must limit our humanity and beneficence by our necessities.

If your honours agree to the conference, this house will afterwards determine what sum of money our finances will permit to be given to Mr. Harford, and the time and mode of payment. If the conferrees should think proper to receive any proposals from Mr. Harford, it would be agreeable to this house. If the senate accede to the proposed conference, we will nominate some of our members to meet such of your body as you may please to appoint for this purpose; and we hope, that by this mode, such measures may be adopted by the general assembly, as will be satisfactory to them and to Mr. Harford.

Which was read.

TUESDAY, December 6, 1785.

The message respecting Henry Harford, Esq; was read the second time, and the question put, That the house assent thereto? The yeas and nays being called for by Mr. Chase appeared as follow:

AFFIRMATIVE.

Messrs Lethrbury, Pearce, Carroll, Edmondson, Waggaman, Chase, Quynn, Sewell, Joseph Dashiell, Purnell, Downes, McMechen,

NEGATIVE.

Messeurs Bond, Somerville, De Butts, Maxwell, B. Worthington, N. Worthington, Hall, Grahame, Taney, Gantt, Fraizer, Jones, Dent, Stone, Ridgely of Wm. Stevenson, Goldsborough, Bracco, Gale, John Dashiell, Adams, Waters, Kirkman, Ennalls, Baker, Oglevee, Miller, W. Bowie, R. Bowie, F. Bowie, John Seney, Jackson, Craille, Mitchell, Faw, Beatty, Carey, Norris, Hughlett, Stull, Cellars, Funk, Oneale, Beall,

So it was determined in the negative.

THURSDAY, December 8, 1785.

Mr. Carroll brings in and delivers to Mr. Speaker the following message:

By the HOUSE of DELEGATES, December 8, 1785.

May it please your honours,

THIS house have heard counsel at its bar on the memorial of Mr. Harford, late proprietary of this state, in which he solicits a compensation or retribution from this government for his confiscated property. We esteem the case of Mr. Harford very important, and of such a nature as to require the united wisdom of both branches of the legislature to decide properly thereon, and do therefore propose a conference with your honours on the subject matter of the said memorial. Should the senate accede to the proposed conference, we will nominate some of our members to meet such of your house as you may please to appoint for the above purpose.

By Order, W. HARWOOD, clk.

Which was read.

The message respecting Henry Harford, Esq; was read the second time, and the question put, That the house assent thereto? The yeas and nays being called for by Mr. F. Bowie appeared as follows:

AFFIRMATIVE.

Bond,	Carroll,	Ridgely of Wm.	Ennalls,	Jackson,	Norris,
Somerville,	Gantt,	Goldsborough,	Baker,	Chaille,	Hughlett,
De Butts,	Frazier,	Gale,	Ramsey,	Mitchell,	Downes,
Maxwell,	Jones,	John Dashiell,	R. Bowie,	Joseph Dashiell,	Stull,
Lethrbury,	Dent,	Adams,	Chase,	Purnell,	Funk,
Graves,	Turner,	Waters,	Quynn,	Faw,	Beall,
Hall,	Stone,	Waggaman,	Sewell,	Carey,	

(Messieurs)

NEGATIVE.

N. Worthington,	Ridgely,	Miller,	F. Bowie,	Beatty,	Cellars,
Grahame,	Bracco,	W. Bowie,	John Seney,	Steret,	Oneale,
Taney,	Oglevee,				

(Messrs.)

So it was resolved in the affirmative.

Sent to the senate by Mr. Fraizer.

WEDNESDAY, December 21, 1785.

Edward Lloyd, Esq; from the senate, delivers to Mr. Speaker the following message and resolution:

BY THE SENATE, DECEMBER 19, 1785.

GENTLEMEN,

UPON the receipt of your message proposing a conference on the memorial of Henry Harford, Esq; we deemed it expedient previously to determine, whether any compensation should be made to the memorialist, for the losses stated in his memorial to have been incurred by him in consequence of the late revolution. For it naturally occurred to us, that it would be mispending time to discuss the quantum and manner of making the compensation, if either house should be of opinion, that no compensation ought to be made to the memorialist. On the fullest inquiry into the subject, and examination of the arguments suggested by the memorialist's counsel in your house (at which most of us were present), and which were again stated to and satisfactorily answered in this house, we are decidedly of opinion, that the memorialist cannot of right ask, or this state, consistently with that justice which is due to others, grant him, any relief or retribution for the losses he has sustained in consequence of the revolution, and the acts of our legislature. That revolution and those acts were occasioned by the prosecution of an unjust war, commenced against this country by the British government, of which the memorialist is a subject. On that government, therefore, to which he remained attached during the whole war, and with whose success his own interests were so intimately connected, he ought only to rely for compensation for his losses. However rigorous the confiscation of the property of British subjects might appear, abstractedly considered, the act for seizing and confiscating that property, under the circumstances and with the restrictions it was passed, we are convinced, was perfectly justifiable. The severity of the measure long delayed its adoption, and that delay mitigated its severity, by affording to every British subject the opportunity of avoiding the consequences of the confiscation act.

The memorialist came of age in the spring of seventeen hundred and seventy-nine, the act of confiscation passed in the beginning of the year seventeen hundred and eighty one, full twelve months after the measure had been warmly and generally agitated in this state, and must have been known in England. Instead of repairing to Maryland and becoming a citizen, the memoralist, confiding in the power and success of his native country, remained in England, attending on the court of chancery, and waiting the adjudication of suits which were to determine the right to the province of Maryland and its dependences, between the memorialist and the heirs at law of the late lord Baltimore, and which adjudication could have no effect unless America should be conquered by the British government. This state of facts leaves not the smallest room to doubt, that the memorialist, both from interest and inclination, continued a British subject, and devoted to his native country, which, although free, endeavoured, by lavishing its blood and treasures, to deprive us of our freedom. We cannot discover a single circumstance in the case of the memorialist, to distinguish him from other British subjects, and which should induce this government to except him out of the general law of confiscation, or partially compensate the losses, which the revolution, that law, and his own conduct, have brought upon him. Every British subject, who did not bear arms against these United States, and whole property has been confiscated, has an equal if not a better claim to our commiseration.

Legislatures, ought to be governed by general rules and principles; their acts should not be liable to the reproach of partiality, or of an undue pretence. If any retribution should be made by this state to the memorialist, a proportionable compensation ought to be given to every other British subject. Will the state of our finances, and the heavy debt we have contracted in the defense of our liberty, suffer such application of public monies? The claims of justice must be satisfied, and we ought to attend to the distresses of our own citizens, occasioned by the depredations of the enemy and other causes in the course of the war; but British subjects, if entitled to any compensation for their losses, must seek redress from that government, whose injustice occasioned them, and of which they are citizens. The attachment of the memorialist to the British government, and the great losses he has incurred, may entitle him to the bounty of a British parliament, but can give him no just claim to any compensation from this legislature. The claim to quit-rents, as a subsisting debt recoverable under the treaty, which was urged as a ground for making a compensation to, or compromise with, the memorialist, has also been considered, and appears to us entirely groundless and inadmissible, being, as we conceive, incompatible with the sovereignty and independence of this state; and we cannot, confidently with the duty we owe to our constituents, do, or suffer to be done, any act, that has the most distant tendency to create a supposition, that any power on earth can place the free people of Maryland in the degraded condition of tenants to a superior lord, a foreigner, and a British subject. We are also clearly of opinion, that the quit-rents reserved upon the grants of the former proprietaries, were hereditaments subject to all the rules and consequences of other real estate, and therefore cannot, consistently with law, be held by an alien; and that no part of the treaty of peace can give the smallest colour to a supposition, that these hereditaments, more than others, were saved or reserved. That the claim of the former proprietary to quit-rents ceased upon the declaration of independence, we have not the smallest doubt, and we think the legislature acted wisely in declaring, that the payment of them even to this government should never be exacted, and that the citizens of this state should hold their lands on equal terms with the citizens of the other states.

Having stated our opinions and the reasons for them, it would be an useless waste of time to confer on the memorial of Henry Harford, Esq; especially as we have no cause to surmise that your opinion may be different from ours, as to the principle of making compensation.

To prevent the public councils from being diverted from more important and necessary concerns, and to save the further loss of time upon this subject, we herewith transmit a resolve, unanimously agreed to in this house, which, if adopted by yours, will effectually obviate the inconveniences just mentioned.

We flatter ourselves, gentlemen, that you do us the justice to believe, that we will cheerfully confer with you at all times, and upon all occasions, in which the public service may be promoted by our assistance, and that our declining the proposed conference, does not proceed from the smallest disrespect, but from an impression and belief, that the mode we have suggested will bring the question of a compensation to the speediest conclusion, and consequently be the most acceptable to both houses.

By order, J. DORSEY, clk.

BY THE SENATE, DECEMBER 19, 1785.

THE memorial of Henry Harford, Esq; stating his losses, and soliciting compensation, being read and considered, the senate were unanimously of opinion, that the memorialist cannot of right ask, or this state consistently with justice to others grant him, any compensation or retribution for the losses he states in his memorial to have been by him sustained in consequence of the revolution and acts of our legislature: Wherefore, RESOLVED, That the memorial and application of the said Henry Harford, Esquire, be rejected.

By order J. DORSEY, clk.

Which were read.

FRIDAY, JANUARY 6, 1786.

On the second reading the message respecting the memorial of Henry Harford, Esq; and the resolution, the question was put, That the house assent to the said resolution? The yeas and nays being called for by Mr. Faw appeared as follow:

AFFIRMATIVE

Messieurs

Key,	Jones,	Edmondson,	Miller,	Chaille,	Wheeler,
Bond,	Dent,	Goldsborough,	W. Bowie,	Purnell,	Driver,
De Butts,	Turner,	Bracco,	Digges,	Faw,	Steret,
B. Worthington,	Stone,	Gale,	R. Bowie,	Beatty,	Stull,
N. Worthington,	Ridgely,	John Dashiell,	F. Bowie,	Bayly,	Cellars,
Hall,	Ridgely of Wm.	Adams,	John Seney,	Carey,	Funk,
Grahame,	Stevenson,	Waters,	Sewell,	Norris,	Oneale,
Taney,	Roberts,	Hooper,	Joshua Seney,	Love,	Wootton.
Frazier,					

NEGATIVE

Mes. Lethrbury, Carroll, Ramsey, Chase, Quynn, Joseph Dashiell
Graves,

So it was resolved in the affirmative.

Extract from the Journal,
W. HARWOOD, Cl.Ho.Del.

APPENDIX C

CASE OF
THE BRITISH AMERICAN CLAIMANTS

Claimants' Letter and Case (1813)

   Ref.: British Museum, Manuscript Room, Documents #38252.F.352, and #38252.F.353.

Letter, House of Lords, Record (1975)
    Office. Outcome of the Case.

Excerpt from Report of March 25. (1812)

   Ref.: Commons Journal, Vol. 67, pages 54–55, 112, and 234.

The Undersigned Committee of British American Claimants present their respectful Compliments to the Earl of Liverpool and beg leave to intimate to his Lordship that it is intended on the part of the Claimants that a motion shall be submitted to the House of Commons on Thursday the 13th Instant to the effect of acknowledging — That the Claimants have made out such a Case as affords an equitable ground for Parliamentary relief.

The Committee of Claimants confidently trust that a motion of the above general nature will not meet with opposition upon the part of His Royal Highness the Prince Regent's Government.

Old Broad Street —
8th May 1813

Henry Harford
Willm Cunninghame
Henry Glassford
John Nutt
Davison
J. T. Watson

CASE

OF THE

BRITISH AMERICAN CLAIMANTS.

VARIOUS misconceptions, with regard to the case of the Claimants, having gone abroad, they think it necessary, to state shortly, the Facts, as established by the Report of the Select Committee of the House of Commons.

The Claim of the Petitioners, is *not* for Losses by War, *but* for Losses occasioned—by the violation, on the part of America, of the Treaty of Peace concluded in 1783; by her subsequent violation of the Treaty of Amity concluded in 1794; and by the Convention between His Majesty and the United States in 1802.

Before the American War, in the year 1776, the relations between Great Britain and her American Colonies, were those of fellow-subjects; and when the War commenced, immense Sums were due from the Colonists, to British Subjects residing in Great Britain, and to such Loyal Subjects of Great Britain residing in America, as took part with the Mother Country, in the Contest which ensued. The present Claimants, consist of both these descriptions of British Subjects.

While the American War continued, the recovery of these Debts was impossible.

By the 4th Article of the Treaty of Peace, it was stipulated, that "Creditors on either side, should "meet with no lawful impediment to the recovery of Debts theretofore contracted."—But this solemn stipulation was violated by America, her Courts of Judicature still remaining closed against British Subjects.—*The evils of War were thus protracted with respect to the Petitioners, while the British Empire enjoyed profound Peace.* When at last, the American Courts were opened, after a lapse of several years, many of the Debtors who had been solvent at the Peace, were found to have become insolvent during this interval, and the Debts were thereby lost for ever to the British Creditors.

By the 6th Article of the Treaty of Amity between Great Britain and the United States, concluded in 1794, America agreed to make *full and complete Compensation,* to British Subjects, for the Losses, which her violation of the former Treaty had thus occasioned.—And by the 7th Article of the said Treaty of 1794, Great Britain, on the other hand, agreed, to make full and complete Compensation to American Citizens, who had sustained Losses, by illegal or irregular Captures of their Vessels and Property, during the then existing War between Great Britain and France.

The Treaty of 1794, was negotiated by Lord Grenville, on the part of His Majesty, and by Mr. Jay, on the part of the United States; and it was in the view of both these Negotiators, that a principle of Reciprocity should be established, by the 6th and 7th Articles, the one, containing stipulations in favour of the Subjects of Great Britain, and the other, containing stipulations in favour of the Citizens of the United States.

A Board of British and American Commissioners met at Philadelphia, in May, 1797, to ascertain the amount, payable under the 6th Article, by the United States, to the British Creditors; but the appointment of this Board was rendered ineffectual, and its proceedings were first interrupted, and afterwards, entirely defeated and closed, by the secession of the American Commissioners. The conduct of the British Commissioners, during the whole of the proceedings of this Board, was approved most highly by the British Government.

When the British Government was apprised of this interruption of the proceedings at Philadelphia, they immediately suspended the execution, on the part of Great Britain, of the 7th Article of the Treaty. And many representations were made by the Petitioners, urging the extreme hardship of their case, and calling on His Majesty's Ministers, to take measures for procuring their just demands from America, and stating, that if this was not done, they must throw themselves on the National Justice, by an application to Parliament.

The Petitioners, at the same time, stated to Government, that in the event of a Compromise being thought advisable, they were willing to take, if properly guaranteed, 2,500,000*l.* in full of their Claims.

In, or soon after December, 1800, during the Negotiation which led to the Convention of 1802, Mr. McDonald, who had been First Commissioner at Philadelphia, at the request of the United Secretary of State for Foreign Affairs, communicated to him, that he conceived, a Sum of between a Million and a Half, and Two Millions, would be a fair Sum to be demanded from America, under the stipulations of the 6th Article of the Treaty of 1794. And afterwards, on *14th May,* 1801, Mr. McDonald, in answer to certain verbal enquiries, made a further communication to Mr. Hammond, that he imagined a fair execution of the Sixth Article of the Treaty of 1794, would have made good *about Two Millions of the sums claimed.*

On the 8th January, 1802, a Convention was signed between His Majesty and the United States, whereby His Majesty, *without the concurrence or privity of the Petitioners,* consented to accept, for the use of the persons described in the 6th Article of the Treaty of 1794, (who are the present Petitioners), the sum of 600,000*l.* Sterling, in satisfaction and discharge, of the Money which the United States might have been liable to pay to them, under the said 6th Article, which His Majesty, *thereby, declared to be cancelled and annulled.*

But by the said Convention, the Stipulations of *the 7th Article* of the Treaty of 1794, *in favour of American* Citizens, were reserved whole and entire: the Commissioners for executing that Article, recommended their sittings, and the Sum of 1,369,448*l.* has been paid to American Citizens, under its provisions.

The considerations, which led to this Convention, are stated in the Evidence of the Earl of Liverpool, by whom it was negotiated, to have been partly of a national nature; and his Lordship further states, that the suspension of the said 7th Article, might certainly have been continued.

As soon, as the Petitioners were apprised of the Convention, they expressed their dissatisfaction, and intimated their intention of applying to Parliament, for Compensation; and in March, 1802, having waited on Mr. Addington, (then First Lord of the Treasury, and Chancellor of the Exchequer), they protested against the Terms of the Convention. Mr. Addington admitted the case of the Petitioners to be a hard one, and said, he had no objections to their applying to Parliament, though he meant to give no opinion on the merits of the Claim. But he thought that Parliament would not entertain any Petition, till the amount of their losses was ascertained. The Petitioners, in consequence, did not then present any Petition to Parliament.

In April, 1803, an Act of Parliament was passed, appointing Commissioners for apportioning and distributing the said Sum of 600,000*l.* among the persons who should be found entitled. These Commissioners finished their Adjudications in May, 1811, and by such Adjudications, the Claims of the Petitioners were fully established, and were found to amount to 1,420,000*l.* as on the first June, 1804.

It thus appears, That by the Convention of 1802, His Majesty was pleased, *in consideration of* 600,000*l. to cancel and annul the 6th Article of the Treaty of* 1794, whereby America would have been bound to pay to the Petitioners 1,120,000*l.*; and by the same Convention, His Majesty's Government was pleased, on the other hand, to stipulate, that Great Britain should, nevertheless, pay to American Citizens, the *full amount of their demands under the*

7th Article; and these demands have been discharged by Great Britain, to the extent of 1,369,448*l.*, as above mentioned.

It is not for the Petitioners, to call in question the wisdom of His Majesty's Government, in concluding this Convention. But they must again observe, that they (the Petitioners), were not privy to it, nor at all consulted, during its progress—That they gave no consent, directly or indirectly, to the conclusion of such a bargain—That they entered their Protest against it, as soon as it was made known to them—That the rights of which they were thereby deprived, were vested rights, coming within the description of Private Property, in the strictest sense of the word—That His Majesty's Government were fully aware, that the Property thus sacrificed, would probably amount to nearly Two Millions Sterling; and that this sacrifice of the rights of the Petitioners, was thus made to the United States, at the same time that a Fund existed in the bands of Great Britain, due to America under the 7th Article of the Treaty, which, in conformity in the principle of Reciprocity between the 6th and 7th Articles, might justly have been retained, in satisfaction of the demands due to the Petitioners, under the 6th Article.

Under such circumstances, it must be presumed, that His Majesty, exercising his undoubted right, of alienating the property of a part of his Subjects, for the public good, had in view, to compensate them for the sacrifice, according to those principles of Public Law, which are universally acknowledged, and have been invariably acted upon by Great Britain.—A reference to former cases, will show, that the claim of the Petitioners, is fortified by analogous Precedents; and they believe, that no similar instance can be adduced, in which Compensation has not been granted.

The Petitioners have, therefore, applied to Parliament, for Compensation, on account of the heavy loss they have sustained, by the above Convention—having as yet received only 659,493*l.*, instead of 1,420,000*l.*, to which they have been found justly entitled.

It is far from the wish of the Petitioners, to press upon the national resources, by a demand of payment at the present moment—they are willing to accept Debentures, or other Securities, to be made payable, at such periods, as may best suit the convenience of the State.

The Claimants commenced this statement, by asserting,—that their Claim is *not* for a Loss occasioned by War.—And it should be known, that besides the Loss now claimed, *arising solely in time of Peace,* and occasioned by America's violation of the Treaty of Peace, they have actually sustained Losses, to the amount of several millions, by the American War, for which they do not ask any Compensation whatever.

Record Office,
House of Lords,
London, SW1A 0PW.

24th July, 1975.

Dear Miss Rollo,

Thank you for your letter of the 16th July. The American Loyalists' Petition was presented to the House of Commons on the 22nd January 1812, and was referred to a Committee which reported on the 25th March of that year (Commons Journal, Vol. 67, pages 54-5, 112 and 234). The report of the 25th March 1812, was again referred to a Committee on the 26th February 1813, and the Committee reported on the 1st March. On the 20th May 1813 there was a motion in the Commons "that the petitioners have established such a case as forms an equitable ground for Parliamentary relief". This motion was defeated in the Commons, and no further action was taken (Commons Journal, Vol. 68, pages 242, 244 and 505).

According to the report of 25th March 1812 the Commissioners dealing with American claims had made adjudications in favour of various claimants to the amount of £1,420,000 and had divided amongst the claimants the sum of £659,493. The claimants were therefore petitioning for the payment of the difference between these two sums, and this was disallowed.

The report contains a list of the individual claimants and sums allowed to them, and I enclose a copy of this.

Yours sincerely,

H.S. Cobb

Deputy Clerk of the Records

Miss Vera F. Rollo,
9205 Tuckerman Street,
Lanham,
Maryland 20801,
U.S.A.

Excerpt from Report of March 25, 1812
Ref.: Commons Journal, Vol. 67, pp. 54–55, 112, and 234.

the same, the first of the said instalments to be paid at the expiration of one year, and the second instalment at the expiration of two years, and the third and last instalment at the expiration of three years next following the exchange of the ratification of the said Convention, and to be paid in money of the said United States, reckoning four dollars and forty-four cents to be equal to one pound sterling: And whereas it is expedient that Commissioners should be appointed for the apportioning, dividing and distributing such sum of money, amongst the several persons who shall by such Commissioners be found entitled to receive compensation out of the same, in proportion to their several and respective claims, so far as the same shall by such Commissioners be approved or adjudged to be good; May it therefore please Your Majesty; that it may be enacted; and be it enacted by the King's Most Excellent Majesty, by and with the advice and consent of the Lords Spiritual and Temporal, and Commons in this present Parliament assembled, and by the authority of the same, That Thomas Macdonald, Esquire, Henry Pye Rich, Esquire, and John Guillemard, Esquire, shall be and they are hereby constituted and appointed Commissioners for the purposes aforesaid; and that the adjudication of such Commissioners, or any two of them, as to all claims made for compensation out of such money, and also as to the apportionment and distribution thereof as aforesaid, shall be final and conclusive. *[Commissioners appointed.]*

Sect. 7. And be it further Enacted, That no claim or request of any person or persons under this Act shall be received after the 1st day of June 1804. *[No Claim to be received after June 1, 1804.]*

Sect. 8. And be it further Enacted, That the said Commissioners shall from time to time, at their discretion, or as often as they shall be *[Commissioners shall give an account of their Proceedings to the Treasury, &c.]*

thereunto required, and as soon as possible for the determination of their examinations and proceedings by virtue of this Act, without any further requisition, give an account of their proceedings in writing to the Lords Commissioners of His Majesty's Treasury, and to His Majesty's principal Secretaries of State for the time being.

Sect. 12. And be it further Enacted, That when and so soon as the said Commissioners, or any two of them, shall have approved and adjudged the claim of any person or persons to any such compensation as aforesaid to be good and valid, in the whole or in part, and ascertained the amount of any dividend or proportion of money to which any such person is, or persons respectively are then entitled, the said Commissioners, or any two of them, shall make out or cause to be made out, in such form as they shall think fit, an Order or Orders for the payment of such sum or sums respectively as shall have been so ascertained as aforesaid, or of such part thereof as shall be in proportion to the amount of the money which shall then have been remitted from America, and paid into the Bank of England in manner hereinbefore directed, and shall annex their hands and seals, or the hands and seals of any two of them, to such Order or Orders, and shall cause the same to be delivered to the person or persons duly authorized, on such receipts acquittances or designments being delivered duly executed by such person or persons, to the extent of the money be by such person or persons respectively received, as the said Comissioners, or any two of them, shall have directed or required.

When Claims are ascertained, orders shall be made out for Payment.

Appendix, No. 39

LIST of ADJUDICATIONS by the Commissioners
appointed under the
Act 43d Geo. III. cap. 39.

GLASGOW CLAIMS.

	£	s.	d.
John Alston, for Alston, Young, and Co.	6,000	—	—
D'---John Alston and Co.	4,800	—	—
Buchanan, Hastie, and Co	61,500	—	—
James Baird, for John Hay and Co.	7,000	—	—
John Buchanan and G. Lawson	15,000	—	—
Bonar, for Allan, Love, and Co.	6,000	—	—
John Ballantine and Co.	3,000	—	—
G. Brown and J. Lawrie	7,000	—	—
Buchannan and Milliken	200	—	—
Andrew Buchanan, for G. and A. Buchanan	7,000	—	—
J. Buchanan, for C. Ried and Co.	4,800	—	—
Cochrane, Donald, and Co.	6,200	—	—
Margaret Coates	5,000	—	—
Wm Calderhead, for Jamieson, Campbell, and Co.	3,500	—	—
Duncan Campbell's Executors	4,000	—	—
Wm Cuninghame and Co.	88,000	—	—
Cuninghame, Findlay, and Co.	5,600	—	—
Alexander Donald and Co.	7,200	—	—
Dinwiddie, Crawford, and Co.	18,000	—	—

66.   Dreghorn,

	£	s.	d.
Dreghorn, Murdoch, and Co.	5,820	—	—
Colin Dunlop and Son, and Co.	13,300	—	—
Thomas and Alexander Donald and Co.	5,500	—	—
James and Robert Donald and Co.	50,500	—	—
Dunlops and Crosse	4,000	—	—
Donald Scott and Co.	20,500	—	—
Dunmore, Blackburne, and Co.	8,000	—	—
Alexander Donald	800	—	—

	£.	s.	d.
Glassford, Gordon, Monteath, and Co.	15,500	—	—
Glassford and Henderson	13,500	—	—
John Glassford and Co.	26,500	—	—
James Gaunnet	5,000	—	—
Henderson, McCall, and Co.	32,500	—	—
Archibald and John Hamilton	48,150	—	—
James Hunter and Co.	1,000	—	—
George Keppen and Co.	28,150	—	—
George Lothian, for N. Menzies Trustees, &c.	5,700	—	—
Isabella Logan	2,110	—	—
Murdoch, Donald, and Co.	10,000	—	—
James Murdoch, for James Murdoch and Co.	2,500	—	—
Do --- for Thomas Yuille, James Murdoch and Co.	3,500	—	—
Robt Muirhead, for Aitcheson Hay and Co.	1,500	—	—
McCall, Dennistown, and Co.	5,440	—	—
McCall, Smellie, and Co.	10,000	—	—
George McCall and Co.	3,500	—	—
McDowall, Stirling, and Co.	13,500	—	—
John McDowall and Co.	16,000	—	—
Helen, McCall, and others	7,000	—	—
William Ogilvy	1,380	—	—
Oswald Dennistown and Co.	16,800	—	—
James Ritchie and Co.	26,500	—	—
James and Henry Ritchie	2,000	—	—
Ramsay Monteath and Co.	3,000	—	—
John Robertson, for P. Telfer's Trustees	1,000	—	—
William Robertson, for Cuming, McKenzie and Co.	12,500	—	—
Andrew Sym and Co.	4,500	—	—
Archibald Speirs, John Bowman, and Co.	87,000	—	—
Archibald Speirs	500	—	—
Thomson, Snodgrass and Co.	7,000	—	—
George Thomson, for Andrew Thomson and Co.	400	—	—
James Wilson and Sons	1,800	—	—
Amount of the Glasgow Claims	£.783,650	—	—

ENGLISH CLAIMS

	£.	s.	d.
The Revd Bennett Allan	2,524	—	—
Andrew Allen	6,977	15	9
Gerard G. Beckman	505	16	3
Garstang Bradstock	110	—	—
Thomas Bell and Joseph Stanfield	1,400	—	—
John and Jane Backhouse	12,000	—	—
Thomas Bibby	2,000	—	—
Daniel Coxe	1,800	—	—
The Revd Robt Cooper	3,000	—	—
Mary Cowper	4,958	4	8
Abraham Cuyler	4,152	8	9
Sir Wm Douglas and others	13,000	—	—
Oliver De Lancey	4,500	—	—
Daniel Dulany	14,193	—	—
Crawford Davison, Executor of J. Simpson	10,072	1	1
D^o - - - - of Storr	3,355	18	5
Samuel Donaldson	17,500	—	—
Samuel Douglas's Executors	7,000	—	—
Matthew Dobson	5,000	—	—
George Folliott	26,099	8	10
General Edmund Fanning	1,800	—	—
Judith Foxcroft	274	14	6
Samuel Gist	5,200	—	—
Adam Gordon	8,818	4	8
Edmund Granger	1,669	10	2
Henry Harford	43,401	—	—
William Hannay	16,187	3	10
James Holmes	834	5	—
James Hume	1,518	—	—
John Harford	1,353	2	7
Mary Hatch, Executrix of Elizabeth Hatch	550	—	—
William Higginson	86,500	—	—
Richard Hanson	3,000	—	—
Capel Hanbury and others	934	5	—
Thomas Hutchinson	300	—	—
Sir Hugh Inglis and Edward Antrobus	12,833	13	10
The Right Revd C. Inglis	1,711	12	3
Ann Jones	1,500	—	—
John Jameson's Executors	2,800	—	—
William Jauncey	37,000	—	—
The Rev. Cavalier Jouet	5,000	10	7

	£.	s.	d.
John Kane	2,000	—	—
J. H. Littler	9,000	—	—
Richard Lechmere	600	—	—
John Lane, for Massachusett's Bay Notes,			
Thoˢ Palmer ---- £.475 8 —			
Thoˢ Hutchinson -- 260 17 —	2,784	5	6
Robert Livie	2,525	19	9
Isaac Low	6,000	—	—
William Robertson Lidderdale	4,000	—	—
Samuel Lyde	1,000	—	—
J. Lloyd, surviving Partner of Hanbury & Co.	3,000	—	—
Dº -- Executor of Osgood Hanbury	5,000	—	—
John Lane, for Jon. Wᵐ Simpson	2,000	—	—
Dº -- for Anthony Lechmere	5,000	—	—
Jon. Mallet, Executor of Kemp	2,300	—	—
P. Martin, for the creditors of J. Bland	9,000	—	—
William Molleson's Executors	15,000	—	—
Joseph Martyr	250	—	—
James Moss	3,500	—	—
Catherine Flood McCall	10,000	—	—
Thomas Main, Executor of Hyndman	1,200	—	—
Dº -- and Robert Bunn	1,700	—	—
William Masterman and Richard Chester	4,000	—	—
John Miller's Executors	700	—	—
C. McIvers, Executor of McIvers	4,000	—	—
Richard Miles and others, Executors of Shoolbred	4,000	—	—
John Nutt	23,639	4	8
Nicholas Ogden	7,439	—	—
Rebecca Ogilvie	4,872	13	—
R. W. Powell	19,000	—	—
John Page and Elias Vanderhost	3,000	—	—
Robert Palmer	294	10	—
Pearke and others, Executors of Waterman	800	—	—
John Rogers and others	15,000	—	—
Morris Robinson's Executors	8,500	—	—
Joseph Rutherford	685	—	—

	£.	s.	d.
Colin Ross, Administrator of Jardine	1,500	—	—
Stephen Skinner	9,000	—	—
D⁰ - - - for Kearney	945	7	2
Joseph Stanfield, Assignee of Syme	1,200	—	—
Anna Jane Simpson	800	—	—
Strahan and M ͨKenzie	2,500	—	—
Charles Shaw	650	—	—
Robᵗ Sheddon & Co.	2,500	—	—
Jon. Simpson's Executors	1,821	9	6
John Savage's Executors	1,171	12	9
Wᵐ Taylor's Executors	500	—	—
Abraham Walton, Administrator of Phillips	6,000	—	—
Wakelin Welsh	8,500	—	—
John Weatherhead	1,136	1	6
John Tyndale Warre	35,000	—	—
Ann White and others, Executors of Thomas White	6,000	—	—
Wᵐ Walton, Administrator of Walton	2,000	—	—

Amount of English Claims ....£.636,350 — —

Total amount of ADJUDICATIONS .£.1,420,000 — —

APPENDIX D

WILL OF
HENRY HARFORD, ESQUIRE

Date of Will, July 16, 1829.

Codicil Added, Dated June 1, 1833.

Will Proved in London, January, 1835.

Ref.: Prob. 10/5516/Sir Henry Harford, C 10977.

Public Record Office, London.

The following is a transcription of the will of Henry Harford, Esquire, made in 1974, from a photocopy of the official copy of the original will. The will was written on parchment, with each page being signed by Henry Harford. The will was obtained from the Public Record Office in London, reference: Prob. 10, Box 5516 Sir Henry Harford. C 10977. Harford's Codicil to his will may be found under the same reference number.

Underlines are added. "Indec.", in brackets, indicates that the preceding word was not clear.

Hyphenations to divide words at the end of a line were not used in the original document. Such hyphenations were introduced by the author. Spaces at the end of lines in the original document were filled in with a graceful line so that extraneous words could not be introduced.

[Cover Sheet]

16 Jan 1835

[From: REGISTER of January 1835 page 241, PROBATE 8/228. British Record Office, Chancery Lane, London.]

HENRY HARFORD, ESQ. 60,000 pounds.

On the sixteenth day [Jan] the Will with a Codicil of Henry Harford late of New Cavendish Street in the Parish of Saint Marylebone in the County of Middlesex and of Down Place in the County of Berks., Esquire deceased was proved by the Oaths of Robert Lambert, Robert Richard Pigou, George William Gillett Potter Esquires the Executors to administration was granted having been first sworn duly to administer.

WILL OF HENRY HARFORD, ESQUIRE

THIS IS THE LAST WILL AND TESTAMENT of me HENRY HARFORD of New Cavendish Street in the Parish of Saint Mary le bone in the County of Middlesex Esquire IN the first place I direct that all my debts funeral expenses and the charges of proving this my Will be paid out of my personal Estate by my Executors hereinafter named   I give and bequeath unto my dear Wife Esther Harford the sum of One Thousand pounds to be paid to her immediately after my decease. I also give to my said dear Wife all her Jewels trinkets and other ornaments of her person with such part of my plate as she shall choose not exceeding One Thousand two hundred Ounces and all my carriages and also all the wine and spirits at my house in New Cavendish Street and likewise the household goods and furniture linen and china pictures books and glasses there to and for her own use I give and bequeath unto George William Killett Potter of Coleman Street London Gentleman the sum of Five hundred pounds for the trouble he may have in the execution of the Trusts of this my Will I give and bequeath unto John Lund, Christian Bouchardt and John Locke three of my Servants or to such one or more of them as shall be living with me at the time of my decease one years wages each I give devise and bequeath unto and to the only proper use and behoof of Robert Lambert Esquire Admiral in His Majestys Navy Robert Richard Pigou of Wimpole Street in the County of Middlesex Esquire and the said George William Killett Potter their heirs and assigns All that my capital messnage [menage] or mansion house called Down Place situate at Water Oakley near Windsor in the County of Berks lately purchased by me of John Huddleston Esquire together with the outbuildings lands and appurtenances thereto belonging UPON TRUST nevertheless that they the said Robert Lambert Robert Richard Pigou and George William Killett Potter or the survivors or survivor of them or the heirs or assigns of such survivor do and shall as soon as conveniently may be after my decease at their or his discretion absolutely sell and dispose of the said hereditaments and premises and the fee simple and inheritance thereof either by public sale or by private Contract and either together or in parcels and at their or his discretion from time to time to buy in and resell the same or any part or parts thereof either by public sale or private contract and either together or in parcels without being subject to any loss that may arise thereby and unto any person or persons that may be willing to purchase the same or any part thereof and for the most money and best price or prices that can or may be reasonably had or obtained for the same And for facilitating such sale or sales I do hereby authorize and empower my said Trustees or the survivors or survivor of them or the heirs or assigns of such survivor to make and execute all such lawful acts deeds conveyances and assurances in the Law as shall or may be necessary or as Counsel shall advise for conveying and assuring to or vesting in such purchaser or purchasers his her and their heirs and assigns or as he or they shall direct the hereditaments and premises so to be purchased by him her or them respectively and I declare that the receipt and receipts of my said Trustees or the survivors or survivor of them or the heirs and assigns of such survivor shall be from time to time a good and sufficient discharge and good and sufficient discharges to all and every such purchaser or purchasers for such sum and sums of money as in such receipt or receipts shall respectively be expressed to be received and that such purchaser or purchasers having paid his her or their purchase money or purchase monies or any part thereof respectively to my said Trustees or the survivors or survivor of them or the heirs or assigns of such survivor and taken such receipt or receipts as aforesaid shall not afterwards be answerable or accountable for the loss misapplication or nonapplication of any sum or sums of money in such receipt or receipts expressed to be received or be in any wise concerned or obliged to see to the application thereof or any part thereof And I direct that all monies to arise by such sale or sales shall after payment and deduction of all expenses attending such sale or sales and all other expenses attending the execution of the aforesaid Trust become and make part of my personal Estate. I give and bequeath unto the said Robert Lambert Robert Richard Pigou and George William Kellett Potter their Executors Administrators and Assigns All that my leasehold messnage or tenement two sets of Stables yard and premises in New Cavendish Street in the County of Middlesex and all my Estate and interest therein upon trust to permit my said dear Wife Esther Harford personally to reside therein or in case she shall decline so to do to permit and suffer her to receive the Rents and Profits thereof during her life or widowhood she paying all rent and taxes in respect of the said premises keeping the same in repair and performing the covenants contained in the Leases thereof during her residence therein and also whether she reside therein personally is to enjoy the rents and profits thereof aforesaid indemnifying my Executors and Estate from such rents taxes repairs and covenants respectively and from and immediately after the decease or marriage of my said Wife or not paying such rents or taxes or any part thereof respectively as aforesaid or not Keeping the same premises in repair or not performing the covenants contained in the said Leases during her residence therein or not indemnifying my Executors and Estate as aforesaid whichever shall first happen Upon Trust that they my said Trustees or the survivors or survivor of them or the Executors or administrators of such survivor do and shall sell and dispose of the same by public sale or private contract and from time to time at their and his discretion do and shall buy in and resell the same either by public sale or private contract without being subject to any loss that may arise thereby and unto any person or persons that may be willing to purchase the same for the most money that can be reasonably obtained for the same And for facilitating such sale I do hereby authorize and empower my said Trustees or the survivors or survivor of them or the Executors or administrators of such survivor to make and execute all such lawful acts deeds conveyances and assurances as shall be necessary or as Counsel shall advise for assigning and assuring to or vesting in such purchaser or purchasers his her or their executors or administrators or as he or they may direct the said Leasehold hereditaments and premises And I declare that the receipt and receipts of my said Trustees or the survivors or survivor of them his Executors or administrators shall be a good and sufficient discharge and good and sufficient discharges to such purchaser or purchasers for so much money as in such receipt or receipts shall be expressed to be received and that such purchaser and purchasers having paid his her or their purchase money and any part thereof to my said Trustees or Trustee and taken such receipt or receipts as aforesaid shall not afterwards be answerable for the loss misapplication or nonapplication of any sum or sums of money in such receipt or receipts respectively expressed to be received or any part thereof And I direct that all monies to arise by such sale or sales shall after payment and deduction of all expenses attending such sale or sales and all other expenses attending the execution of the aforesaid Trust become and make part of my personal Estate AND WHEREAS under and by virtue of a certain deed of gift and declaration of Trust bearing date on or about the thirtieth day of March One Thousand eight hundred and thirteen under the hands and seals of Sir Nelson Rycroft Baronet Henry Rycroft Esquire and George Burley Gentleman It is declared that as to Two thousand pounds like annuities then standing in their names in the Books of the Governor and Company of the Bank of England they should stand possessed thereof Upon Trust to pay the dividends thereof unto my said dear Wife Esther Harford and her assigns for her life for her sole use notwithstanding her coverture and after her decease Upon Trust to transfer the same unto me the said Henry Harford my Executors Administrators or Assigns NOW I DO hereby in virtue of all powers in me vested give and bequeath limit and appoint the said Two Thousand pounds four per cent annuities unto my said Wife Esther Harford her Executors and Administrators to and for her and their own use absolutely AND

WHEREAS Frederick Pigou late of Wimpole Street Cavendish Square in the County of Middlesex Esquire deceased did by his last Will and Testament in writing bearing date the thirty first day of May One Thousand eight hundred and four give to Frederick John Pigou Robert Richard Pigou and the said Robert Lambert the sum of Four thousand pounds UPON TRUST to invest the same in the public stocks or funds of Great Britain or on real securities in England at interest and from time to time to alter vary and transpose the same And upon further Trust to pay the interest and dividends thereof to me the said Henry Harford during my life and after my decease to pay or transfer the said sum of Four thousand pounds or the stocks funds or securities on which the same should be invested unto or amongst all and every or such one or more of the children of me the said Henry Harford on the body of <u>his the Testators</u> Daughter Louisa my late Wife deceased begotten at such age or time or respective ages or times and in such shares and proportions and subject to such conditions and limitations over such limitations over being for the benefit of some or one of such children as I the said Henry Harford by deed or will executed in the presence of and to be attested by two or more credible witnesses shall direct or appoint And the said <u>Testator also gave unto his Brother William Henry Pigou</u>, me the said Henry Harford, and the said Robert Lambert, the residue of his personal Estate UPON TRUST after the decease of his the Testators Wife Jemima Pigou* to raise thereout the sum of Thirty thousand pounds and to stand possessed of Six thousand pounds part thereof Upon Trust to invest the same in the public stocks or funds of Great Britain or on real securities in England at interest with liberty of transposing the same when and as often as they or he should deem it expedient and to stand possessed thereof and of the dividends or interest of the same upon such of the same Trusts as he the said Testator

*[Note: Underlines added to indicate items of particular interest.]

had before directed to be performed with respect to the said Legacy of four thousand pounds before given for the benefit of me the said Henry Harford and my children by the said Louisa my late Wife deceased and the stocks funds or securities on which the same should be invested and the dividends and interest arising therefrom or such or so many of them as should be subsisting or capable of taking effect AND WHEREAS I have four children by my said late Wife Louisa Harford deceased that is to say <u>Frederick Paul Harford Louisa Ann Harford Frances Harford and Frederica Elizabeth Harford</u> AND WHEREAS my Son Frederick Paul Harford is amply provided for under the settlement made on my marriage with my said late Wife Louisa Harford and otherwise by this my Will AND WHEREAS the said sum of Four thousand pounds does now consist of forty shares of one hundred pounds each in the capital stock of the Globe Insurance Company in London AND WHEREAS by a deed Poll or Instrument in Writing under the hand and seal of me the said Henry Harford bearing date the twenty seventh June One thousand eight Hundred and twenty nine and sealed and delivered by me in the presence of two credible witnesses by virtue and in part execution of the power and authority to me for that purpose given by the hereinbefore in part recited Will of the said Frederick Pigou Have directed and appointed that the one third equal part of the said forty shares of the said capital of the said Globe Insurance Company (subject to the life interest of me the said Henry Harford) and the one third equal part of the said sum of Six thousand pounds subject to the life interest of her the said Jemima Pigou and me the said Henry Harford should go and be in trust for my Daughter Frederica Elizabeth <u>now the Wife of Robert Thomas John Glyn Esquire</u> and be an interest vested in her immediately after the sealing and delivery of the said Deed Poll now in recital NOW THEREFORE I the said Henry Harford in further exercise of the powers to me given by the said Will of the said

Frederick Pigou deceased and of all other powers in me thereto enabling do by this my Will duly made and published for that purpose give direct and appoint the two remaining equal third parts of the said forty shares of the said Capital of the said Globe Insurance Company and also the remaining two equal third parts of the said sum of Six thousand pounds subject as aforesaid and the stocks funds and securities in which the same are or shall be invested and all interest dividends and accumulations thereof unto and between them my said daughters Louisa Ann Harford and Frances Harford in equal shares and proportions and to be an interest vested or interests vested in her or them immediately after my decease AND WHEREAS by <u>Indenture</u> bearing date the <u>fourth day of June One thousand eight hundred and six</u> and made between me the said Henry Harford of the first part <u>Esther</u> my now Wife <u>then Esther Rycroft Spinster</u> of the second part Sir Nelson Rycroft Baronet Henry Rycroft Esquire and Robert Richard Pigou Esquire of the third part (being the settlement made previous to and in contemplation of the marriage which afterwards took effect between me and my said now wife) It is (amongst other things) declared that they the said Sir Nelson Rycroft Henry Rycroft and Robert Richard Pigou should stand possessed of Seven thousand seven hundred pounds Bank three pounds per cent reduced annuities therein mentioned to have been transferred into their names Upon Trust after the decease of the survivor of them the said Henry Harford and Esther his now wife that they the said Trustees or the survivors or survivor of them his executors or administrators should pay transfer and assign the said trust monies stocks funds and securities and the interest dividends and annual produce thereof unto all and every or such one or more exclusively of the Child or Children of the said Henry Harford by the said Esther his now Wife or unto all and every or such one or more exclusively of the others or other of the issue born in the lifetime of the said Henry Harford and Esther his now wife or the survivor of them of any of the said Children or both unto such one or more of the said Children and such one or more of their or any of their issue born in the life time of the said Henry Harford and Esther his now wife or the survivor of them at such ages or respective ages from fifteen inclusive to twenty one inclusive happening after the decease of them the said Henry Harford and Esther his now Wife or at any age or ages happening in the life time of the said Henry Harford and Esther his now wife or the survivor of them in such manner and if more than one in such shares and proportions as I the said Henry Harford by Deed in writing to be executed as therein mentioned or by my last Will and Testament in writing to be by me signed and published in the presence of and attested by two or more credible witnesses should from time to time direct or appoint AND WHEREAS I have four children by my said present Wife now living that is to say George Harford Esther Harford Emily Harford and Charles Harford NOW I the said Henry Harford in exercise of the powers to me given by the said recited Indenture of Settlement and of all other powers in me thereto enabling do by this my Will duly made and published for that purpose give direct and appoint that from and after the decease of the survivor of me the said Henry Harford and Esther my now wife the said seven thousand seven hundred pounds Bank three per cent annuities and the stocks funds and securities in which the same are and shall be invested shall be paid transferred and assigned unto and amongst all and every of them the said George Harford Esther Harford Emily Harford and Charles Harford in equal shares and proportions and to be an interest vested or interests vested in the said George Harford and Charles Harford on the day next before he or they shall attain his or their age or ages of twenty one years and in the said Esther Harford and Emily Harford on the day next before she or they shall attain her or their age or ages of twenty one years or on the day or respective days of her or their marriage which [ever] shall first happen but not to be payable to him her or them respectively until after the decease of the survivor of us the said Henry Harford and Esther my now Wife I GIVE AND BEQUEATH to the said Robert Lambert Robert Richard Pigou and George William Killett Potter so much of my personal estate as will be sufficient to purchase twenty one thousand eight hundred and thirty three pounds six shillings and eight pence three pounds per cent consolidated Bank annuities clear of all deductions for Legacy duty Brokers Charges and other expenses Upon Trust that they my said Trustees do and shall as soon as conveniently may be after my decease therewith purchase and cause to be transferred into their names or name of the survivors or survivor of them his executors or administrators twenty one thousand eight hundred and thirty three pounds six shillings and eight pence three pounds per cent Consolidated Bank annuities and do and shall stand possessed thereof and of the interest dividends and annual produce thereof upon and for the trusts intents and purposes herein after mentioned that is to say UPON TRUST by and out of the interest dividends and annual produce of the said trust fund from time to time as the same interest dividends and annual produce shall be received to pay the several annuities or yearly sums herein after mentioned that is to say ONE annuity or clear yearly sum of five hundred pounds to my said Wife Esther Harford during her natural life if she shall so long continue my Widow such annuity to cease immediately after her death or marriage which shall first happen and such annuity to be paid to the said Esther Harford personally or to such person as she shall by writing from time to time appoint to receive the same such writing to be from time to time signed after the respective days on which the dividends shall become payable and not by way of anticipation ONE other annuity or clear yearly sum of thirty pounds to Elizabeth Broughton of

Windsor in the County of Berks during her natural life ONE other annuity or clear yearly sum of twenty five pounds to my late Servant Sarah Lish during her natural life ONE other annuity or clear yearly sum of One hundred pounds to Henrietta Emily Calvert—Spinster during her natural life ONE other annuity or clear yearly sum of fifty pounds to my Servant John Parrot during his natural life if he should be living with me at the time of my decease ONE other annuity or clear yearly sum of twelve pounds unto my Servant Christopher Parsons during his natural life if he should be living with me at the time of my decease, such several annuities to be paid to the said Elizabeth Broughton Sarah Lish and Henrietta Emily Calvert John Parrot and Christopher Parsons respectively or to such person or persons as they shall respectively from time to time by writing under their respective days on which the dividends of the said Trust funds shall from time to time become payable and not by way of anticipation it being my intention that such several annuities shall be for the sole and separate personal use of them the said Elizabeth Broughton Sarah Lish and Henrietta Emily Calvert [names are inserted but then crossed out: John Parrot and Christopher] respectively free and independent of any present or future Husband or Husbands of them respectively and not to be subject to the debts engagements disposal or control of any such husband or husbands AND I declare that the several receipts and discharges of the said Elizabeth Broughton Sarah Lish and Henrietta Emily Calvert John Parrot and Christopher Parsons or of such persons as they shall respectively from time to time appoint as aforesaid shall from time to time be good and effectual discharges to my Trustees for so much money as in such receipts shall be respectively acknowledged to be received AND I do hereby direct that from time to time from and immediately after the ceasing of any of the annuities herein-before directed to be paid to my said Wife Esther Harford or to the said Elizabeth Broughton Sarah Lish and Henrietta

Emily Calvert John Parrott and Christopher Parsons respectively in manner aforesaid such part of the Capital of the said trust fund as shall be unnecessary to be reclaimed for securing the payment of the remaining annuities or annuity charged on the said trust fund shall become part of the residue of my personal estate and shall be paid or transferred by my said Trustees or the survivors or survivor of them his executors or administrators to such person or persons and in such manner as is directed with regard to the said residue of my personal estate I GIVE and BEQUEATH unto the said Robert Lambert Robert Richard Pigou and George William Killett Potter and the survivors and survivor of them the sum of twenty four thousand pounds sterling free of Legacy duty Upon Trust that they my said Trustees do and shall as soon as conveniently may be after my decease lay out the same in the names or name of my said Trustees or the survivors or survivor of them his executors or administrators in some or one of the public funds or parliamentary stocks of Great Britain or at interest upon Government or real Securities in England and do and shall alter and vary the same from time to time as to them or him shall seem meet — And do and shall pay assign and transfer the said trust monies stocks funds and securities unto and amongst all the every of them my said Sons and Daughters Louisa Ann Harford Frances Harford and Frederica Elizabeth the wife of Robert Thomas John Glyn and George Harford Esther Harford Emily Harford and Charles Harford in such shares and proportions and manner as hereinafter as immediately mentioned that is to say to Louisa Ann Harford four thousand pounds to Frances Harford two thousand pounds to Frederica Elizabeth the wife of the said Robert Thomas John Glyn two thousand pounds (this last mentioned sum of Two thousand pounds I direct my said Trustees or Trustee for the time being to pay to the Trustees or Trustee named in and appointed by a certain Deed bearing date the twenty ninth day of June one thousand eight hundred and twenty nine being the Settlement made previous to the marriage of my Daughter the said Frederica Elizabeth with the said Robert Thomas John Glyn as it is my intention that the same shall be in full satisfaction and discharge of the Covenant therein entered into by me for payment of a sum of two thousand pounds on or before the expiration of six months, next after my decease to George Harford five thousand pounds to Charles Harford five thousand pounds to Esther Harford three thousand pounds and to Emily Harford three thousand pounds AND as to the shares and proportions of my four last mentioned Sons and Daughters I direct the same to be an interest vested and interests vested in the said George Harford and Charles Harford at his or their age or ages of twenty one years (and in the said Esther Harford and Emily Harford at her or their age or ages of twenty one years) or day or respective days of marriage which shall first happen and in case these events shall happen to my said Sons and Daughters in my lifetime then immediately on my decease the above mentioned proportions of my said Daughters Louisa Ann Harford Frances Harford and Frederica Elizabeth the wife of the said Robert Thomas John Glyn to be an interest vested in them immediately on my decease PROVIDED ALWAYS that if any one or more of them my said sons and daughters shall depart this life before the share or shares of him her or them so dying of and in the said trust funds and premises shall have become vested THEN I direct that the share intended to be hereby provided for each son and daughter so dying of and in the said trust funds and premises or so much thereof as shall not have been raised and paid or applied for the preferment or advancement in the World of any such son or daughter or sons or daughters so dying in pursuance of the power or authority for that purpose herein after contained shall sink into and become part of the residue of my personal estate PROVIDED ALSO and I hereby declare that it shall and may be lawful to and for my said Trustees and the survivors and survivor of them his executors and administrators at any time or times and from time to time when and as often as they or he shall think fit to raise by said disposal or transfer of the said trust monies stocks funds or securities or any part or parts thereof any sum or sums of money for each Child not exceeding in the whole for any one Child the share to which each such Child if a son or sons would be entitled to on his or their attaining his or their age or ages of twenty one years and if a daughter or daughters to which each such Daughter would be entitled to on her or their attaining her or their age or ages of twenty one years or day or days of marriage which shall first happen and to pay and apply the sum or sums so from time to time to be raised for each such child in and for the preferment advancement or benefit of each such Child in such manner and so often as they my said Trustees or the survivors or survivor of them his executors or administrators shall in their or his discretion think fit notwithstanding the share or shares of such child or children shall not have become vested or payable PROVIDED ALSO and I do hereby direct and declare that it shall and may be lawful to and for my said Trustees and the survivors and survivor of them his executors and administrators by and out of the interest dividends and annual produce of the said trust monies stocks funds and securities to pay and apply for the maintenance and education of my said sons and daughters in the mean time and until his her or their share or shares of and in the said trust monies stocks funds and securities shall become vested and payable such yearly sum and sums of money as they my said Trustees or the survivors or survivor of them his executors or administrators shall in their or his discretion from time to time think fit and do and shall lay out and invest the residue of such interest dividends and produce if any in augmentation of the principal of the said trust monies stocks funds and securities which augmentation I do hereby direct shall be considered as part of the said trust monies stocks funds and securities and shall be paid applied and disposed of to and amongst the same persons and in such and the same manner as is by this my will directed with respect to the said principal trust monies funds and securities AND AS TO all the rest residue and remainder of my real and personal estate whatsoever and wheresoever and of whatever nature or kind the same may be I GIVE DEVISE and BEQUEATH the same unto and to the only proper use and behoof of my said Son Frederick Paul Harford his heirs executors and administrators to and for his and their own use and benefit AND I DO hereby bequeath the custody or guardianship of the persons of such of my children as shall be under the age of twenty one years at the time of my death to my said present Wife Esther Harford the said Robert Lambert Robert Richard Pigou and George William Killett Potter during the minorities of my said Children respectively AND I do hereby nominate and appoint the said Robert Lambert Robert Richard Pigou and George William Killett Potter Executors of this my WILL hereby revoking all former Wills by me at any time heretofore made PROVIDED ALWAYS and I do hereby declare it to be my Will and intention that (in order to facilitate the execution of the several dispositions and trusts herein in this my Will contained) it shall and may be lawful to and for my said Trustees and the survivors and survivor of them and the heirs executors administrators and assigns of such survivor and also to and for the Trustees or Trustee for the time being to be appointed and acting under this my Will as hereinafter mentioned at their or his discretion either by public sale or by private contract to make sale and dispose of and to buy in and resell all or any part of the aforesaid trust estates mortgages funds or securities and to lay out and invest the money arising by any such sale or disposition or resale in the names or name of them the said Trustees or Trustee for the time being acting under this my Will either in the public funds or parliamentary stocks of Great Britain or at interest upon Government or real securities in England and to alter vary and transfer the same as to them or him shall from time to time seem meet and reasonable AND I do hereby direct that the receipt or receipts in writing of them the said Trustees or Trustee for the time being acting under this my Will for any sum or sums of money whatever payable or to be paid as or for the consideration money for the sale of any lands tenements or hereditaments to be sold by virtue of the powers contained in this my Will or for the sale of any stocks funds or securities or for any mortgage or other money laid out at interest or for any other sum or sums of money whatsoever shall effectually discharge the persons to whom such receipt or receipts shall be given from seeing to the application or being answerable for the misapplication of the money therein to be mentioned to be received or from inquiring into the necessity or expediency of any such sale or transfer PROVIDED ALWAYS and I do hereby direct and declare that if the Trustees hereby nominated and appointed or any of them their or any of their heirs executors administrators or assigns or any future Trustee or Trustees to be appointed in the place of them or any of them as hereinafter is mentioned shall happen to die or be desirous of being discharged of and from or refuse or decline or be incapable of act in the trusts hereby in them respectively reposed or shall reside abroad before the said trusts shall be fully executed Then and in such case and when and so often as the same shall happen it shall be lawful to and for the said Trustees or the survivors and survivor others and other of them acting under this my Will their his or her heirs executors administrators or assigns by any writing or writings under their his or her hands and seals or hand and seal and to be attested by two or more credible witnesses from time to time to nominate substitute or appoint any other person or persons to be a Trustee or Trustees in the stead or place of the Trustee or Trustees so dying or desiring to be discharged or refusing declining or becoming incapable to act or residing abroad as aforesaid TO THE INTENT there may be always three Trustees acting under this my Will and that when and so often as any new Trustees or Trustee shall be nominated and appointed as aforesaid all the trust estates monies and premises which shall then be vested in the Trustee or Trustees so dying or desiring to be discharged or refusing declining or becoming incapable to act or residing abroad as aforesaid either solely or jointly with the other Trustee or Trustees shall be thereupon with all convenient speed conveyed assigned and transferred in such sort or manner and so as that the same shall be legally and effectually vested in the surviving or continuing Trustee or Trustees of the same trust estates monies and premises respectively and such new or other trustee or trustees Or if there shall be no such surviving or continuing Trustee as aforesaid then in such new Trustee or Trustees only to the same uses and upon the same trusts as are herein before declared of and concerning the same trust estates monies and premises respectively the Trustee or Trustees whereof shall so die or be discharged or refuse decline or be incapable to act or reside abroad as aforesaid or such of them as shall or may be then subsisting or capable of taking effect AND I do hereby direct and declare that every such new Trustee or Trustees jointly or solely as herein before is mentioned shall and may in all things act and assist in the management carrying on and execution of the trusts to which he or they shall be so appointed in conjunction with the other then surviving or continuing trustee of the said Trust estates monies and premises respectively if there shall be any such surviving or continuing Trustee if not then by himself and themselves respectively as fully and effectually and with all the same power and powers authority and authorities whatsoever as if he or they had been originally in and by this my Will nominated or appointed Trustee or Trustees and as the trustee or trustees herein named his or their heirs executors or administrators in or to whose place such new Trustee or

Trustees shall respectively come or succeed are or is enabled to do or could or might have done under or by virtue of the powers herein contained if then living and continuing to act in the trusts hereby in them reposed anything herein contained to the contrary thereof in anywise notwithstanding PROVIDED ALSO and I do hereby direct that the several trustees hereby nominated and appointed and such future Trustee and Trustees to be appointed as aforesaid and each and every of them and the heirs executors administrators and assigns of them each and every of them shall be charged and chargeable respectively only for such monies as they shall respectively actually receive withstanding his their or any of their giving or signing or joining in giving or signing any receipt or receipts for the sake of conformity and any one or more of them shall not be answerable or accountable for the other or others of them or for the acts receipts neglects or defaults of the other or others of them but each and every of them for his and their own acts receipts neglects and defaults respectively and that they or any of them shall not be answerable or accountable for any Banker Goldsmith broker or any other person with whom or in whose custody or hands any part of the said trust estates monies and premises shall or may be deposited or lodged for safe custody or otherwise in the execution of the trusts herein contained and that they or any of them shall not be answerable or accountable for the defect of title of any lands tenements or hereditaments or for the insufficiency or deficiency of any security or securities stocks or funds in or upon which the said trust monies or any part thereof shall be placed out or invested or for any loss on the buying in and reselling all or any part of the said trust estates stocks funds or securities or for any other misfortune loss or damage which may happen in the execution of the trusts herein contained or in relation thereto except the same shall happen by or through their own willful default respectively and also that it shall and may be lawful to and for them my said

Trustees or Trustee and such future Trustee and Trustees to be appointed as aforesaid and every and any of them their and every of their heirs executors administrators and assigns by and out of the monies which shall come to their respective hands by virtue of the trusts aforesaid to retain to and reimburse himself and themselves respectively and also to allow to his and their co-trustee and co-trustees all costs charges damages and expenses which they or any of them shall or may suffer sustain expend disburse be at or be put unto in or about the execution of the aforesaid trusts or in relation thereto IN WITNESS whereof I the said Henry Harford the Testator have to this my last Will and Testament contained in sixteen sheets of paper set my hand and seal that is to say my hand to the first fifteen sheets thereof and my hand and seal to this sixteenth and last sheet thereof this sixteenth day of July — in the year of Our Lord One thousand eight hundred and twenty nine.

/s/ Henry Harford /seal/

SIGNED SEALED PUBLISHED AND DECLARED by the said Henry Harford the Testator as and for his last Will and Testament in the presence of us who in his presence at his request and in the presence of each other have hereto subscribed our names as witnesses hereto — the alteration in the Top of the 3d page being previously made

/s/ Charles Collingridge of Coleman Street London Gentleman
/s/ Joseph Price of the same place Gentleman
/s/ Benj^m Price of the same place Gentleman

Turn this Sheet up to preserve the SEAL.

[End of parchment page 16.]

[Codicil added - Cover Sheet]
CODICIL TO THE WILL OF HENRY HARFORD ESQUIRE
Prob 10 Box 5516 Sir Henry Harford.
WILL   COD^L Middx
                       of
                       Berks
     28 (?)
HENRY HARFORD
    Esquire
January 1835
35
/110/
   Reg ^{d}
   J.H.
   [indecipherable initials]

[The above information is shown on the cover sheet for the Codicil to the will of Sir Henry Harford. Note — he is specifically labeled "Sir Henry" — here. The Codicil is filed in the Public Record Office, London, under reference: Prob. 10 Box 5516 Sir Henry Harford C. 10977]

     [Codicil of the will of Henry Harford.]
         [Undecipherable word]
   THIS IS A CODICIL TO THE LAST WILL and TESTAMENT of me Henry Harford of New Cavendish Street in the parish of Saint Marylebone in the County of Middlesex Esquire bearing date the Sixteenth day of July One thousand Eight hundred and twenty nine and which I desire may be considered as part thereof WHEREAS by my said Will I gave devised and bequeathed unto and to the only proper Use and behoof of Robert Lambert Esquire Admiral in His Majestys Navy Robert Richard Pigou, Esquire and George William Killett Potter Esquire their heirs and assigns ALL that my Capital messnage, or Mansion house called Down Place situate at Water Oakley near Windsor in the County of Berkshire lately purchased

by me of John Huddleston Esquire together with the Outbuildings lands and Appurtenances thereto belonging Upon certain trusts and with such powers of Sale as therein is mentioned. Now I do hereby revoke and make void such powers of Sale as therein is mentioned and bequeath the same Capital Messnage or Mansion House hereditaments and premises unto and to the only proper use and behoof of the said Robert Lambert Robert Richard Pigou and George William Killett Potter their heirs and assigns UPON TRUST to permit and suffer my dear Wife Esther Harford to have the Use thereof and personally to reside therein in and during the term of her natural life or Widowhood if she shall think fit so to do She the said Esther Harford keeping the same Estate and Premises in a proper state of repair And from and immediately after the decease or marriage of my said Wife or in case of her decline to reside in the same premises UPON TRUST that my said Trustees or the Survivors or Survivor of them or the heirs or assigns of such Survivor do and shall at their or his discretion absolutely sell and dispose of the said hereditaments and premises and the fee simple and inheritance thereof either by Public Sale or by Private Contract and either together or in parcels and at their or his discretion or from time to time to buy in and resell the same in any part or parts thereof either by public Sale or private contract and either together or in parcels without being subject to any loss that may arise thereby and unto any person or persons that may be willing to purchase the same or any part thereof and for the most money and best price or prices that can or may be reasonably had or obtained for the same AND for facilitating such Sale or Sales I do hereby authorize and empower my said Trustees or the Survivors or Survivor of them or the heirs or assigns of such Survivor to make and execute all such lawful Acts Deeds Conveyances and Assurances on the Same as shall be or may be necessary or as Counsel shall advise for conveying or assuring to and vesting in Such Purchaser or Purchasers his her or their heirs and assigns or as he or they shall direct the hereditaments and premises so to be purchased by him her or them respectively AND I declare that the receipt and receipts of my said Trustees or the Survivors or Survivors of them or the heirs or assigns of such Survivors shall be from time to time a good and sufficient discharge and good and sufficient discharges to all and every such purchaser and purchasers for such Sum and Sums of money as in such receipt or receipts shall respectively be expressed to be received AND that such purchaser or purchasers having paid his her or their purchase money or purchase monies or any part thereof respectively to my said Trustees or the Survivors or Survivors of them or the heirs or assigns of such Survivor and Taken [?] such receipt or receipts as aforesaid shall not afterwards be answerable or accountable for the loss misapplication or nonapplication of any Sum or Sums of money in such receipt or receipts expressed to be received or be in any wise concerned or obliged to see to the application thereof or any part thereof AND I direct that all monies to arise by such Sale or Sales shall after payment and deduction of all expenses attending the execution of the aforesaid Trust become and make part of my personal Estate And Whereas by my said Will I Give and bequeath unto the Said Trustees therein named then Executors administrators and assigns All that my Leasehold messnage or tenement two sets of Stables Yard and Premises in New Cavendish Street in the County of Middlesex and all my Estate and interest therein Upon certain Trusts therein mentioned NOW I do hereby revoke and make void so much of such bequest as respects the permission of my said dear Wife Esther Harford to reside on the Said Premises during her life or Widowhood AND I do hereby direct that they my said Trustees or the Survivors or Survivor of them or the executors or administrators of such Survivor as soon as conveniently may be after my decease do and shall sell and dispose of the same by Public Sale or Private Contract in the manner as the same is in my said Will directed to be done hereby confirming all such part and parts of my said Will as related to such Sale or Sales the giving receipts and indemnification of my Trustees and the Purchasers of such Property And I direct that all money to arise by such Sale or Sales shall after payment and deduction of all expenses attending such Sale or Sales and all other expenses attending the execution of the aforesaid Trust become and make part of my personal Estate AND WHEREAS by my Said Will I Gave and bequeathed to my said Trustees so much money as would be sufficient to purchase Twenty One Thousand Eight hundred and thirty three Pounds Six Shillings and Eight pence Three Pounds per Cent Consolidated Bank Annuities UPON Trust that they my said Trustees should as soon as conveniently might be after my decease purchase or cause to be purchased [word crossed through] transferred into their Names or the Names or Name of the Survivors or Survivor of them his Executors or Administrators Twenty One thousand Eight hundred and Thirty three Pounds Six Shillings and Eight pence Three Pounds per Cent Consolidated Bank Annuities AND should stand possessed thereof and of the interest dividends and annual produce UPON TRUST (amongst other things, to pay one Annuity or clear yearly Sum of 500 pounds to my said Wife Esther Harford during her natural life if she should so long continue my Widow and to be paid to her at such times and in such manner as therein mentioned. NOW I do hereby revoke and make void such bequest AND WHEREAS since the date and execution of my said Will Emily Harford therein named has intermarried with The Reverend William Henry Wentworth Bowyer Clerk NOW my Will and intention is that such bequests as made for the said Emily Harford in my said Will shall not be paid to her but I do hereby give and bequest unto the said Trustees in my Will named and the Survivors and Survivor of them his executors and administrators all or any Legacies Sum or Sums of money which she the said Emily now the Wife of the said William Henry Wentworth Bowyer Clerk — may become entitled under and by virtue of my said Will — as the sum bequeathed to her — UPON TRUST that they my said Trustees do and shall as soon as conveniently may be after my decease lay out the Same in the names or name of my said Trustees or the Survivors or Survivor of them his executors or administrators in some or one of the Public funds or Parliamentary Stocks of Great Britain or at Interest on real Securities in England and do and shall alter and vary the Same from time to time as to them or him shall seem meet AND do and shall stand possessed thereof and of the interest dividends and annual produce thereof UPON (and for?) the trusts intents and purposes hereinafter mentioned that is to say UPON TRUST to receive and take the interest dividends and annual produce of such Stocks funds or Securities and to pay the same into the hands of the said Emily Bowyer for her sole and separate use or to such person as she shall by writing direct or appoint AND not to be subject to the debts control or engagements of the Said William Henry Wentworth Bowyer or any husband with whom she may intermarry AND I do hereby direct that the receipt or receipts of the said Emily Bowyer or of such person or persons as she shall direct to receive the Same shall be a good and sufficient discharge and good and sufficient discharges to my said Trustees or the Survivors or Survivor of them his Executors or Administrators for such Sum or Sums of money as in Such receipt or receipts shall be respectively acknowledged to be received and from and immediately after the decease of the said Emily Bowyer to pay assign and transfer the said Stock funds and Securities and the interest dividends and annual produce thereof into and amongst such person and persons and in such parts shares and proportions as She the said Emily Bowyer shall by her last Will and

Testament in writing or any Codicil or Codicils thereto or any thing in the nature of her last Will and Testament such last Will or Codicils thereto to be executed in the presence of two or more Witnesses shall direct limit and appoint AND in default of any such direction limitation or appointment to pay assign and transfer the said Trust monies, Stocks funds and Securities unto and amongst all and every Child and Children ~~which shall be living~~ [words written, then elided] of the said Emily Bowyer which shall be living at her decease (if any) and to be equally divided between or amongst them if more than One (share and share alike and if but one such Child to such One) but if there shall be no such Child or Children of the Said Emily Bowyer living at her decease and she shall make no appointment of the said Trust fund then UPON TRUST to pay and assign over the said principal Stocks funds or Securities Interest and dividends unto the said William Henry Wentworth Bowyer if he should Survive the Said Emily Bowyer and in default thereof to her next of kin AND I do hereby ratify and confirm my said Will in all respects not hereby revoked or altered AND I declare this to be Codicil to my last Will and Testament bearing date the Sixteenth day of July — One thousand Eight hundred and Twenty nine IN WITNESS whereof I have put my hand to the first three Sheets thereof and my hand and Seal to this fourth and last sheet thereof this First . . . . day of June — One thousand eight hundred and thirty three.

Sealed published and declared by me Henry Harford as a Codicil to my last Will and Testament in the presence of us who in his presence at his request and in the presence of each other have hereunto subscribed our Names and Witnesses hereto

/s/ Rupert Raries [Last name is unclear]
   of Lombards Street London
                    Sol^r [Solicitor]
/s/ Chas Collingridge Basinghall Street London
                            (SEAL)

                              Sol^r
/s/ Benjamin Price Clk to Potter & Collingridge
    of the same place
                              /s/ HENRY HARFORD
[End of Page 4 of the Codicil.]

Papers referring to proving of Henry Harford's Will and its Codicil following his decease.
File number Prob. 10, Box 5516, Sir Henry Harford, Public Record Office, Chancery Lane, London. Ref. C 10977

                              January 9th 1835
~~Richard~~ [corrected] Robert Lambert Esquire, ~~a line Admiral in His Majesty's Navy,~~ [corrected] Robert Richard Pigou Esquire and George William Killett Potter Esquire, the Executors named in this Will were sworn to the Trust and due Performance thereof and of the Codicil thereto and as usual; also that the Testator died on or about the Eighth day of December last and that his Goods Chattels and Credits do not amount in value to Sixty Thousand Pounds
                    Before me
Pritchard
                    Cav
Sub 60,000 pounds. Com
                    Col   /s/ [A blurred signature -
                                 Indecipherable]
                         16 January
The Testator Henry Harford was late of New Cavendish Street in the Parish of Saint Marylebone in the County of Middlesex and of Down Place in the County of Berks Esquire, and died at the latter place.
    PROVED at LONDON (with a Codicil) 16th January 1835 before the Worshipful Jesse Addams Doctor of Laws and Surrogate by the Oaths of Robert Lambert Robert Richard Pigou, and George William Killett Potter Esquires the Executors to whom Administration was granted

having been first sworn duly to administer.

(Not to be Registered)

In the Prerogative Court of Canterbury

In the Goods of HENRY HARFORD Esquire deceased

(STAMP)

(crown)

Appeared personally Charles Collingridge of Basinghall Street in the City of London Solicitor and made Oath that he was present at the Execution of and is one of the subscriber Witnesses to the last Will and Testament with one Codicil thereto of Henry Harford late of New Cavendish Street in the Parish of Saint Marylebone in the County of Middlesex and of Down Place in the County of Berks Esquire deceased the said Will being now hereunto annexed and beginning thus — "This is the last Will and Testament of me Henry Harford" ending thus "in the Year of our Lord One Thousand eight hundred and twenty nine" and thus subscribed "Henry Harford" and having the following Obliterations and Interlineations therein and words written on Erasures or otherwise in addition to the said Will as originally written viz an erasure at the beginning of the eleventh line of the first Sheet of the said Will and the word "Ounces" written on part of such erasure the partial obliteration of the word "or" at the end of the fifteenth line of the second Sheet of the said Will and the word "and" written immediately over such obliteration, the words "or in case she shall decline so to do to permit and suffer her to receive the rents and profits thereof" — written immediately over that which was originally the first line of the third Sheet of the said Will and Words "if she shall think fit so to do" partially obliterated in the line which was originally the second line of the said third Sheet the words "whether she reside therein personally or enjoy the Rents and profits thereof as aforesaid" interlined between the lines which were originally the fourth and fifth lines of the said third Sheet the partial obliteration of the words "or in case of her declining to reside in the said Messnage or Tenement and Premises" in the lines which were originally the seventh eighth and ninth lines of the said Third Sheet the word or name "Paul" interlined between the twenty fifth and twenty sixth lines and also between the twenty seventh and twenty eighth lines of the fifth Sheet of the said Will the Erasure at the beginning of the twenty second line of the eighth Sheet of the said Will and the words "thereof upon and" written on such Erasure the Interlineation of the Words "as the same" between the twenty third and twenty fourth lines of the said eighth Sheet the partial obliteration of the words "John Parrot and Christopher" between the twentieth and twenth first Lines of the ninth Sheet of the said Will an erasure in the twenty sixth line of the eleventh Sheet of the said Will and the Word "each" written thereon the interlineation of the Word or name "Paul" between the twenty seventh and twenty eighth lines of the twelfth Sheet of the said Will and the interlineation of the word "sixteenth" between the twenty third and twenty fourth lines of the sixteenth and last Sheet of the said Will AND he further made Oath that immediately preceding the Execution of the said Will the same was examined by this Deponent and George William Killett Potter Esquire one of the Executors therein named, with the Draft thereof from which it had been copied, by one of them reading one part thereof aloud in the presence and hearing of the other and of the said Testator and he the said George William Killett Potter then made such Alterations therein as were necessary to make the same conform to the said Draft and such other alterations as were then dictated by the said deceased AND also added to the said Will the Date thereof. AND having now viewed and perused the said Will and carefully observed the several Interlineations Obliterations and Words written on Erasures and otherwise in addition to the said Will hereinbefore recited he the Deponent saith that the same were all made and written either previous to the Examination of the said Will as aforesaid or by the said George William Killett Potter at the time of such Examination and in particular that the Interlineation of the said Word Sixteenth forming part of the Date of the said Will in the sixteenth and last Sheet thereof was then written by the said George William Killett Potter previous to the Execution of the said Will by the said deceased and in conformity with his wishes and directions AND he further made Oath that from his recollection of the said word "Sixteenth" forming part of the Date of the said Will having been interlined as aforesaid on the day of the Execution thereof and previous to such Execution taking place he is enabled to depose and does depose that the said Will was executed on the sixteenth of July One thousand eight hundred and twenty nine being the Day on which it purports by the said Date to have been so executed.

On the Tenth day of January 1835 the said Charles Collingridge was duly sworn to the truth of this Affidavit /s/ Charles Collingridge
  Before me
    /s/ C. Cooke
    /s/ [Another signature, not clear,
       possibly "Thomas Crullwell".]

APPENDIX E

WILL OF
ESTHER RYECROFT HARFORD

Public Record Office, London.
Ref.: Prob. 11/2174:

WILL OF ESTHER RYECROFT HARFORD*

I, ESTHER HARFORD, of Down Place in the parish of Bray in the County of Berks., Widow, hereby revoking all wills by me of any time heretofore made to Declare this to be my last Will and Testament in manner following, that is to say I give and bequeath to Louisa Ann Harford one of the daughters of my late husband by a former marriage if she shall be living at the time of my decease the sum of twenty pounds and I also give and bequeath to Frances Harford another daughter of my late husband by a former marriage if she shall be living at the time of my decease, the sum of twenty pounds, the above legacies to be considered as tokens of my regard and affection for them. I give and bequeath to my Grand Daughter, Fanny Emily Bowyer if she shall be living at the time of my decease, the sum of fifty pounds. I give and bequeath to my maid servant, Esther Willis, if she shall be living with me at the time of my decease the sum of nineteen guineas over and above any wages that may be due to her. I give and bequeath to Frederick Paul Harford the son of my late husband by a former marriage as head of the family, all the family Diamonds consisting of necklace, earrings, and sprig which I leave him in token of my gratitude for his having allowed me the use of his furniture at Down Place AND I also give and bequeath to the said Frederick Paul Harford all and whatsoever articles of furniture there may be at Down Place belonging to me at the time of my decease and which I may have added at any time during my residence there. I give and bequeath to my son Charles Harford my large Diamond ring together with all various spirituous liquors, ale and beer of which I may die possessed. I give and bequeath to my sister Elizabeth Askew if she shall be living at the time of my

---

*London, Public Record Office, Ref. Prob. 11/2174. The will is dated 9 March 1849 and was proved 16 June 1853.

decease, my Diamond ring with [two indecipherable words] together with the sum of twenty pounds. I give and bequeath to my son George Harford the sum of eight hundred pounds AND as to all the REST AND RESIDUE of my property and effects of whatsoever nature or kind the same may consist at the time of my decease, I give and bequeath the same (after payment thereout of all my Debts funeral and testamentary expenses the foregoing legacies and the legacies hereafter given to my Executors) to be equally divided between my Daughter Esther Fitzmaurice and my son Charles Harford. I request that should I die at no great Distance from Down Place, I may be buried in the family vault in Bray Church my funeral to be as private and as little expensive as security will permit, AND lastly, I do hereby appoint my Step-son, the said Frederick Paul Harford, my son Charles Harford and Charles Henry Moore of Sirolus [?] Far Fields, Esquire EXECUTORS of this my last Will and Testament. AND I give and bequeath to each of them my said Executors the sum of fifty pounds for their trouble and I request that all the foregoing legacies may be paid within six calendar months after my Decease in Witness Whereof I the said Esther Harford have to this my last Will and Testament set my hand this ninth day of March one thousand eight hundred and forty nine—
/s/ ESTHER HARFORD
Signed and Declared by the said Esther Harford the testatrix as and for her last Will and Testament in the presense of us both present at the same time who in her presense at her request and in the presense [sic] of each other have hereunto subscribed our names as witnesses this ninth Day of March one thousand eight hundred and forty nine /s/ John Stead, Butler to Mrs. Askew of Wimpole Street /s/ Charles Lawes, Footman to Mrs. Askew of Wimpole Street.

PROVED at London 16th June 1853 before the Judge by the oaths of Frederick Paul Harford, Esquire, Charles Harford, Esquire, her son and Charles Henry

Moore Esquire the Executors to whom Admon was granted they having been first sworn to wit the said Frederick Paul Harford and Charles Henry Moore before the Worshipful John Elliott Pasley Robertson and the said Charles Harford before the Worshipful Robert Joseph Phillimore respectively, Doctors of Law and Surrogates Duly to administer.

APPENDIX F

WILL OF
FRANCES MARY
HARFORD WYNDHAM

Petworth House Archives, Document
#PHA 1608.

COPY from

The following exact copy of the last Will of the late Honble Mrs. Wyndham was taken by Anthony Andrew one of the subscribing witnesses to the said Will on Monday the eighteenth of March 1822 a few hours after the Decease of the Testatrix at Florence.

COPY

I, the Honble Frances Mary Wyndham at this time residing in Florence in perfect Health of Body and Mind do give and bequeath by this my last Will and Testament to my Daughter Mrs. Laura Boultbee the Sum of £15,000 Sterling which according to my Marriage Settlements I have a right to dispose of after my Death among my Children in such proportions as I think fit. I repeat, I give the above mentioned Fifteen thousand pounds Sterling to my Daughter Laura Boultbee on the following Conditions— That she pays to Lord Holland a Debt I owe him of two hundred pounds Sterling or to his Heirs—likewise that she pays annually to the Abbê Jean Blaise Biagini a Succhese Priest who manages my Affairs and is a perfectly honest Man, the Sum of one hundred Sequins, each Sequin making two Scudi of ten Pauls each, and during his Life— The payment of the above mentioned Debt of £200 Sterling to Lord Holland and the above mentioned Pension of one hundred Sequins to the Abbê Jean Blaise Biagini, are to commence from the time in which Mrs. Laura Boultbee is in Possession of the above mentioned £15,000 Sterling—The Pension to the Abbê Jean Blaise Biagini is to be paid half yearly.

I have at this time between Four and Five thousand Tuscan crowns placed out at Interest—I have besides some Trinkets, a very few Diamonds—I have household Furniture, some Plate, Linnen [sic] Procelaine clocks V.Vc which I dispose of in the following way

To Madame Josephine Fournier a French Lady at this time residing with me, I give the Sum of One thousand crowns—all my Household Furniture, Linnen,

Books, musical Instruments, Porcelaine, both useful and ornamental—Miniatures framed and half my plate— I say I give to Madame Josephine Fournier one thousand crowns and the beforesaid Articles—But it is in Case and provided that she is still residing with me at the time of my Death, should she have left me, all I give to her, is to be sold and the produce to belong to my Daughter Mrs. Laura Boultbee, whom I give everything I die possessed of and which I have not bequeathed by this my last Will and Testament to other Persons. I give the Abbê Jean Blaise Biagini half my Plate—my carriages are to be sold. My Maids are to have my Clothes divided between them except Shalls [shawls] and Lace—and three months wages— There is a Will of mine at Drummonds my Bankers in which I have bequeathed to Mrs. Laura Boultbee the £15,000 Ster'g, which this will confirm. She must pay my funeral expenses and whatever debts I may have at the time of my Death, and spend one hundred Sequins for a Stone or an Urn where ever I am buried— AND, I appoint Executors of this my last Will and Testament, my Son George Wyndham and Mr. Boultbee, Husband of my Daughter Laura Boultbee.

      Florence Nov. the 1st, 1820
      /s/S/ Frances Mary Wyndham

Witnesses—
[Indecipherable name] of Hoveton Hall, Co. Norfolk in the Commission of the Peace for that County.
 John Biddulph of Burton Park Sussex.
/s/ Geo. Anthony Andrew Halfpay 20th Lt. Dragoons
Certified to be a correct Copy— Florence 20 March 1822 E. S. Dawkins
     H.M. Charge D'affaires in Tuscany

(Author's 1974 photograph)

Kiplin Hall, home of the First Lord Baltimore, in Yorkshire. This is a view of the back of the old Calvert home. The wings to the left and right are later additions.

APPENDIX G

THE GOVERNORS OF MARYLAND

THE COLONIAL GOVERNORS OF MARYLAND

1633-1647   Leonard Calvert
1647-1649   Thomas Greene
1649-1652   William Stone
1652   Parliamentary Commissioners
1652-1654   William Stone
1654-1657   William Fuller and Council
(Appointed by the Parliamentary Commissioners)
1657-1660   Josias Fendall (Appointed by Lord Baltimore)
1660-1661   Philip Calvert
1661-1676   Charles Calvert
1676   Cecilius Calvert Since Cecilius Calvert was a minor, the actual governing was done by first the Deputy Governor Jesse Wharton, and later, by Deputy Governor Thomas Notley.
1676-1679   Thomas Notley
1679-1684   Charles Calvert returned as Governor. He now was the Proprietor of Maryland and held the title of the Third Lord Baltimore.
1684-1688   Benedict Leonard Calvert. He was only a young child at the time and the actual governing was done for him by a Council of Deputy Governors.
1688-1689   William Joseph, President of the Council of Deputies
1689-1690   John Coode, Leader of Protestant Associators
1690-1692   Nehemiah Blackiston

In 1692 the English crown sent Royal Governors to Maryland. Charles Calvert, the Third Lord Baltimore, who was Proprietor at that time, lost the right to appoint Governors. He did retain the legal right to Maryland and certain benefits and profits from the Province.

ROYAL GOVERNORS

Sir Lionel Copley	1692-1693
Sir Thomas Lawrence	1693
Sir Edmund Andros	1693
Nicholas Greenberry President of Council	1693-1694
Sir Edmund Andros	1694
Sir Thomas Lawrence President of Council	1694

Francis Nicholson	1694-1699
Nathaniel Blackiston	1699-1702
Thomas Tench	
President of Council	1702-1704
John Seymour	1704-1709
Edward Lloyd	
President of Council	1709-1714
John Hart	1714-1715

PROPRIETARY GOVERNORS

(In 1715 the right to appoint Governors of Maryland was returned to the Calvert family, Proprietors of Maryland.)

1715-1720	John Hart
1720	Thomas Brooke, President of Council
1720-1727	Charles Calvert
1727-1731	Benedict Leonard Calvert
1731-1732	Samuel Ogle
1732-1733	Charles Calvert, Lord Propriotor
1733-1742	Samuel Ogle
1742-1747	Thomas Bladen
1747-1752	Samuel Ogle
1752-1753	Benjamin Tasker, President of Council
1753-1769	Horatio Sharpe
1769-1776	Robert Eden

GOVERNORS OF THE STATE OF MARYLAND

Elected Under the Constitution of 1776 by the Legislature for One Year:

Thomas Johnson	1777-1779
Thomas Sim Lee	1779-1782
William Paca	1782-1785
William Smallwood	1785-1788
John Eager Howard	1788-1791
George Plater[1]	1791-1792
John H. Stone	1794-1797
John Henry	1797-1798
Benjamin Ogle	1798-1801
John Francis Mercer	1801-1803
Robert Bowie	1803-1806
Robert Wright[2]	1806-1809
Edward Lloyd	1809-1811
Robert Bowie	1811-1812
Levin Winder	1812-1816
Charles Ridgely of Hampton	1816-1819
Charles Goldsborough	1819-
Samuel Sprigg	1819-1822
Samuel Stevens, Jr.	1822-1826
Joseph Kent	1826-1829
Daniel Martin[3]	1829-1831
Thomas King Carroll	1830-1831
George Howard	1831-1833
James Thomas	1833-1836
Thomas W. Veazey	1836-1839

Elected by the People for Three Years Under the Constitution of 1776 as amended in 1838:

William Grason	1839-1842
Francis Thomas	1842-1845

Thomas G. Pratt	1845-1848
Philip Francis Thomas	1848-1851
Enoch Louis Lowe	1851-1854

Elected Under the Constitution of 1851 by the People for Four Years:

Thomas Watkins Ligon	1854-1858
Thomas Holliday Hicks	1858-1862
Augustus W. Bradford	1862-1866

Elected Under the Constitution of 1864 by the People for Four Years:

Thomas Swann	1866-1869

Elected Under the Constitution of 1867 by the People for Four Years:

Oden Bowie[4]	1869-1872
William Pinkney Whyte[5]	1872-1874
James Black Groome	1874-1876
John Lee Carroll	1876-1880
William T. Hamilton	1880-1884
Robert M. McLane[6]	1884-1885
Henry Lloyd	1885-1888
Elihu E. Jackson	1888-1892
Frank Brown	1892-1896
Lloyd Lowndes	1896-1900
John Walter Smith	1900-1904
Edwin Warfield	1904-1908
Austin L. Crothers	1908-1912
Phillips Lee Goldsborough	1912-1916
Emerson C. Harrington	1916-1920
Albert C. Ritchie[7]	1920-1935
Harry W. Nice	1935-1939
Herbert R. O'Conor[8]	1939-1947
William Preston Lane, Jr.	1947-1951
Theodore R. McKeldin	1951-1959
J. Millard Tawes	1959-1967
Spiro T. Agnew[9]	1967-1969
Marvin Mandel[10]	1969-

1 James Brice of Annapolis, a member of the Governor's Council, became Acting Governor upon the death of Governor Plater on February 10, 1792. He served until April 2 of the same year when he was suceeded by Thomas Sim Lee.
2 Governor Wright resigned on May 6, 1809. James Butcher, a member of the Governor's Council, became Acting Governor and served for one month, or until June 5, 1809, when his successor, Edward Lloyd, qualified.
3 Governor Martin died in office on July 11, 1831. George Howard, a member of the Governor's Council, succeeded him. Governor Howard was subsequently elected by the Legislature for a one-year term in January, 1832.
4 Governor Bowie served three years by special provision of the Constitution.
5 Governor Whyte resigned on March 4, 1874. Governor Groome was elected and assumed office on the same day. Because of a family business disagreement, Governor Whyte changed the spelling of his surname to distinguish his branch of the family.
6 Governor McLane resigned on March 27, 1885. Henry Lloyd, as President of the Senate, succeeded him as Acting Governor until January, 1886, when the Legislature elected him to complete the remainder of Governor McLane's term which expired in January, 1888.
7 Because of a 1922 constitutional amendment which provided for quadrennial elections, the Governor elected in 1923 served for three years. Thereafter gubernatorial terms began in odd years.
8 Governor O'Conor resigned on January 3, 1947 to accept a seat in the United States Senate. William Preston Lane, Jr. was elected by the Legislature to fill the unexpired term. Governor Lane was inaugurated on January 3, 1947 for the remainder of Governor O'Conor's term and on January 8, 1947 for the full four-year term.
9 Governor Agnew, having been elected Vice President of the United States at the general election of November 5, 1968, resigned on January 7, 1969. Marvin Mandel, then the Speaker of the House of Delegates, was elected on the same day to fill the balance of Governor Agnew's unexpired term.
10 Governor Mandel was elected by the people in November of 1970 for a full four-year term. He was inaugurated for this term in January, 1971.

APPENDIX H

ESSAY:

SITES IN ENGLAND ASSOCIATED WITH THE PROPRIETARY FAMILY OF MARYLAND

SITES IN ENGLAND ASSOCIATED WITH THE PROPRIETARY FAMILY OF MARYLAND

Two hundred years have passed since Maryland became a state and so deposed Henry Harford, Esquire, her last Proprietor. Nearly 350 years have passed since the idea of planting an English colony in America took form in the mind of George Calvert, first Lord Baltimore. Yet, many buildings and sites associated with the proprietary family may still be found in England today, for though the lengths of time mentioned above seem long to Americans, they are but yesterday to the English.

Kiplin Hall

As it has for three and a half centuries, Kiplin Hall stands today in its gardens surrounded by Yorkshire fields. True, since George Calvert re-built his old home in the early seventeenth century, there have been several large additions, yet the main building still stands. The first Lord Baltimore incorporated a portion of the solid walls of his old family home in the core of this main block. When he completed his building at Kiplin around 1625, he had evolved a strong, rather tall, structure Jacobean in style.[*] It is believed to have been built from plans designed by Inigo Jones.[+] Traces of an imposing avenue remain to the east of Kiplin Hall.

Upon entering the building one finds tall doors leading to a small flagged vestibule. Next one may enter a large room paneled in age-darkened oak. On the western wall of this room is a great fireplace which once warmed the "hall," and around the room are hung portraits of persons associated with Kiplin, for example Lady Charlotte Fitzroy, natural daughter of

---

[*] Nikolaus Pevsner, *The Buildings of England* (Harmondsworth, Middlesex, G.B.: Penquin Books, Ltd., 1966), pp. 38, 208.

[+] G. Bernard Wood, *Historic Homes of Yorkshire*, (London: Oliver & Body, 1957), p. 79.

Charles II and of her husband, Edward Henry, 1st Earl of Litchfield. (These were the parents of Benedict Leonard Calvert's wife, also named Charlotte.)*

To the left of the entrance door is a room used as a dining room and named the Canaletto Room for the paintings by that artist that hang there.+

Within and without one can see the central block of George Calvert's building of Kiplin Hall. Around a central core there are four towers with ogee caps and eight gables. These are rather lost in additions made by later owners, yet if one observes closely, the original structure may be detected.*

The Calvert family kept Kiplin Hall after the establishment of their American colony in Maryland. In fact, it was not until after the death of the fourth Baron that Kiplin passed out of the direct line of descent of Calvert family members.

The widow of Benedict Leonard Calvert (Charlotte, granddaughter of Charles II) traveled to Europe. There she met and married a gentleman, Christopher Crowe. When they returned to England, Crowe was delighted with Kiplin. He arranged with its owner, his stepson, Charles Calvert (II), to purchase the old mansion with much of its acreage in 1722 for 7,000 pounds.+

One may see Crowe, in a portrait of that interesting man painted by Canaletto, wearing a turban and scarlet cloak. Crowe brought the Canalettos to Kiplin.#

For a century Crowes enjoyed Kiplin, then passed it on, by the marriage of a daughter, to the Carpenter family. Sarah Crowe married George (Carpenter), Earl of Tyrconnel, who added the great library wing to

---

*Observed by Vera Rollo, during the summer of 1974.
+G. Bernard Wood, p. 79.
*James W. Foster, "George Calvert: His Yorkshire Boyhood," *Maryland Historical Magazine,* Vol. 55, No. 4 (December, 1960), p. 262.
+G. Bernard Wood, pp. 79-81.
#Ibid.

the south side of Kiplin Hall in the nineteenth century.**

Kiplin remained a private home occupied in turn by relatives of the Carpenter family, by Walter Cecil Talbot, and by the last private owners, Mrs. Christopher Turnor and Miss Bridget Talbot. Since large houses of this ilk were increasingly unsuitable as private residences in the twentieth century, Kiplin went on the market and there was speculation that it might be pulled down. During pre-World War II years it was used as a school, and later, during the war, by the Royal Air Force.

Following the war, its roof crumbling, its acres threatened, the old mansion was rescued by a group of public-spirited persons, known today as the Trustees of Kiplin Hall.* The Trustees engaged Mr. H. T. Prime as curator and began the battle of halting the deterioration of Kiplin Hall in order to make it available to persons interested in British and American history. In the summer of 1975 a new roof was placed on the building, just in time to preserve the fabric of the structure, through the financial assistance of a member of the Maryland Historical Society.

Kiplin Hall may be visited by appointment. Plans are, as soon as possible, to open the Hall at regular times. It is located about 40 miles north-northwest of the city of York, and lies east of the town of Catterick.

Epsom and Woodcote Park

From Yorkshire one might journey southward, seeking Calvert family locales, passing London, traveling into Surrey, and the town of Epsom. Epsom little resembles the rural village that once existed there, for it has been enveloped by the twentieth-century sprawl of the London suburbs. Still, one can still view the old

---

**Ibid.
*Trustees of Kipling Hall, 1974: Captain Hugh Chetwynd-Talbot, M.B.E.; Lt. Colonel Maurice J. B. Burnett, D.S.O., DL; Mrs. Janet Adams; Hon. Mrs. Lavender Garnier; Margaret, Lady Beresford-Peirse; and Chief-Superintendent George Thompson.

parish church, St. Martin's, and the churchyard where members of the Calvert family are laid to rest.

St. Martin's Parish Church resembles a Gothic structure and is made of brick with a curious facing of broken flintstone.[+] By the church, the last Baron of Baltimore, Frederick Calvert, sixth Lord Baltimore, was interred in the late eighteenth century.[++]

About a mile south of Epsom is Woodcote Park. This estate came into the Calvert family in 1691, willed to Cecil, Lord Baltimore, by Mrs. Elizabeth Evelyn, a relation.[#] Cecil Calvert having died in 1675, the property came to his heir Charles Calvert (I), third Lord Baltimore.

For generations Woodcote Park remained a Calvert home until it was sold, as mentioned above, by Frederick, sixth Baron, around 1768.

Charles Calvert (II), before Frederick's time, added a great deal of embellishment to the mansion and enjoyed entertaining there. Nearby was another large property, "Durdans," used by Frederick, Prince of Wales, between 1737 and 1747. As we have mentioned, the fifth Lord Baltimore and the Prince had a long and close association.

Woodcote Park showed four floors above ground level, the first encased in stone, the upper three floors stuccoed. Twin staircases mounted and met at an entrance on the second story. From the center portion of the building wings extended out, providing an imposing frontage.

Inside the mansion was a large room, a "hall," with corinthian columns supporting a frieze. There were five principal apartments; many of the rooms boasting ornately decorated ceilings of considerable artistic merit. There was a splendid library, profusely ornamented with gilding on a blue ground, and graced by a

---

[+] Gordon Home, *Epsom, Its History and Surroundings* (Epsom and London, 1901, republished, York: S. R. Publications, Ltd., 1971), p. 65.

[++] "An Inhabitant," *History of Epsom* (Epsom: W. Dorling, also by J. Hearne, London, 1825), p. 22.

[#] Gordon Home, p. 81.

ceiling painted by Verrio. That artist did, as well, the ceiling of the family chapel at Woodcote Park. All in all, during its tenure by the Calverts it was an impressive residence.*

Once disposed of by Frederick the mansion and its lands passed through several hands until, in 1913, it was sold to the Royal Automobile Club for use as a country club. After World War I the work of converting the estate into a club was completed. Club members for many years enjoyed golf, tennis, croquet, squash, and swimming, and their handsome clubhouse until, August 1, 1934, a disastrous fire destroyed the old building with its beautiful ceilings and other elaborate decorative details.

Today a new building, opened in 1936, stands on the site, its facade an exact replica of the former Calvert home. The interior has been modernized, of course, and with its lighting and air conditioning would appear strange indeed to its former owners, yet it is now admirably suited to the needs of the R.A.C. members in the twentieth century.[+]

London

In spite of the damage done to the city by the bombing raids of World War II, and in spite of the building projects in London, there are still many sites there that Henry Harford might find familiar.

His street is there, "New Cavendish Street in the Parish of Saint Marylebone in the County of Middlesex." Nearby is another street that also figured in his life, Berners Street, the home of Louisa, daughter of Peter Pigou, Esquire, who was to be his first wife.

Many of the great public buildings of London, Harford would find familiar. True, large towers of glass and steel are rising there, yet the British are zealously preserving many of the old landmarks. London goes to sleep at night and is quiet, unlike many American

---

*Gordon Home, p. 80.
[+]Royal Automobile Club, *Jubilee Book,* ed., Dudley Noble (London: R.A.C., 1947), pp. 65-73.

cities which continue to rumble and hum. How quiet a city it must have been in Harford's day! The same parks are there, as well, that existed in his time. Today more of these are open to the public, no longer reserved for the pleasure of owners of the surrounding houses. These green and pleasant plots which Harford enjoyed two hundred years ago, are still in use.

Eton and Windsor

At Eton College, only a footbridge apart from the city of Windsor, one can see college buildings that Harford once knew. He did not wear the frock coat and top hat worn today by "Eton boys," for these were adopted later, upon the death of the friend of the college, King George III.* Yet Harford did tread these same Etonian streets and enjoyed the same river and its meadows.

When Harford attended Eton the grey mass of Windsor Castle loomed, as it does now, above Eton. King George III enjoyed living at Windsor and during his reign made it a royal home. The castle is still used by the royal family as a residence. It is open to the public and is a most rewarding place to visit. Extensive royal parks surround the castle, but are used now more for the pleasure of the public than as private royal hunting grounds. The green acreage around the castle provides a welcome open space for royalty and commoner alike. In Windsor town itself, one can find streets and several buildings dating back to the eighteenth century, ones that Henry Harford must have known.

Down Place

Down Place, Henry Harford's country home near Windsor, remained a Harford home until the 1930's. The last Proprietor's great-grandson, Frederick Reginald Harford, sold it at that time to Colonel and Mrs. George Davies. When the writer visited Down Place in the summer of 1974, Mrs. Davies was still living in an apartment in one wing of the old mansion.

---

*Christopher Hollis, *Eton: A History,* (London: Hollis and Carter, 1960), p. 180.

(Author's 1974 photograph.)

An old building often passed by Maryland's young Proprietor as he walked the main street of Eton.

She remarked that she and her husband had sold Down Place and its remaining acreage, to a motion picture company. This company, via a series of mergers, is now known as the Bray Film Services, with studios located at Down Place.

The film company has put Down Place to utilitarian use. Dressing rooms are installed in former servants' quarters, while the stables and barns shelter film-making equipment. Offices now fill the tall rooms of the mansion, with only a graceful cornice here and there remaining to hint at former grandeur. Behind the old Harford home looms the bulk of a sound stage.

Down Place may be seen by appointment only. Seemingly, there is little there now to reward one in search of a Maryland Proprietor, yet the Thames is still there by the lawn, a peaceful stream. There are still open fields about the house. At the rear of the mansion tall, carved oak doors open into a high, flagstoned entry room. In odd corners other carvings and stonework remain from Harford's time.

Visiting Down Place proved to be most rewarding for the writer, since via a casual remark made by Mrs. Davies, she was able to locate and to meet the last direct descendants of the Proprietor to bear the Harford name.

The Town of Bray

Henry Harford often visited the town of Bray, near Down Place. He attended church there with his family. Inside the parish church, in its vestibule, one can see a framed document commemorating the names of members who donated funds for "re-pewing" the church. One of the names is that of Harford's second wife, Esther Harford, with the date, "4 Feb. 1839."

Though not visible today due to the installation of an organ, there are, on a wall of the parish church at Bray, two markers that read:

Sacred to the memory of Hester [sic], wife of the late Henry Harford, Esqr, of Down Place, who departed this life May 17th 1853, aged 78 years.

Sacred to the memory of Henry Harford, Esqr, of Down Place, Berks., who departed this life on the 8th of December, 1834, in the 76th year of his age.*

Both Henry Harford and his wife Esther were buried in the Bray Church cemetary, according to old parish registers, yet the exact location is not certain.⁺ Esther Harford mentioned "the family vault," in her will (Appendix E). There are many old grave markers and tombs whose inscriptions are completely worn away by wind and rain.

Perhaps Harford lies near his son who is buried in the churchyard of Bray Church near a roadway that provides access to homes called, "Berkeley's-Vicarage," located on the river behind Bray Church. Here one may find a well-preserved stone that reads:

> In Memory of Frederick Paul Harford of Down Place, Berks.
> Formerly an officer of the Scots
> Fusilier Guards who died February
> 21, 1860. Aged 57 years.
> and
> Also of
> Eliza Louisa
> Wife of the Above
> Who died July 28, 1876. Aged 66.

*Charles Kerry, *The History and Antiquities of the Hundred of Bray* (London: author, 1861), p.46.
⁺Berkshire County Record Office, Reading. Bray Church Burial Registers: D/P23/1/11 Burials 1813–1837, and 1850–1860.

The village of Bray has buildings and roadways that existed in Harford's day. Several old cottages and the village inn remain. Giant trees shade the narrow streets of the town and only now are the fields being taken over by modern housing and a new roadway. Two hundred years have changed Bray, of course, but in many ways it remains the charming country town that Harford knew.

Often members of the Harford family called for their carriages and journeyed to Bray to attend church and social functions. Many a Harford squire called for his coach and drove to meet his friends at the inn. The town has long been a favorite spot, too, for romantic hide-a-ways, being close to Windsor and not very far from London. Further back in its history Normans use the present parish church site as a place of worship. During the Roman occupation of Briton, Bray was used by Romans as traces of buildings attest. Indeed, the same Roman connection is true of Down Place, near Bray.*

Petworth House

Following her marriage to the Hon. William Frederick Wyndham, fourth son of the first Earl of Egremont, Frances Mary Harford lived near Petworth House in Sussex, at the village of Bignor. She must have visited Petworth House and walked to the same huge tree that tops a hill today, near an ornamental lake on the grounds of the mansion.

Petworth House is an all-but-royal residence, with murals on the ceilings, gorgeous paneling, and an outstanding art collection. The chapel has a most unique "drapery" and other exquisite work done by artists in wood carving. Carving, sculpture, and paintings adorn Petworth House. The house is regularly opened to visitors and is a most interesting place to see.

---

*Nan Birney, *Bray: Today and Yesterday* (Maindenhead and Trowbridge: Thames Valley Press, 1973), pp. 13–17, also, Charles Kerry, p. 153.

From the Petworth House Archives came valuable clues as to the life and death of Henry Harford's sister, as well as new information about the length of his stay in America. Surely, it seemed to the writer, there would be in the Petworth House Archives letters from Henry Harford, yet none came to light.

One can only speculate as to whether Harford journeyed to Petworth House and nearby areas, visiting his sister and viewing the lovely cathedral town of Chichester a few miles away. One may stroll the pathway that tops parts of the old city wall, visit the Cathedral, and walk the narrow streets of this ancient city as perhaps Maryland's last Proprietor did nearly 200 years ago.

Oxford

Henry Harford knew well many of the buildings, streets, and river meadows that one may see in Oxford today. The city is larger now, but still it lies cupped in the Oxfordshire hills, and is still laced by rivers flowing from the Berkshires eastward toward London. It is a small city of great charm with cobbled sidewalks and narrow streets overhung by tall houses.

Students still race through the streets, black robes flapping, though there are girl students among them now. Automobiles now move along Oxford's streets, yet scarcely faster than horses and carriages once moved. After examinations, friends of students still meet them at the door of the college with bottles of wine to celebrate the completion of the examination.

Exeter College of Oxford University was attended by Maryland's last Proprietor. It boasts a beautiful and lofty dining hall of great age where Henry Harford dined. There is a lovely Chapel which he attended, and he must often have strolled the uniquely green English turf of the College courtyard.

The buildings of the University which existed in his day are there to be admired, by the visitor.

Exeter and Exmouth

On a raw, grey, Sunday afternoon, during a holiday in the summer of 1973, the writer entered Exeter Cathedral while on a holiday in England. She stood by a vault containing the remains of "Bishop James Berkeley, 1377," and waited for her daughter to complete a methodical circuit of the various plaques and monuments in the great cathedral. Idly the writer looked at a wall plaque, near where she happened to be standing, and read the inscription: "Louisa the wife of Henry Harford, Esqr d. at Exmouth Nov. 1st, 1803, aged 34 years." Surely this could not be the same Henry Harford the writer had been studying for several years now, the coincidence was too unlikely. Still, she jotted down the inscription on a scrap of paper and once back in Maryland found that the dates did match!

The following year the writer returned to Exeter Cathedral to find, not only records of Henry Harford's first wife being interred at the Cathedral, but connections with other relatives of Louisa Pigou Harford.* These connections were of such note that Louisa had been buried with considerable pomp at the great cathedral.

Research revealed that she had been visiting nearby Exmouth for her health, for the mild salt air of the little fishing village was believed to be beneficial to persons suffering respiratory ailments.

Again, the writer hoped that in some collection of local papers that letters or documents might be found to reveal more about Henry Harford, but save for the scant details of Louisa's stay and demise at Exmouth, no correspondence was discovered. Surely Harford must have written to his wife, perhaps he accompanied her to Exmouth in person, or came occasionally to visit her there. We can but speculate, and know only the

---

*J. W. Hewett, B.A., *A Complete Monumentarium of the Cathedral Church of St. Peter, Exeter,* Vol. I., (Exeter: Exeter Diocesan Architectural Society, 3 vols., 1849), p. 24. *Gentleman's Magazine,* Vol. LXXIII (November, 1803).

poignant fact that Louisa died shortly after the birth of her son, "at Exmouth, aged 34 years."

Other Sites

In England and Ireland there are several other sites associated with the colonial period of Maryland's history. In England, for example, one may visit the Isle of Wight, departure point for the *Ark* and the *Dove* bound for Maryland. In Ireland one might seek out the Baltimore estates.

So rooted are we in the history of both England and Ireland that the American traveler reaches these islands with a sense of homecoming. For the Marylander, in particular, it is a most worthwhile journey.

(Author's 1974 photograph.)

Side view of Kiplin Hall.

BIBLIOGRAPHY

I. PRIMARY SOURCES

Documents in Manuscript Form

Bray Inclosure Award Map of 1817. Berkshire Record Office, Shire Hall, Reading, England.

Burial Register, Parish of Bray. January 1850 to October 1860. Record Office, County of Berkshire, Reading, England. #253,32.

Burial Register, Parish of Bray. 1813–1837. Record Office, County of Berkshire, Reading England. D/P23/1/11.

Calvert Papers. Manuscripts Division. Maryland Historical Society. Microfilm Roll #2.

Calvert Family Bible. Contains entries of births beginning with that of Frederick Calvert and continuing to the present Misses Harford. Personal papers, Misses Harford, Buckinghamshire.

Dulany Papers Collection. Manuscripts Division. Maryland Historical Society.

Estate Act of 1781. Microfilm, 100 pages. Record Office, House of Lords, London.

Executors' Statement regarding the settlement of the fifth Lord Baltimore's estate. Addressed to the courts of England. Calvert Papers, microfilm roll 2, Items 480, 481. MS Div., Maryland Historical Society.

Fauquier County, Virginia. Record of Land Causes, Book 2, p. 297.

Frederick County, Virginia, Will Book 4, Frederick County, Virginia.

"Henry Harford Letter and Case, 8 May 1813." Items 38252.F.352, and 38252.F.353. Manuscripts Room, British Museum, London.

Harford Family Pedigree. Engrossed by College of Arms, London. In the private papers of the Misses Harford, Buckinghamshire.

Jonas Clapman, accounts books, from May 21, 1785 to January 21, 1818. Scharf Papers, Manuscripts Division, Maryland Historical Society.

Lee, John W. M. letters, May 1888. Regarding third Manuscripts Division, Maryland Historical Society.

Marriage Settlement of Charles Calvert, fifth Lord Baltimore and Mary Janssen. Microfilm roll 2, Calvert Papers. Manuscripts Division, Maryland Historical Society.

Marriage Settlement of William Frederick Wyndham and Frances Mary Harford, July 1784. Petworth House Archives No. 51, file #3027. Courtesy Lord Egremont.

Society of Genealogists, letter from Secretary of the Society, C. M. Mackay, to Vera Rollo, Lanham, Md., dated October 28, 1974.

Will of Charles Calvert, fifth Lord Baltimore, 7 November 1750. Calvert Papers, microfilm roll 2, MS#174. MS Div., Maryland Historical Society.

Will of Frederick Calvert, sixth Lord Baltimore. Public Record Office, London. Taverner 5. Proved, London, January, 1772.

Will of Esther Rycroft Harford. Public Record Office, London. Prob./11/2174.

Will of Henry Harford, Esquire. Public Record Office, London. Prob./10/5516.

Will of Hester Rhelan Harford Prevost. Public Record Office, London. Prob./11/1530/p.91.

Will of Peter Prevost. Public Record Office, London. Prob./11/1176/p.109.

Will of Frances Mary Harford Wyndham. Petworth House Archives. PHA Document N 16/A a 2.

Documents: In Printed Form

Archives of Maryland. Vols. 31, 47, 48, 62, and 64. Baltimore: Maryland Historical Society. Continuing series.

The Calvert Papers, 3 vols. Baltimore: Maryland Historical Society, 1889–1899.

Case of the British American Claimants. MS Room, British Museum, London. Document #38252.F.353.

English Consistory Reports, 1788–1821. Harford v. Morris portion, pp. 792–797, vertical files, MS Div., Maryland Historical Society, ref. under date of December 2, 1776.

Eton College Register: 1698–1752. Richard Arthur Austen-Leigh, ed. Eton: Spottiswoode, Ballantyne & Co., Ltd., 1927.

Eton College Register: 1753–1790. Richard Arthur Austen-Leigh, ed. Eton: Spottiswoode, Ballantyne & Co., Ltd., 1921.

Henry Harford Memorial, and related proceedings of the Maryland House of Delegates, dated January 6, 1786. Vertical files, MS Div., Maryland Historical Society.

Minutes of the Supreme Executive Council of Pennsylvania: From its Organization to the Termination of the Revolution.
Vol. 14, Jan. 1, 1784 - April 3, 1786. Harrisburg: State of Pennsylvania, 1853.
Vol. 16, Feb. 7, 1789 - December 20, 1790. Harrisburg: State of Pennsylvania, 1853.

Revised Code of Virginia, Vol. 2. Richmond: Commonwealth of Virginia, 1819.

Periodicals and Newspapers

Gentleman's Magazine. Vols. 38, 41, 54, 58, 73, 76, 98, and vol. 3, new series. Bound volumes located in Periodicals Room, British Museum, London.

Maryland Gazette. June 25, 1767 issue, and handbill following; June 8, 1769; August 14, 1783; December 25, 1783; and March 2, 1786, issues. Microfilm. Maryland Hall of Records, Annapolis, Maryland.

II. SECONDARY SOURCES

Books

Andrews, Matthew Page. *History of Maryland: Province and State*. Garden City, N.Y.: Doubleday, Doran & Co., Inc., 1929.

Barker, Charles Albro. *The Background of the Revolution in Maryland*. New Haven: Yale University Press, 1940.

Bramwell, George. *An Analytical Table of the Private Statutes Passed 1727–1782*. London: np, 1837.

Brooke, John. *King George III*. New York: McGraw-Hill Book Co., 1972.

Browning, Charles. *An Appeal to the Citizens of Maryland*. Baltimore: np, 1821.

———. *The Granting of Lands in Maryland*. Baltimore: "For the Proprietor," 1825.

Burke's Genealogy and Heraldic History of the Landed Gentry. London: Burke's Peerage, Ltd., 1937.

Carr, Lois and David Jordan. *Maryland's Revolution of Government, 1689–1692*. Ithaca, N.Y.: Cornell University Press, 1974.

The Complete Peerage, G. E. C., Vol. 5. London: St. Catherine Press, 1926.

Conway, Moncure Daniel. *Barons of the Potomack and the Rappahannock*. New York: Grolier Club, 1892.

Debrett's Complete Peerage, Vol. 1. London: Dean & Sons, Ltd., 1922.

Dickinson, Josiah Look. *The Fairfax Proprietary*. Front Royal, Va.: Warren Press, 1959.

Dorling, W. and J. Hearns, *History of Epsom*. London: np, 1825.

Dulany, Daniel. *Maryland and the Empire, 1773: The Antilon—First Citizen Letters*. Introduction and ed. by Peter S. Onuf. Baltimore: Johns Hopkins University Press, 1973.

Edgar, Lady Matilda Ridout. *A Colonial Governor in Maryland*. London: Longmans, Green & Co., 1912.

Fishwick, Marshall W. *Gentlemen of Virginia*. New York: Dodd, Mead & Co., 1961.

Foster, Joseph. *Alumni Oxonienses: The Members of the University of Oxford, 1715–1886*. Oxford: Parker & Co., 1887.

Hall, Clayton C. *The Lords Baltimore and the Maryland Palatinate*. Baltimore: Nunn, 1904.

Hewett, J. W. *A Complete Monumentarium of the Cathedral Church of St. Peter, Exeter*. Exeter: Exeter Diocesan Architectural Society, 1849.

Hoffman, Ronald. *A Spirit of Dissension: Economics, Politics, and the Revolution in Maryland*. Baltimore: Johns Hopkins University Press, 1973.

Holdsworth, Sir William. *An Historical Introduction to the Land Law*. Oxford: Oxford University Press, 1935.

Hollis, Christopher. *Eton: A History*. London: Hollis and Carter, 1960.

Home, Gordon. *Epsom, Its History and Surrounds*. Epsom: np, 1901. Republished, York, England: S. R. Publishers, Ltd., 1971.

Jenks, Edward. *The Book of English Law*. Athens, Ohio: Ohio University Press, 1967.

Kerry, Charles. *The History and Antiquities of the Hundred of Bray: In the County of Berkshire*. London, n.p., 1861.

Land, Aubrey C. *The Dulanys of Maryland*. Baltimore, Maryland Historical Society, 1955.

―――. "Provincial Maryland," Chapter III, *Maryland: A History—1632 to 1974*. Richard Walsh and William Lloyd Fox, eds. Baltimore: Maryland Historical Society, 1974.

Lyte, Sir. H. C. Maxwell. *A History of Eton College: 1440–1910*. London: Macmillan & Co., Ltd., 1911.

Morris, John G. *The Lords Baltimore*. Baltimore: Maryland Historical Society, 1874.

Nelson, William H. *The American Tory*. Oxford: Clarendon Press, 1961.

Norton, Mary Beth. *The British-Americans: The Loyalist Exiles in England, 1774–1789*. Boston: Little, Brown, 1972.

Onuf, Peter S., intro. and ed. *Maryland and the Empire, 1773: The Antilon—First Citizen Letters*. Baltimore: Johns Hopkins University Press, 1973.

Pound, Arthur. *The Penns of Pennsylvania and England*. New York: Macmillan Co., 1932.

Radoff, Morris L. *The Bank Stock Papers*. (Calender of Maryland State Papers, No. 2). Annapolis: State of Maryland, 1947.

Scharf, J. Thomas. *History of Maryland*, 3 vols. Hatboro, Penna.: Tradition Press, 1967. A facsimile reprint of the 1879 edition.

Steiner, Bernard Christian. *Life and Administration of Sir Robert Eden*. Baltimore: Johns Hopkins Press, 1898.

Walsh, Richard. "The Era of Revolution," Chapter II, *Maryland: A History—1632 to 1974*. Richard Walsh and William Lloyd Fox, eds. Baltimore; Maryland Historical Society, 1974.

Ward, Thomas and W. Roberts. *Romney*. London: T. Agnew & Sons, 1904.

Wood, G. Bernard. "Kiplin: Birthplace of Maryland," Chapter 16, *Historic Homes of Yorkshire*. London: Oliver and Boyd, 1957.

Wyndham, George. *The Life and Letters of George Wyndham*. London: Hutchinson & Co., 1925.

Wyndham, Hugh Archibald. *A Family History: 1688–1837—The Wyndhams of Somerset, Sussex and Wiltshire*. London: Oxford University Press, 1950.

Articles

Ammerman, David. "Annapolis and the First Continental Congress: A Note on the Committee System in Revolutionary America." *Maryland Historical Magazine*, Vol. 66, No. 2 (Summer 1971), pp. 169–180.

Bolton, Sidney Charles. "The Anglican Church in Maryland Politics." Master's thesis. University of Wisconsin, 1968. Chapter 2.

Cox, Richard J. "Notes on Maryland Historical Society Manuscript Collections: Some Personal Letters of Frederick Calvert, Last Lord Baltimore." *Maryland Historical Magazine,* Vol. 70, No. 1 (Spring 1975), pp. 98–103.

Fisher, Josephine. "Bennet Allen, Fighting Parson," *Maryland Historical Magazine,* Vol. 38 (December 1943), pp. 299–322; and Vol. 39 (March 1944), pp. 49–72.

Foster, James W. "George Calvert: His Yorkshire Boyhood," *Maryland Historical Magazine,* Vol. 55, No. 4 (December, 1960), pp. 261–274.

Gipe, George A. "A Moderator in Immoderate Times," *Maryland Magazine,* Vol. 6, No. 3 (Spring 1974), pp. 26–29.

Haw, James. "Maryland Politics on the Eve of the Revolution: The Provincial Controversy, 1770–1773," *Maryland Historical Magazine,* Vol. 65 (Summer 1970), pp. 103–129.

"Henry Harford, Etonian." *Etoniana,* Vol. 109 (December, 1950), pp. 135–136.

Jenkins, Howard M. "The Family of William Penn," *Pennsylvania Magazine of History and Biography,* Vol. 21, No. 4, 1897, pp. 421–429.

Nicklin, John B. C. "The Calvert Family," *Maryland Historical Magazine,* Vol. 16, No. 1 (March, 1921), pp. 50–59.

Notes and Queries, "Portrait of Miss Harford," *Maryland Historical Magazine,* Vol. 35, No. 1 (March, 1940), pp. 86, 87.

Overfield, Richard A. "The Patriot Dilemma: The Treatment of Passive Loyalists and Neutrals in Revolutionary Maryland." *Maryland Historical Magazine,* Vol. 79, No. 2 (Summer, 1973), pp. 140–159.

(Author's 1976 photograph)

A view of Spa Creek, much as it must have looked in Henry Harford's day. Harford and Robert Eden could see the water from the Upton Scott House, during their stay in Annapolis.

(M. E. Warren Photograph. Maryland Department of Economic Development)

On St. Clements Island today there is a modern cross commemorating the landing of the English settlers who were members of the Calvert colony.

Maryland Historical Society

The Ark and The Dove
— by Mall

YOUR MARYLAND COUNTIES

County Name and 1960 and 1970 Population Figures	Date Founded	County Seat	Origin of the County Name
Allegany 84,169 84,044	1789	Cumberland	From the Indian word meaning "Beautiful Stream."
Anne Arundel 206,634 297,539	1650	Annapolis	Named for the wife of Cecil Calvert, Second Lord Baltimore.
Baltimore 492,428 621,077	1659	Towson	Named for the Irish Barony belonging to the Calvert family.
Baltimore City 939,024 905,759	1729	(Incorporated 1797)	Named for the Irish Barony belonging to the Calvert family.
Calvert 15,826 20,682	1654	Prince Frederick	This county was known as Patuxent County until 1658 when it was renamed in honor of the Calvert family.
Caroline 19,462 19,781	1773	Denton	Named for Lady Caroline, sister to the Sixth Lord Baltimore.
Carroll 52,785 69,006	1836	Westminster	Named in honor of "The Signer" (of the Declaration of Independence) Charles Carroll of Carrollton.
Cecil 48,408 53,291	1674	Elkton	Named for Cecil Calvert, Second Lord Baltimore.
Charles 32,572 47,678	1658	La Plata	Named for the Third Lord Baltimore, Charles Calvert.
Dorchester 29,666 29,405	1668	Cambridge	Named for the Earl of Dorset, a friend of the Calverts.
Frederick 71,930 84,927	1748	Frederick	Named, probably, for Frederick Calvert, who became the Sixth Lord Baltimore.
Garrett 20,420 21,476	1872	Oakland	Named for John W. Garrett, a prominent banker.
Harford 76,722 115,378	1773	Bel Air	Named for the last Proprietor of Maryland, Henry Harford.

County	Population	Founded	County Seat	Origin of Name
Howard	36,152 / 61,911	1851	Ellicott City	Named in honor of the Maryland patriot, John Eager Howard.
Kent	15,481 / 16,146	1642	Chestertown	Called after the English county of the same name.
Montgomery	340,928 / 522,809	1776	Rockville	Named for General Richard Montgomery, who served in the American Revolution.
Prince George's	357,395 / 660,567	1695	Upper Marlboro	Named for the husband of Queen Anne, Prince George of Denmark.
Queen Anne's	16,569 / 18,422	1706	Centreville	So named in honor of Queen Anne of England.
St. Mary's	38,915 / 47,388	1637	Leonardtown	Named in honor of the Virgin Mary.
Somerset	19,623 / 18,924	1666	Princess Anne	So named for Mary Somerset the sister-in-law of Cecil Calvert, Second Lord Baltimore.
Talbot	21,578 / 23,682	1661	Easton	Named for Grace Talbot, the sister of Cecil Calvert, Second Lord Baltimore.
Washington	91,219 / 103,829	1776	Hagerstown	Named for George Washington.
Wicomico	49,050 / 54,236	1867	Salisbury	Named for the Indian words for house (wicko) and for building (mekee), and also for the Wicomico River.
Worcester	23,733 / 24,442	1742	Snow Hill	Named for the Earl of Worcester.

THE TOTAL POPULATION OF MARYLAND IN 1960 WAS 3,100,689.
BY 1970 THE POPULATION HAD INCREASED TO A TOTAL OF 3,922,399 PERSONS.

THE GREAT SEAL OF MARYLAND

OBVERSE   REVERSE

In the middle 1600's Cecil Calvert, Second Lord Baltimore, sent out a new Great Seal to his colony to replace that lost to Ingle. Though new seals were adopted later, in 1876 the original seal sent by Lord Baltimore was selected as the official Great Seal of Maryland.

The obverse side of the seal shows Lord Baltimore on horseback in full armor, holding a sword. Around the edge the Latin words meaning "Cecilius, Absolute Lord of Maryland and Avalon, Baron of Baltimore" appear.

On the reverse side of the seal is a coat of arms, supported on one side by a fisherman, and on the other side by a plowman. It rests on a scroll bearing the motto, "Deeds males, words females" as literally translated from the Latin, or it might be translated in meaning as "Manly deeds, womanly words." The top half of this side of the seal shows a special cap with a ducal crown and a flowing mantle inscripted around with words that possibly refer to the good will of the English crown, "Thou hast crowned us with the shield of thy good will."

The fisherman shown on the seal probably refers to the fishing industry of the Avalon colony belonging to Lord Baltimore. This colony was founded in the early 1620's in Newfoundland and much of the prosperity of the settlement depended on fishing.

Maryland, Lord Baltimore's other colony, is represented by the figure of a farmer with a spade in one hand, since Maryland's wealth lay in her agriculture.

MARYLAND STATE FLAG

Reprinted courtesy Department of Economic Development

Maryland's flag bears the arms of the Calvert and Crossland families. Calvert was the family name of the Lords Baltimore who founded Maryland. Crossland was the family of the mother of the first Lord Baltimore. The escutcheon or shield in the Maryland Seal bears the same arms. This flag in its present form was first used about 1886. It was officially adopted in 1904.

MARYLAND STATE FLOWER

The Black-eyed Susan is the flower emblem of the State of Maryland.

INDEX

Annapolis, 48, 49, 55, 56, 74, 76, 78, 79, 81, 86.
Bank of England stock, xii, 91-92, 94.
Bray, 111, 112, 215, 216, 217.
British American Claimants, 92-93; Appendix C, 151-164.
Browning, Charles, xii, 42, 45n, 66, 117-119, 120, 126n, 128.
Browning family, xii, xiii, xiv, 19, 40, 42, 44, 46n, 61, 65, 78, 91, 117-119, 120, 126n.
Browning, John, 40, 42, 61, 65-66, 91, 117, 120.
Browning, Louisa Calvert. See Calvert, Louisa.
Calvert, Benedict Leonard (Fourth Lord Baltimore), 13-15, 120, 204, 209.
Calvert, Caroline (Dame Caroline, wife of Sir Robert Eden), 19, 36, 40, 41, 45n, 47, 65-66, 78, 91, 120.
Calvert, Cecil (Second Lord Baltimore), 10-12, 120, 204, 211.
Calvert, Charles (I), (Third Lord Baltimore), 11-13, 120, 211.
Calvert, Charles (II), (Fifth Lord Baltimore), 15, 18, 19, 41, 42, 43, 117, 120, 204, 209, 211.
Calvert, Frederick (Sixth Lord Baltimore), xi, 17-34, 35-44, 45n, 47, 51, 52, 57, 59, 66, 95, 98, 120, 128, 211; Appendix A, 131-140.
Calvert, George (First Lord Baltimore), 5-9, 120, 208.
Calvert, Louisa (Mrs. John Browning), 19, 36, 40-42, 45n, 46n, 66, 78, 91, 117, 118, 120.
Calvert Papers, 121-126.
Carroll, Charles of Carrollton, 53, 82, 77, 83, 84, 87.
Chase, Samuel, 83, 84, 87.
Church of England, 1, 2, 6, 9, 14, 25, 29, 32, 51.
Down Place, xiv, 108-111, 113, 119-125, 213, 214-215, 217.
Eden, Caroline Calvert. See Calvert, Caroline.
Eden, Sir Robert, after Revolution in Maryland, 79-81, 82, 86, 90n; in Maryland as Governor, 47-58; re. contested proprietorship 65-66, 78; 40, 91, 95, 120, 205.
Epsom, xiv, 19, 23, 24, 43, 45n, 60, 61, 210-212.

Estate Act of 1781, xiii, xiv, 65-68, 68n, 78, 91, 119, 128.
Eton College, xii, xiv, 59, 61-63, 129, 213, 214.
Fairfax, Denny Martin, 72-74, 88, 89.
Fairfax, Lord (Thomas), 70-74, 89.
Hammersley, Hugh, 40, 95.
Harford County, Maryland, viii, x, xi, xv, 52.
Harford, Esther Ryecroft. See Ryecroft, Esther.
Harford, family, xv, 107-116, 115n, 116n, 119-127; ancestry 120; 129, 213.
Harford, Florence M., 120, 125, 126, 127.
Harford, Frances Mary, xii, 21, 41, 45n, 59, 63; 95-106; 107, 107n, 110, 120, 130; will, Appendix F, 199-201; 217.
Harford, Frederick Henry, 119-125.
Harford, Frederick Paul, 108, 111, 113, 114, 119, 120, 216.
Harford, Frederick Reginald, 120, 125-126, 213.
Harford, Henry, viii, x, xi, xii, xiii, 1, 6, 26, 29, 35, 38, 39, 45n, 47, 48, 105; birth, 21, 59, 81, 85, 116n, 120, 130; descendants, 119-126; epilogue, 128-130; his English background, 59-68; in Maryland, 75-90; is willed fortune, 40, 41-44; obtains restitution from Britain, 91-94, 128-129; proclaimed Proprietor, 51, 52, 57; sites, 208-220; his will, 110-114, Appendix D, 165-194.
Harford, Hester Rhelan (later Mrs. Peter Prevost), 20, 21, 36, 40, 59, 61, 95, 110, 120.
Harford, Louisa Pigou. See Pigou, Louisa.
Harford, Pamela V., 120, 125, 126, 127.
Ireland, 8, 9, 19, 59, 220.
Kiplin Hall, xiv, xvii, 6, 7, 10, 15, 202, 208-210, 220.
Loyalists, 71, 72, 75-77, 79, 85, 94n, 130.
Maryland, colonization, 10, 11; during French and Indian War, 27, 28, 31, 32; treatment of Loyalists, 75-77.
Maryland Convention, 55, 56, 75.
Maryland Gazette, 23, 29, 53, 87-89, 89n, 90n, 118, 119.
Maryland General Assembly, 18, 19, 26, 30, 31, 49, 52, 55, 56, 70, 75, 79, 80, 122; re. Harford's claims in Maryland, 81-90.
Maryland Historical Society, xiv, 121-126.

235

Morris, Robert, 40, 41, 63, 95, 96, 98-99.
Oxford University, xiv, 8, 59, 63, 64, 65, 129, 218.
Penn, John, of Stoke, 69-74, 88, 89, 111n.
Pennsylvania, 23, 29, 67, 69-74, 81, 88, 89, 128.
Petworth House, xiv, 100, 101, 102-103, 217-218.
Pigou, Louisa (Henry Harford's first wife), xiv, 107, 108, 129, 212, 219-220.
Prevost, Hester Rhelan Harford. See Harford, Hester Rhelan.
Prevost, Peter, 40, 41, 95, 110. See Harford, Hester Rhelan.
Rhelan, Hester. See Harford, Hester Rhelan.

Roman Catholic Church, 1-3, 6, 9, 14, 17.
Ryecroft, Esther (Henry Harford's second wife), 108, 111, 113, 114, 116n, 215, 216, 129; her will, Appendix E, 195-198.
Scott, Dr. Upton, 79, 81, 82.
Sharpe, Governor Horatio, 23, 25-28, 30, 36, 37, 47, 55, 205.
Stamp Act, 25, 30, 31, 54, 55.
Virginia, 9, 29, 67, 69-74, 81, 88-89, 128.
Wyndham, Frances Mary Harford. See Harford, Frances Mary.
Wyndham, George Francis ("Wyndham"), 103, 104, 120, 121.
Wyndham, William Frederick, 99, 100, 103-106, 217, 218.